BOOK OF
DEATH

ROBERT VENDITTI | ROBERT GILL | DOUG BRAITHWAITE
DAVID BARON | BRIAN REBER

CONTENTS

Collection Cover Art: Robert Gill with Brian Reber

Associate Editor: Kyle Andrukiewicz (#1-4)
Editors: Warren Simons (#1-4),
Tom Brennan ("Chapter Zero")

VALIANT.

Peter Cuneo
Chairman

Dinesh Shamdasani
CEO & Chief Creative Officer

Gavin Cuneo
Chief Operating Officer & CFO

Fred Pierce
Publisher

Warren Simons
VP Editor-in-Chief

Walter Black
VP Operations

Hunter Gorinson
Director of Marketing,
Communications & Digital Media

Atom! Freeman
Director of Sales

Matthew Klein
Andy Liegl
John Petrie
Sales Managers

Josh Johns
Digital Sales & Special Projects Manager

Travis Escarfullery
Jeff Walker
Production & Design Managers

Alejandro Arbona
Tom Brennan
Editors

Kyle Andrukiewicz
Associate Editor

Peter Stern
Publishing & Operations Manager

Andrew Steinbeiser
Marketing & Communications Manager

Danny Khazem
Editorial Operations Manager

Ivan Cohen
Collection Editor

Steve Blackwell
Collection Designer

Lauren Hitzhusen
Editorial Assistant

Rian Hughes/Device
Trade Dress & Book Design

Russell Brown
President, Consumer Products,
Promotions and Ad Sales

Geeta Singh
Licensing Manager

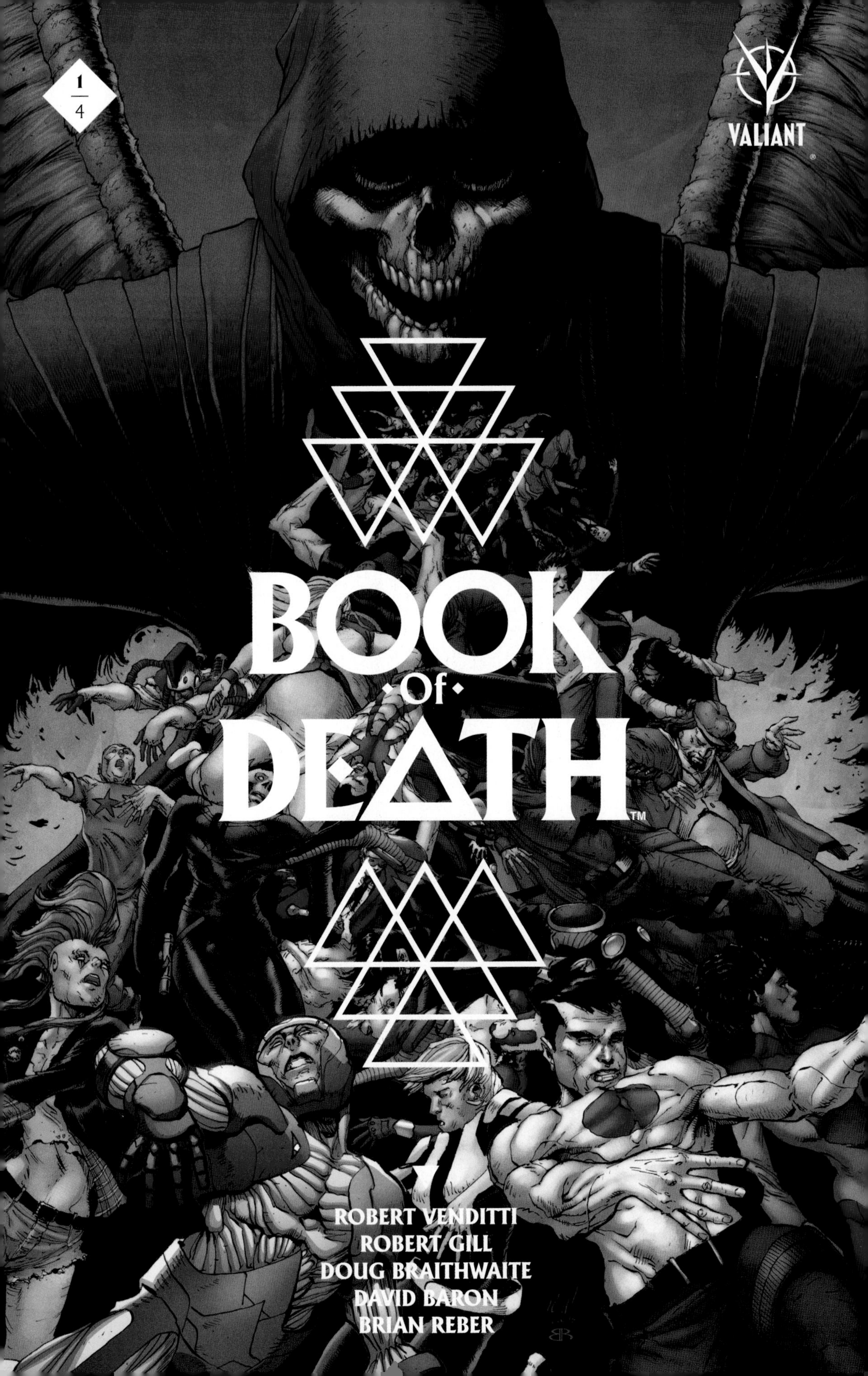
1/4
VALIANT
BOOK
·of·
DEATH™
ROBERT VENDITTI
ROBERT GILL
DOUG BRAITHWAITE
DAVID BARON
BRIAN REBER

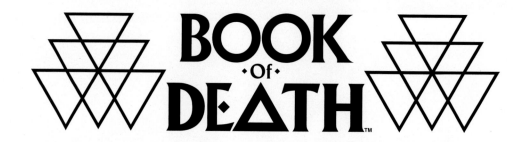

BOOK ·of· DEATH

For millennia, the Eternal Warrior has protected the Geomancers—enigmatic mystics who guide mankind and protect the Earth. But the arrival of Tama—a new Geomancer from the future—has caused great division in the Valiant Universe...especially as she carries the Book of the Geomancer—a tome which foretells an impending dark age...

ETERNAL WARRIOR

A master of ancient and modern combat, Gilad Anni-Padda has wandered the Earth for thousands of years in service to the Geomancers. He is also a member of Unity, the world's most elite superteam.

TAMA, THE GEOMANCER

The latest in a long line of mystics who speak for the Earth and shepherd humanity to new heights, this eleven-year-old girl comes from the future with the Book of the Geomancer.

X-O MANOWAR

Aric of Dacia was a fifth-century Visigoth warrior before he was abducted by aliens and stranded in our time with a sentient suit of armor. He is a member of Unity.

NINJAK

Calculating, mysterious, and wealthy, this British superspy often freelances for the highest bidder, but his personal code of ethics sometimes aligns Ninjak with MI-6 and Unity.

LIVEWIRE

Once the pawn of a megalomaniacal billionaire, Livewire now uses her technopathic ability to control any electronic device. She leads Unity.

NEVILLE ALCOTT

The MI-6 liaison for Unity, little is known about the man who pulls the strings of the most powerful team on Earth.

COL. JAMIE CAPSHAW

Commanding officer of G.A.T.E., the Global Agency for Threat Excision. She works with her British counterpart, MI-6's Neville Alcott, to address unfolding crises around the world.

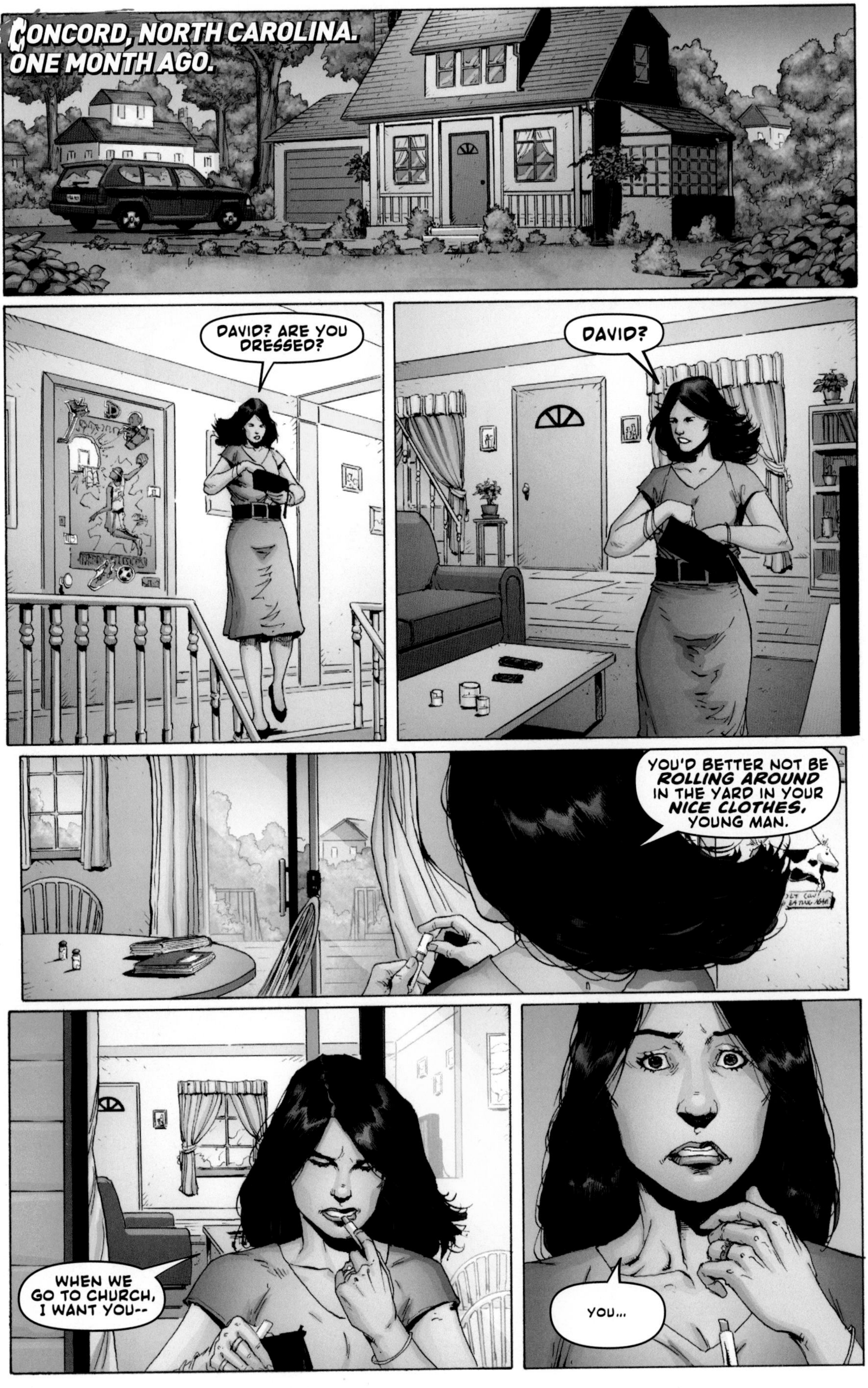
CONCORD, NORTH CAROLINA.
ONE MONTH AGO.
DAVID? ARE YOU DRESSED?
DAVID?
YOU'D BETTER NOT BE ROLLING AROUND IN THE YARD IN YOUR NICE CLOTHES, YOUNG MAN.
WHEN WE GO TO CHURCH, I WANT YOU--
YOU...

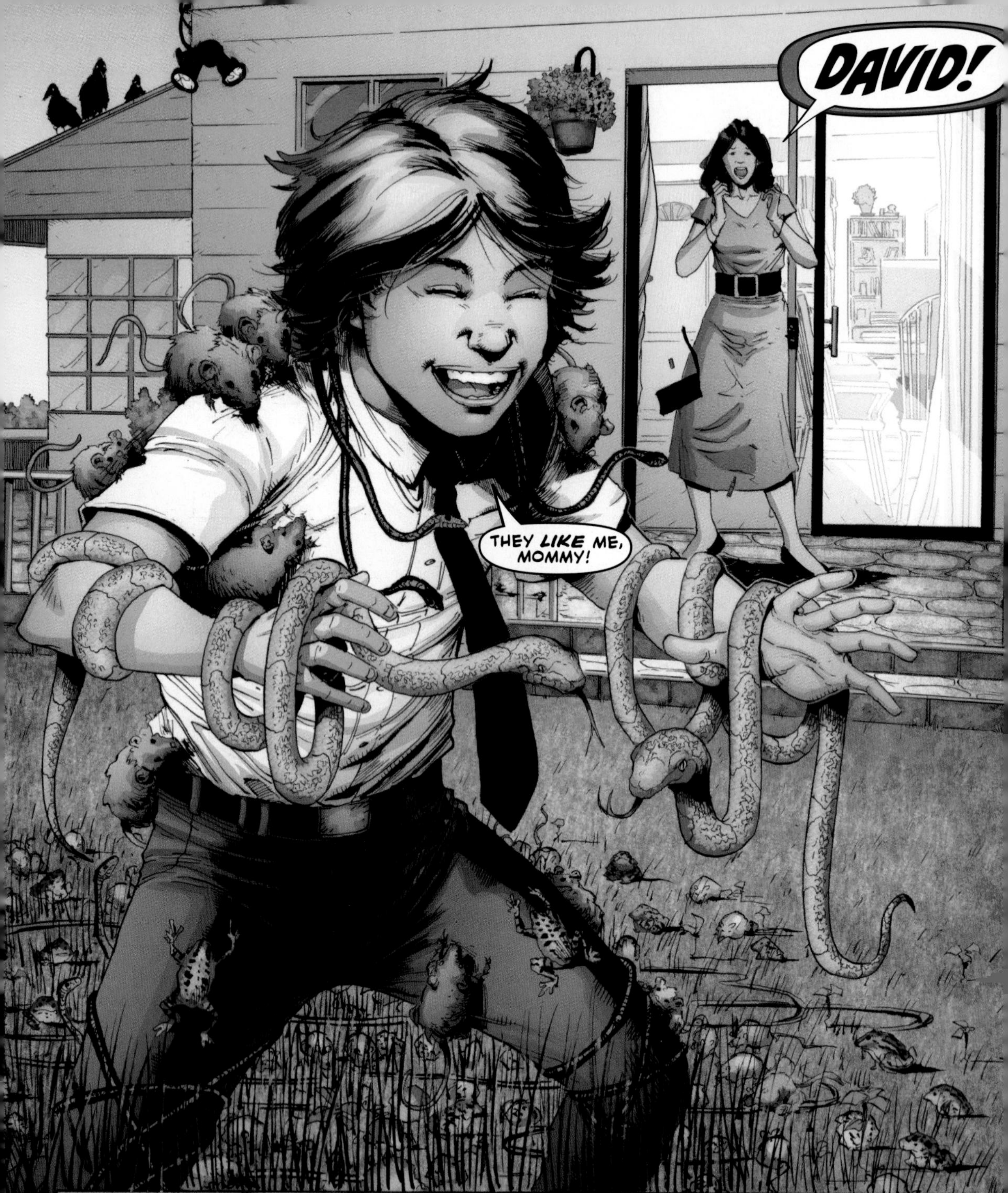
DAVID!
THEY LIKE ME, MOMMY!

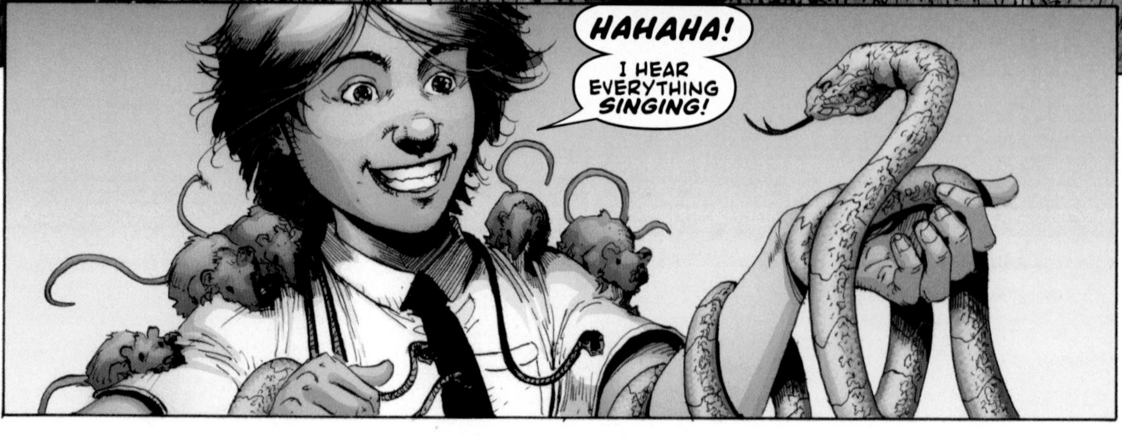
HAHAHA!
I HEAR EVERYTHING SINGING!

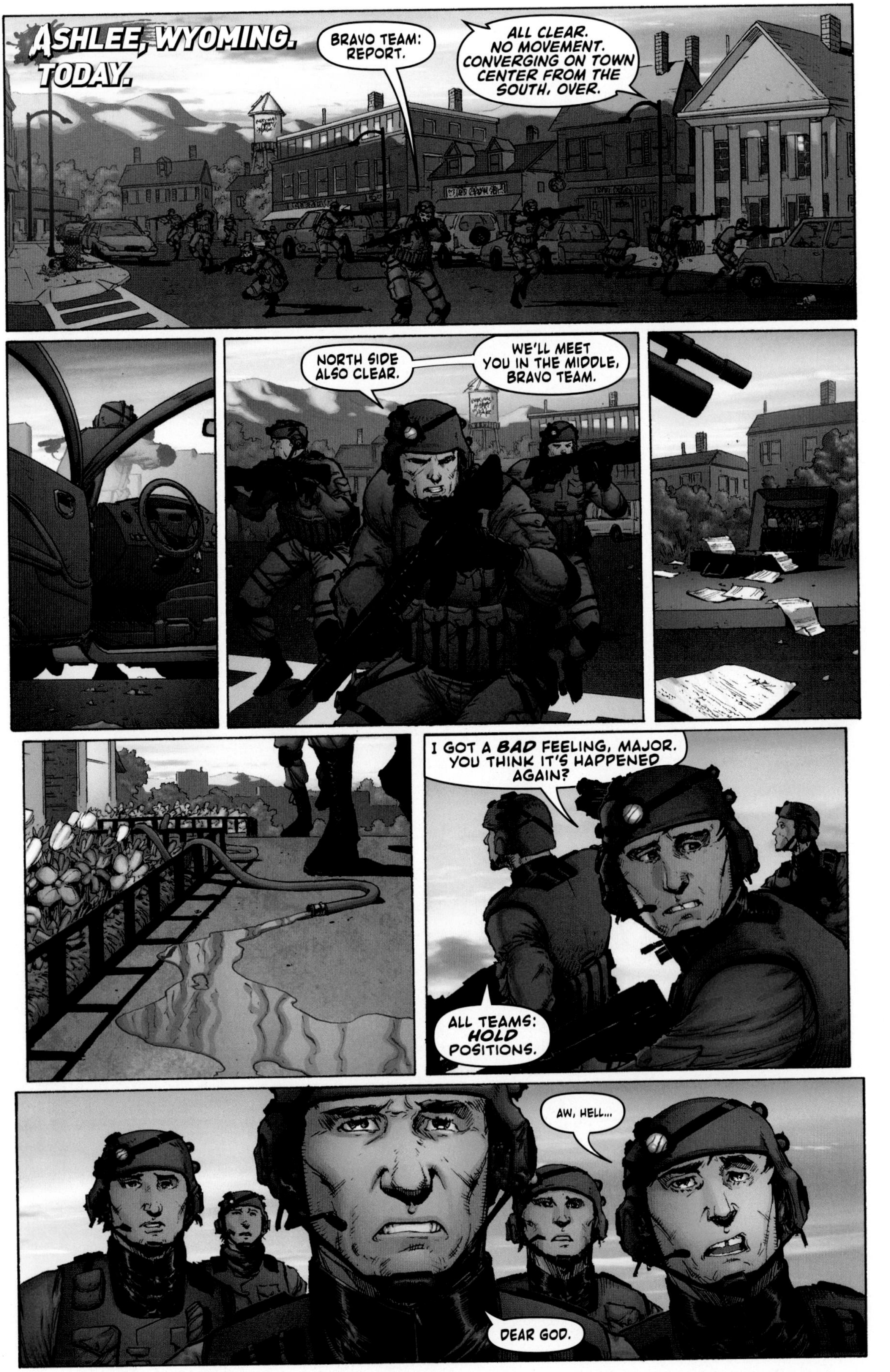
ASHLEE, WYOMING. TODAY.
BRAVO TEAM: REPORT.
ALL CLEAR. NO MOVEMENT. CONVERGING ON TOWN CENTER FROM THE SOUTH, OVER.
NORTH SIDE ALSO CLEAR.
WE'LL MEET YOU IN THE MIDDLE, BRAVO TEAM.
I GOT A BAD FEELING, MAJOR. YOU THINK IT'S HAPPENED AGAIN?
ALL TEAMS: HOLD POSITIONS.
AW, HELL...
DEAR GOD.

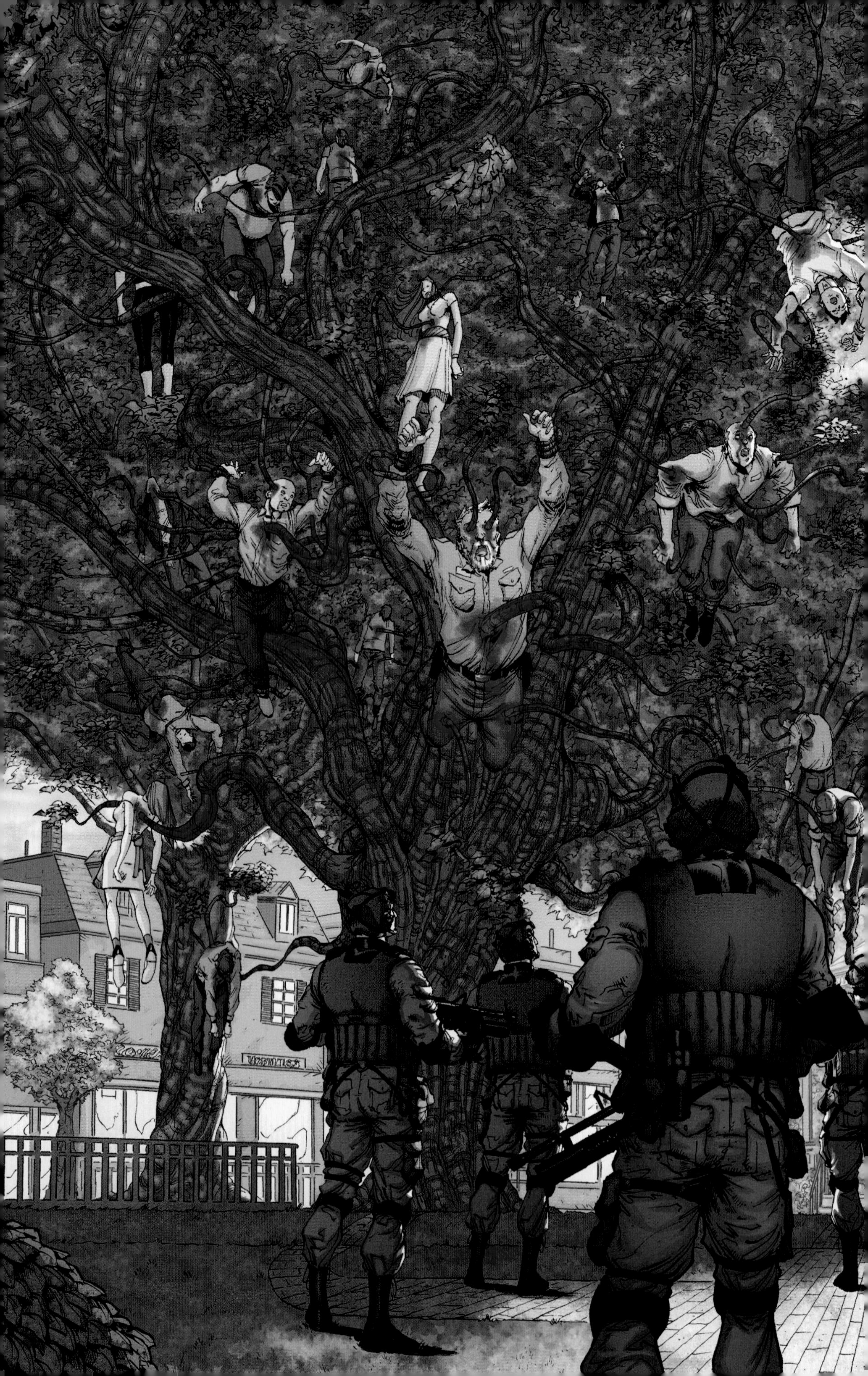

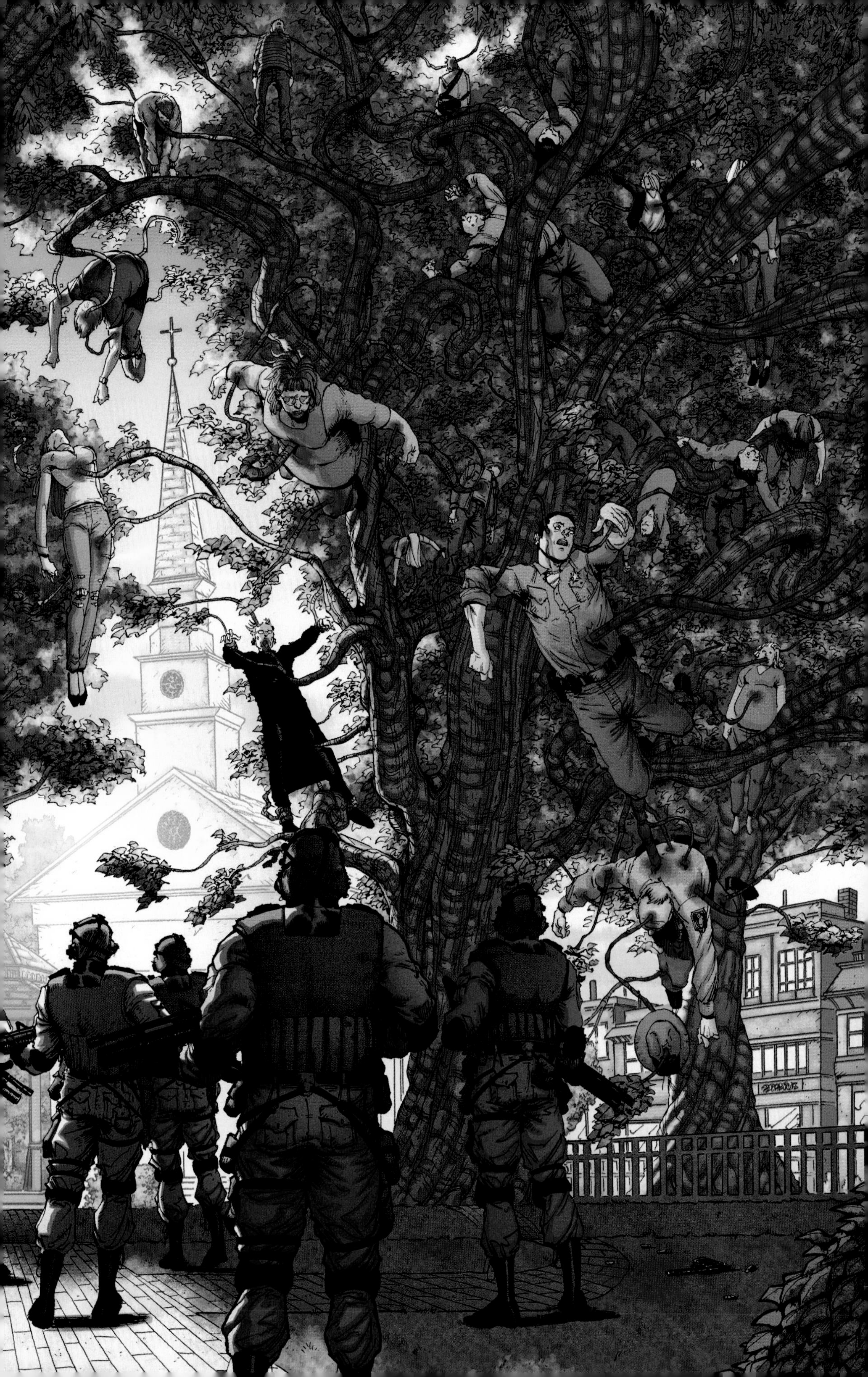

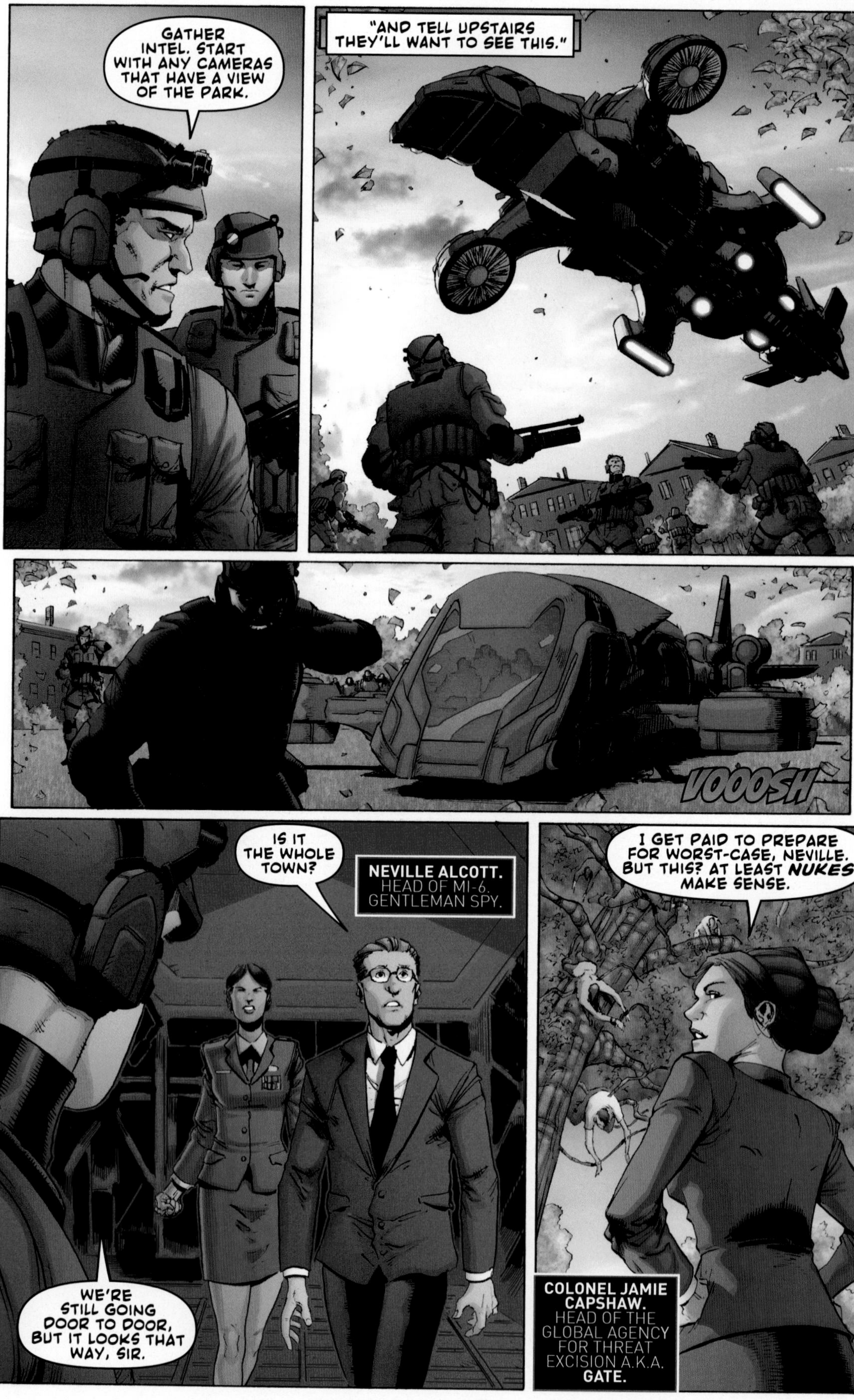
GATHER INTEL. START WITH ANY CAMERAS THAT HAVE A VIEW OF THE PARK.
"AND TELL UPSTAIRS THEY'LL WANT TO SEE THIS."
VOOOSH
IS IT THE WHOLE TOWN?
NEVILLE ALCOTT. HEAD OF MI-6. GENTLEMAN SPY.
WE'RE STILL GOING DOOR TO DOOR, BUT IT LOOKS THAT WAY, SIR.
I GET PAID TO PREPARE FOR WORST-CASE, NEVILLE. BUT THIS? AT LEAST NUKES MAKE SENSE.
COLONEL JAMIE CAPSHAW. HEAD OF THE GLOBAL AGENCY FOR THREAT EXCISION A.K.A. GATE.

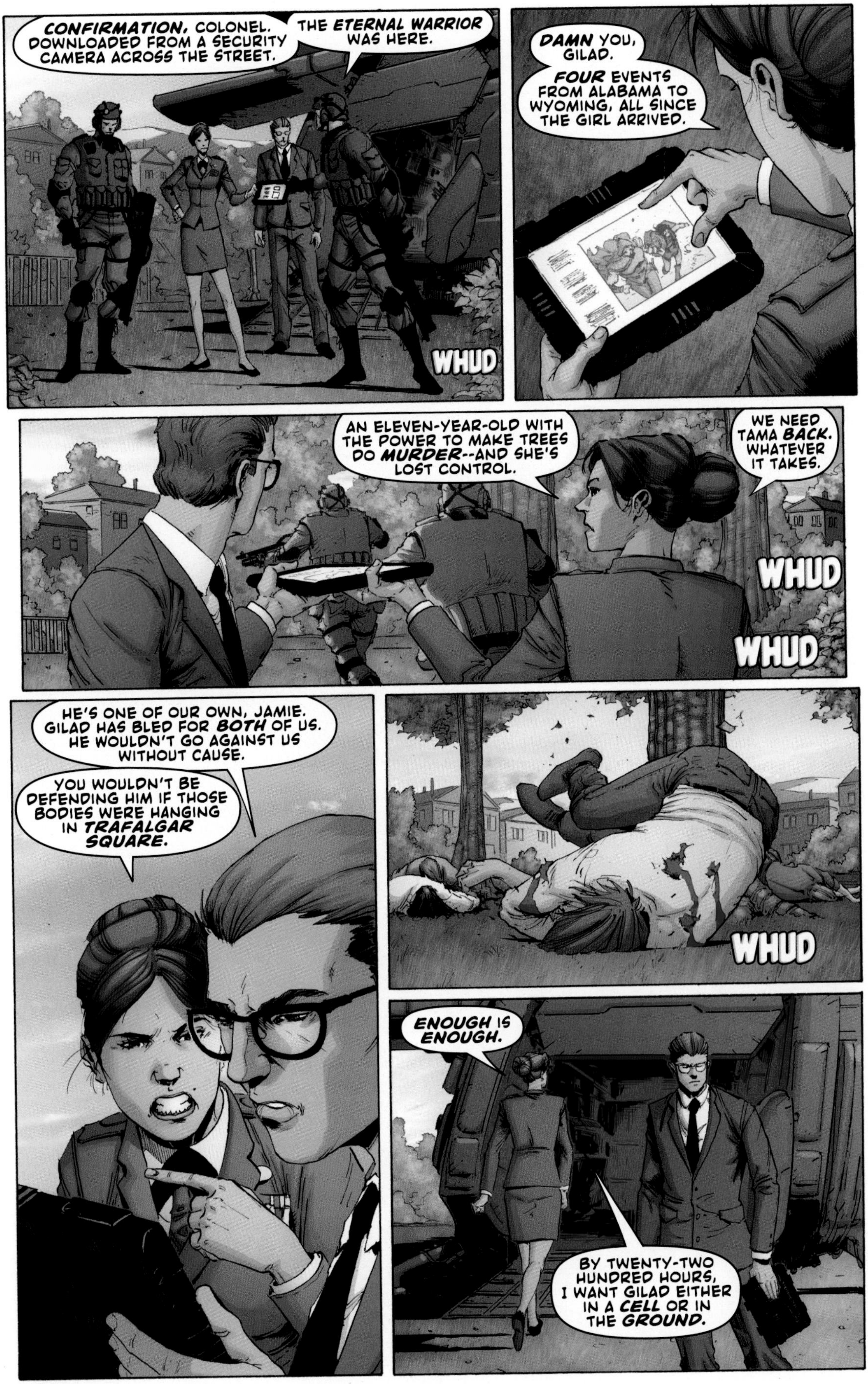
CONFIRMATION, COLONEL. DOWNLOADED FROM A SECURITY CAMERA ACROSS THE STREET.
THE ETERNAL WARRIOR WAS HERE.
WHUD
DAMN YOU, GILAD.
FOUR EVENTS FROM ALABAMA TO WYOMING, ALL SINCE THE GIRL ARRIVED.
AN ELEVEN-YEAR-OLD WITH THE POWER TO MAKE TREES DO MURDER--AND SHE'S LOST CONTROL.
WE NEED TAMA BACK. WHATEVER IT TAKES.
WHUD
WHUD
HE'S ONE OF OUR OWN, JAMIE. GILAD HAS BLED FOR BOTH OF US. HE WOULDN'T GO AGAINST US WITHOUT CAUSE.
YOU WOULDN'T BE DEFENDING HIM IF THOSE BODIES WERE HANGING IN TRAFALGAR SQUARE.
WHUD
ENOUGH IS ENOUGH.
BY TWENTY-TWO HUNDRED HOURS, I WANT GILAD EITHER IN A CELL OR IN THE GROUND.

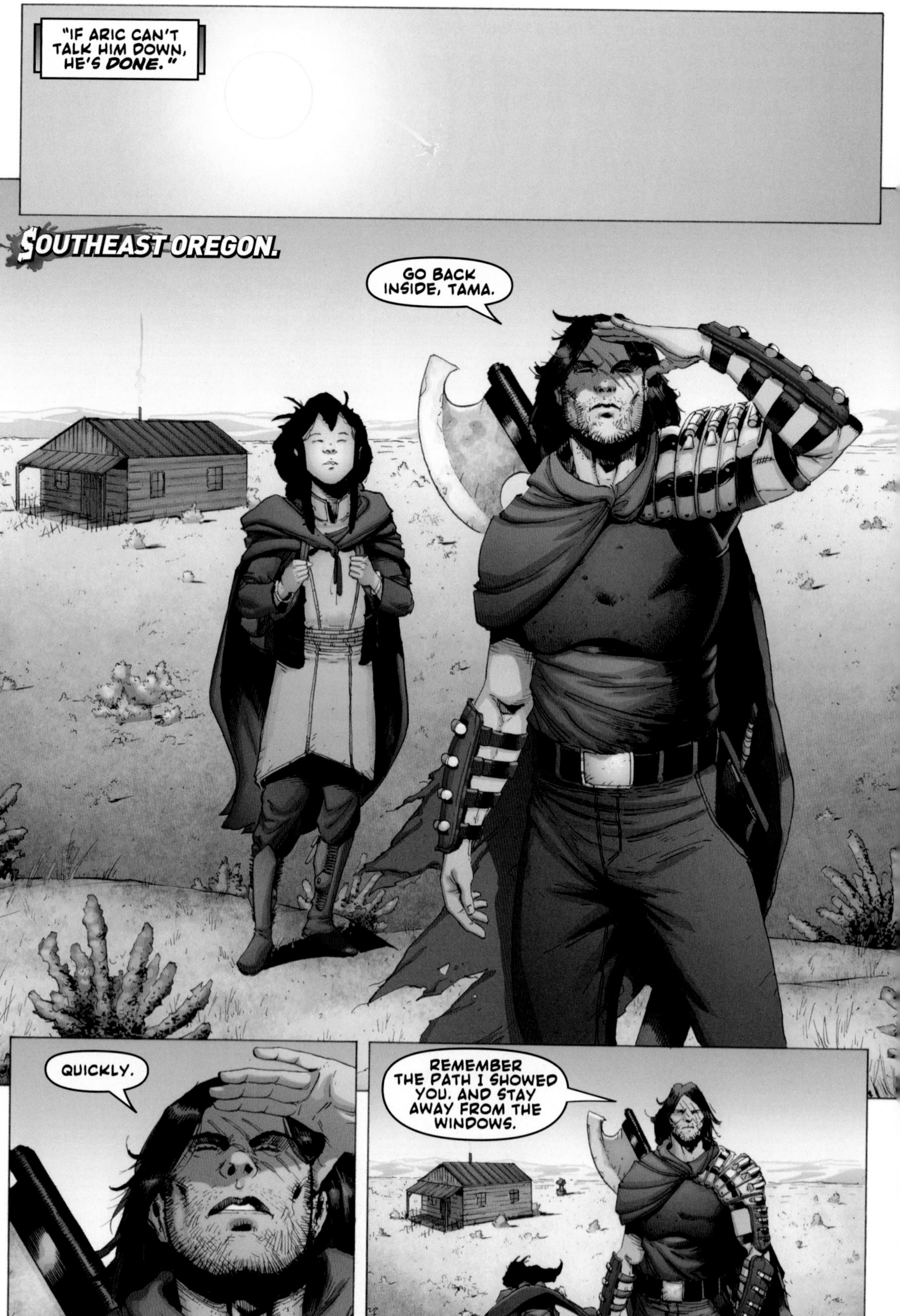
"IF ARIC CAN'T TALK HIM DOWN, HE'S DONE."
SOUTHEAST OREGON.
GO BACK INSIDE, TAMA.
QUICKLY.
REMEMBER THE PATH I SHOWED YOU. AND STAY AWAY FROM THE WINDOWS.

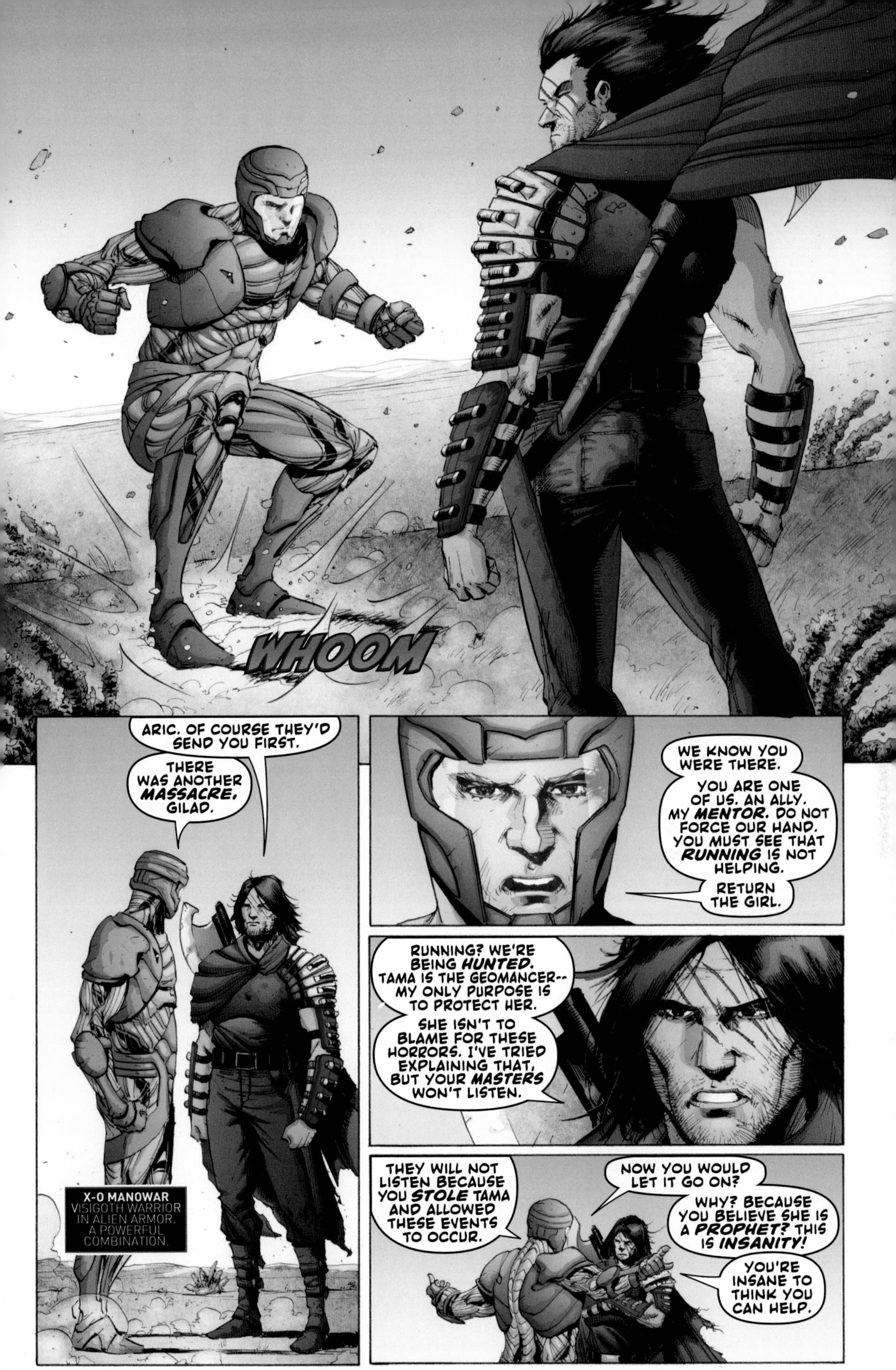
WHOOM
ARIC. OF COURSE THEY'D SEND YOU FIRST.
THERE WAS ANOTHER MASSACRE, GILAD.
X-O MANOWAR VISIGOTH WARRIOR IN ALIEN ARMOR. A POWERFUL COMBINATION.
WE KNOW YOU WERE THERE.
YOU ARE ONE OF US. AN ALLY. MY MENTOR. DO NOT FORCE OUR HAND. YOU MUST SEE THAT RUNNING IS NOT HELPING.
RETURN THE GIRL.
RUNNING? WE'RE BEING HUNTED. TAMA IS THE GEOMANCER-- MY ONLY PURPOSE IS TO PROTECT HER.
SHE ISN'T TO BLAME FOR THESE HORRORS. I'VE TRIED EXPLAINING THAT, BUT YOUR MASTERS WON'T LISTEN.
THEY WILL NOT LISTEN BECAUSE YOU STOLE TAMA AND ALLOWED THESE EVENTS TO OCCUR.
NOW YOU WOULD LET IT GO ON?
WHY? BECAUSE YOU BELIEVE SHE IS A PROPHET? THIS IS INSANITY!
YOU'RE INSANE TO THINK YOU CAN HELP.

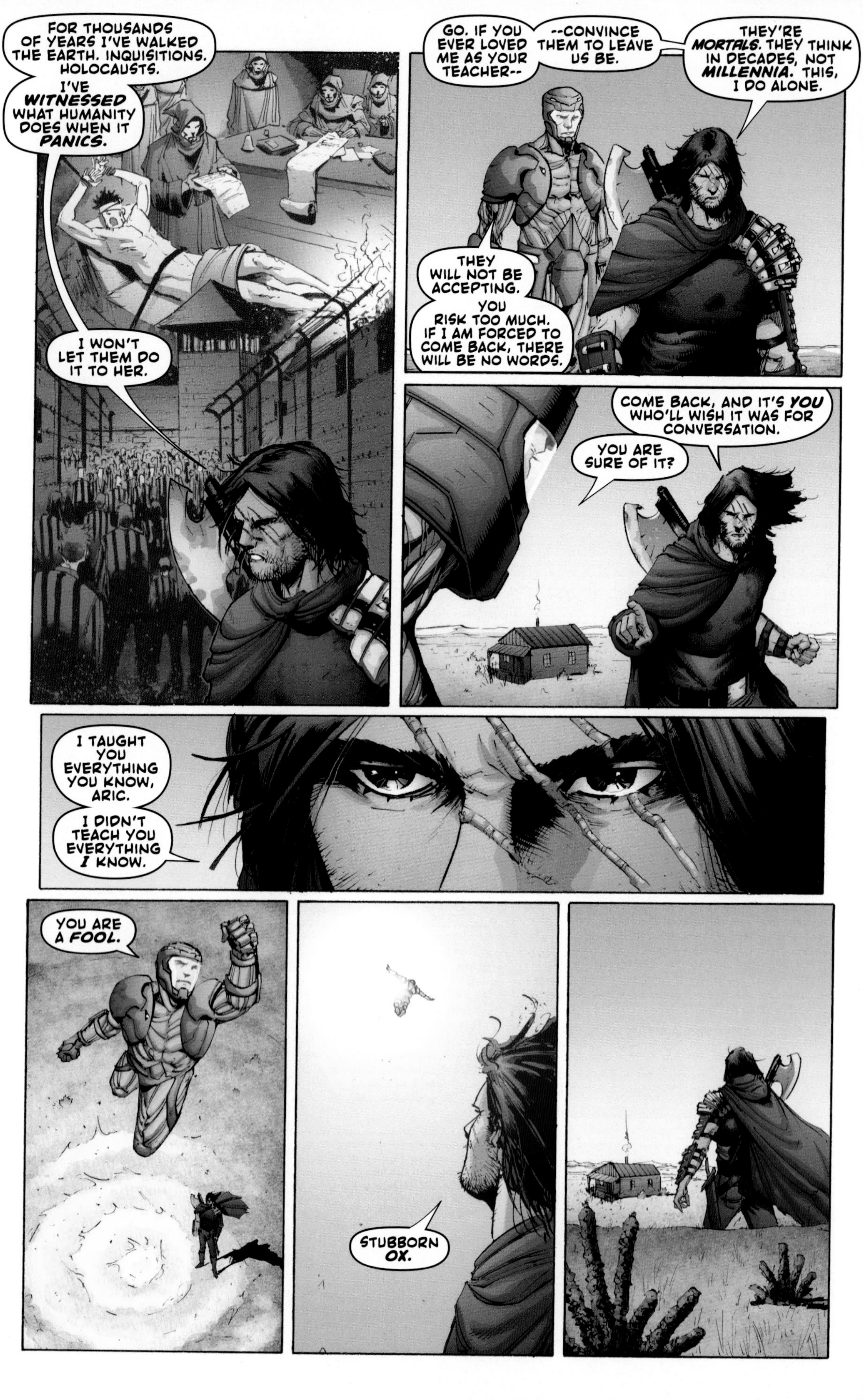
FOR THOUSANDS OF YEARS I'VE WALKED THE EARTH. INQUISITIONS. HOLOCAUSTS.
I'VE WITNESSED WHAT HUMANITY DOES WHEN IT PANICS.
I WON'T LET THEM DO IT TO HER.
GO. IF YOU EVER LOVED ME AS YOUR TEACHER--
--CONVINCE THEM TO LEAVE US BE.
THEY'RE MORTALS. THEY THINK IN DECADES, NOT MILLENNIA. THIS, I DO ALONE.
THEY WILL NOT BE ACCEPTING.
YOU RISK TOO MUCH. IF I AM FORCED TO COME BACK, THERE WILL BE NO WORDS.
COME BACK, AND IT'S YOU WHO'LL WISH IT WAS FOR CONVERSATION.
YOU ARE SURE OF IT?
I TAUGHT YOU EVERYTHING YOU KNOW, ARIC.
I DIDN'T TEACH YOU EVERYTHING I KNOW.
YOU ARE A FOOL.
STUBBORN OX.

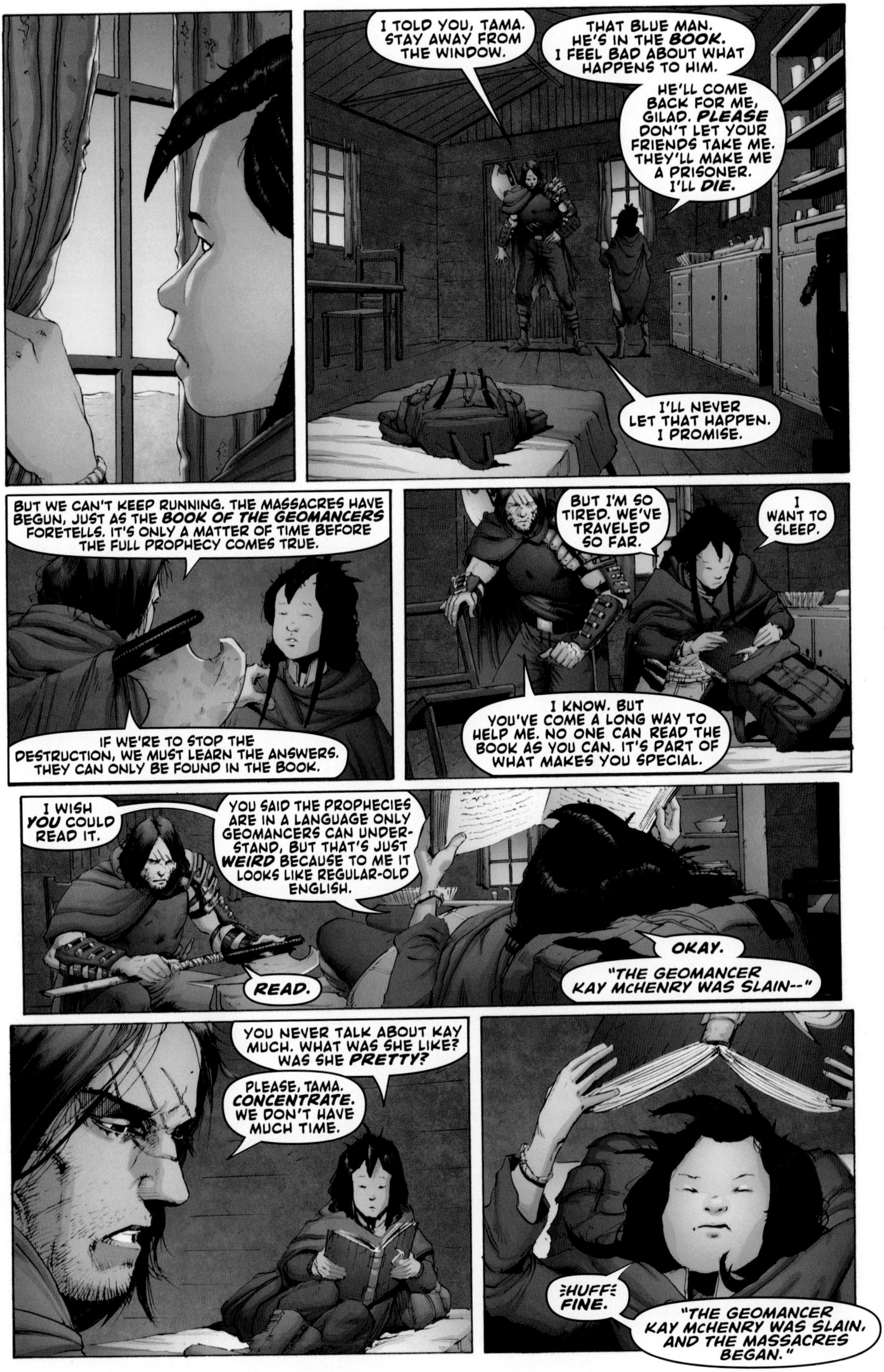
I TOLD YOU, TAMA. STAY AWAY FROM THE WINDOW.
THAT BLUE MAN. HE'S IN THE BOOK. I FEEL BAD ABOUT WHAT HAPPENS TO HIM.
HE'LL COME BACK FOR ME, GILAD. PLEASE DON'T LET YOUR FRIENDS TAKE ME. THEY'LL MAKE ME A PRISONER. I'LL DIE.
I'LL NEVER LET THAT HAPPEN. I PROMISE.
BUT WE CAN'T KEEP RUNNING. THE MASSACRES HAVE BEGUN, JUST AS THE BOOK OF THE GEOMANCERS FORETELLS. IT'S ONLY A MATTER OF TIME BEFORE THE FULL PROPHECY COMES TRUE.
IF WE'RE TO STOP THE DESTRUCTION, WE MUST LEARN THE ANSWERS. THEY CAN ONLY BE FOUND IN THE BOOK.
BUT I'M SO TIRED. WE'VE TRAVELED SO FAR.
I WANT TO SLEEP.
I KNOW. BUT YOU'VE COME A LONG WAY TO HELP ME. NO ONE CAN READ THE BOOK AS YOU CAN. IT'S PART OF WHAT MAKES YOU SPECIAL.
I WISH YOU COULD READ IT.
YOU SAID THE PROPHECIES ARE IN A LANGUAGE ONLY GEOMANCERS CAN UNDERSTAND, BUT THAT'S JUST WEIRD BECAUSE TO ME IT LOOKS LIKE REGULAR-OLD ENGLISH.
READ.
OKAY.
"THE GEOMANCER KAY McHENRY WAS SLAIN--"
YOU NEVER TALK ABOUT KAY MUCH. WHAT WAS SHE LIKE? WAS SHE PRETTY?
PLEASE, TAMA. CONCENTRATE. WE DON'T HAVE MUCH TIME.
HUFF FINE.
"THE GEOMANCER KAY McHENRY WAS SLAIN, AND THE MASSACRES BEGAN."

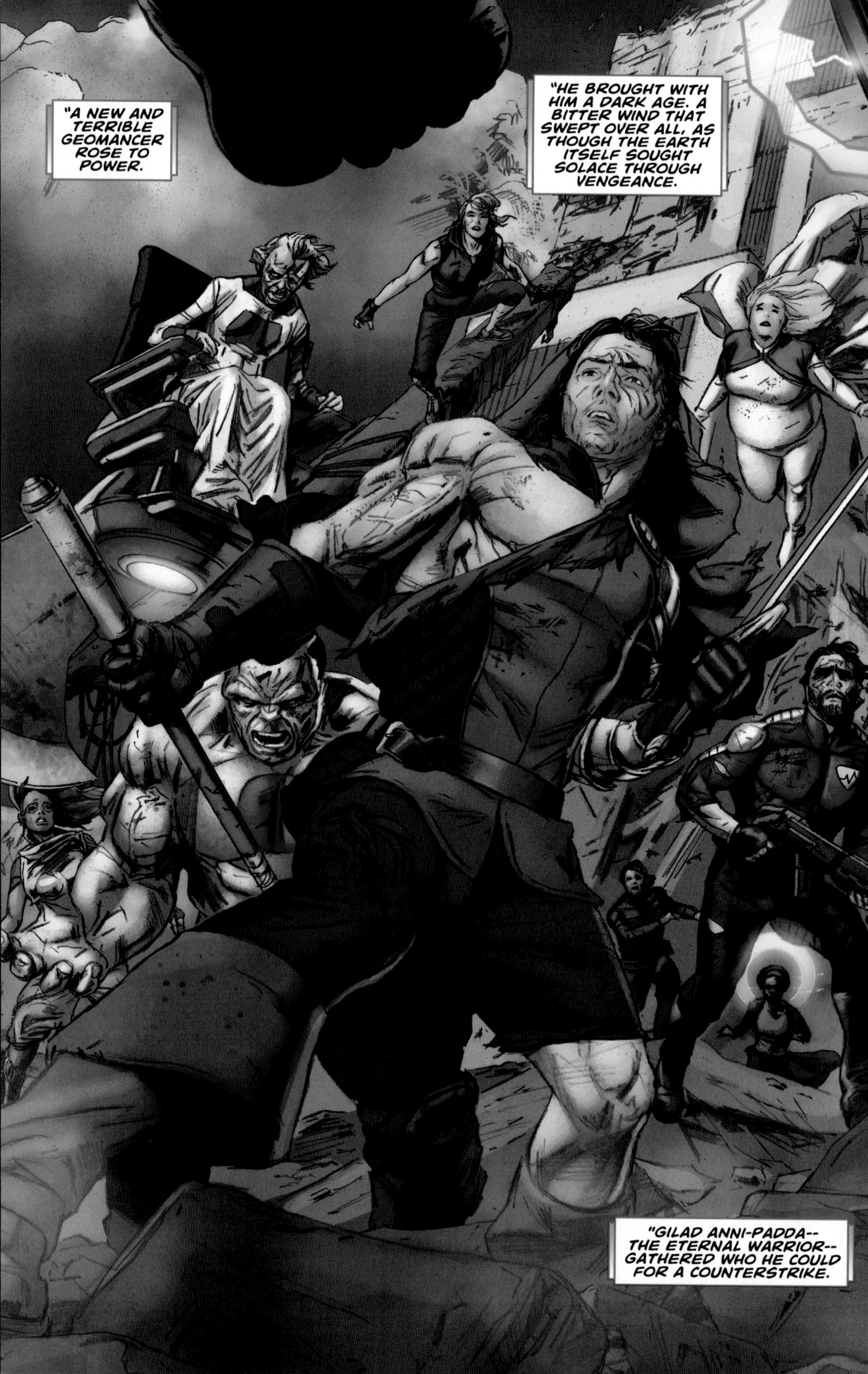
"A NEW AND TERRIBLE GEOMANCER ROSE TO POWER.
"HE BROUGHT WITH HIM A DARK AGE. A BITTER WIND THAT SWEPT OVER ALL, AS THOUGH THE EARTH ITSELF SOUGHT SOLACE THROUGH VENGEANCE.
"GILAD ANNI-PADDA-- THE ETERNAL WARRIOR-- GATHERED WHO HE COULD FOR A COUNTERSTRIKE.

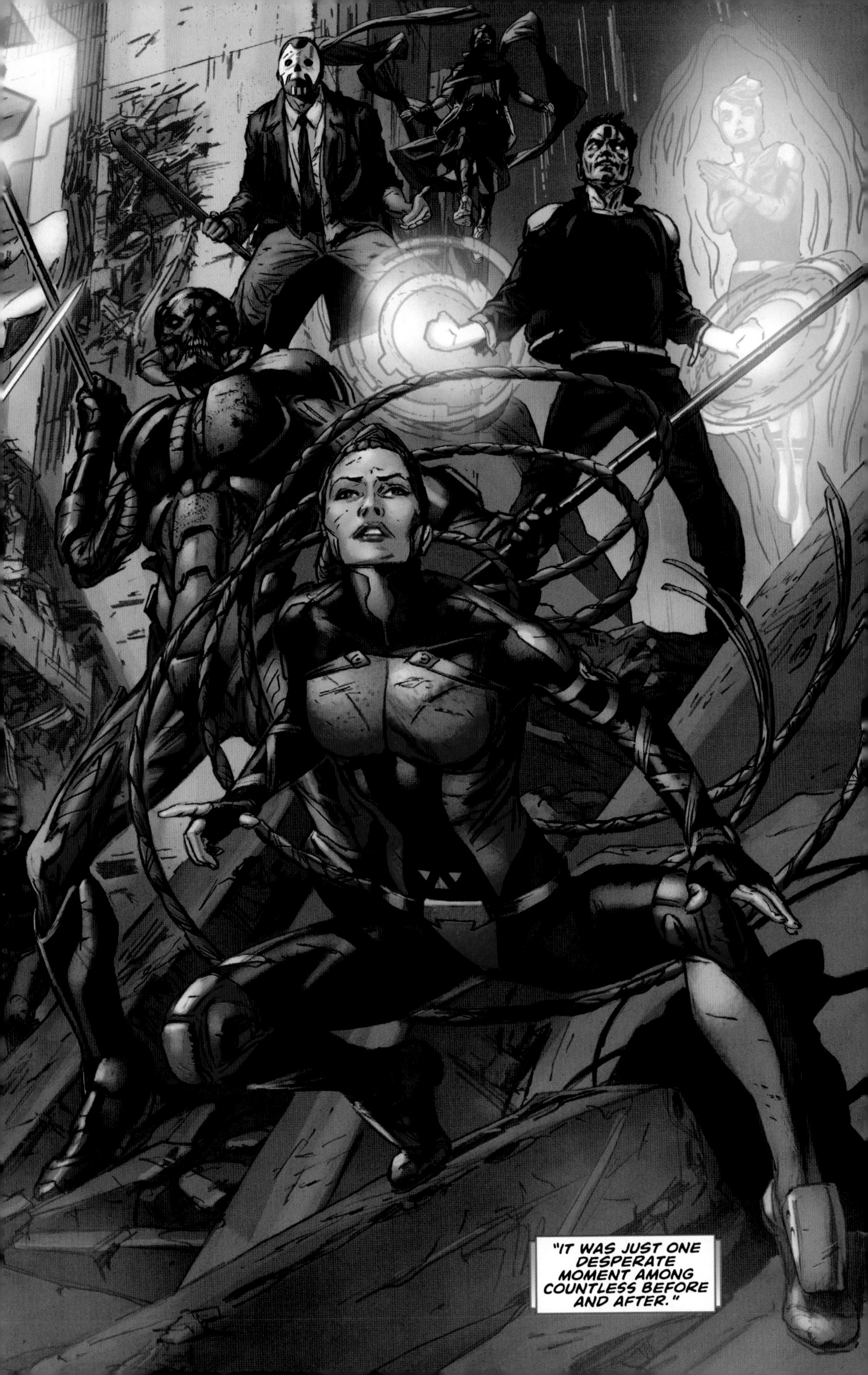
"IT WAS JUST ONE DESPERATE MOMENT AMONG COUNTLESS BEFORE AND AFTER."

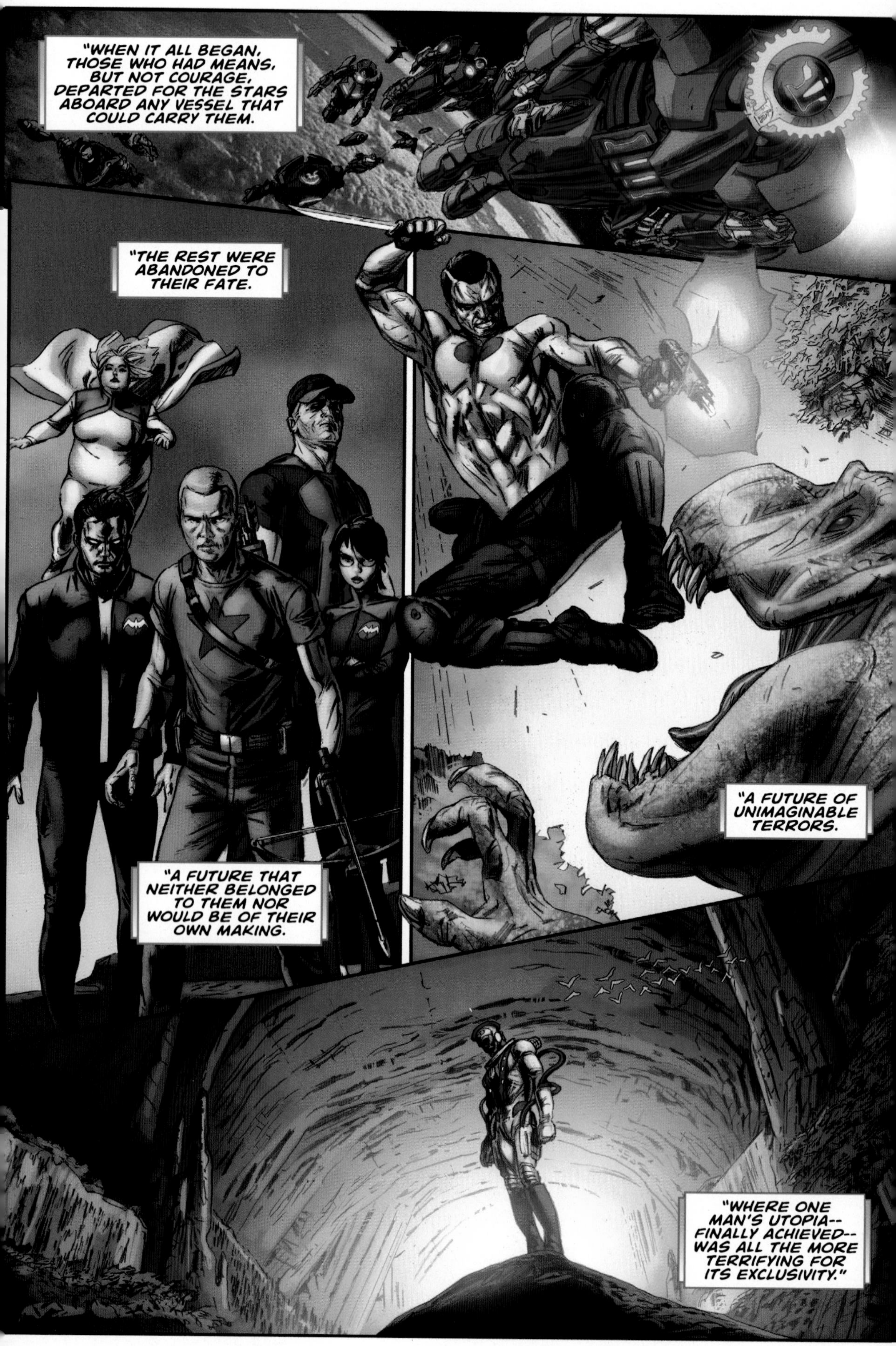
"WHEN IT ALL BEGAN, THOSE WHO HAD MEANS, BUT NOT COURAGE, DEPARTED FOR THE STARS ABOARD ANY VESSEL THAT COULD CARRY THEM.
"THE REST WERE ABANDONED TO THEIR FATE.
"A FUTURE THAT NEITHER BELONGED TO THEM NOR WOULD BE OF THEIR OWN MAKING.
"A FUTURE OF UNIMAGINABLE TERRORS.
"WHERE ONE MAN'S UTOPIA-- FINALLY ACHIEVED-- WAS ALL THE MORE TERRIFYING FOR ITS EXCLUSIVITY."

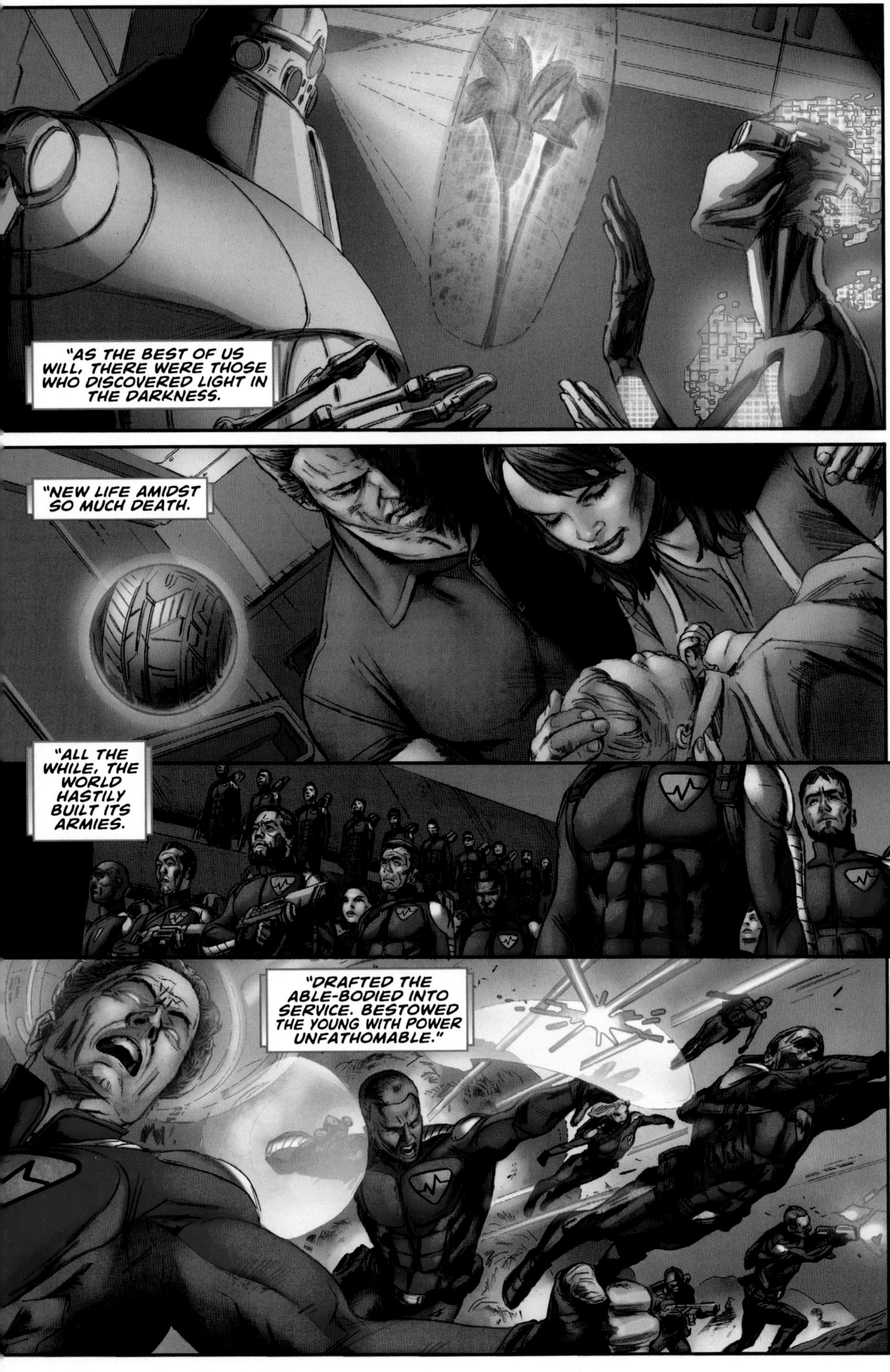
"AS THE BEST OF US WILL, THERE WERE THOSE WHO DISCOVERED LIGHT IN THE DARKNESS.
"NEW LIFE AMIDST SO MUCH DEATH.
"ALL THE WHILE, THE WORLD HASTILY BUILT ITS ARMIES.
"DRAFTED THE ABLE-BODIED INTO SERVICE. BESTOWED THE YOUNG WITH POWER UNFATHOMABLE."

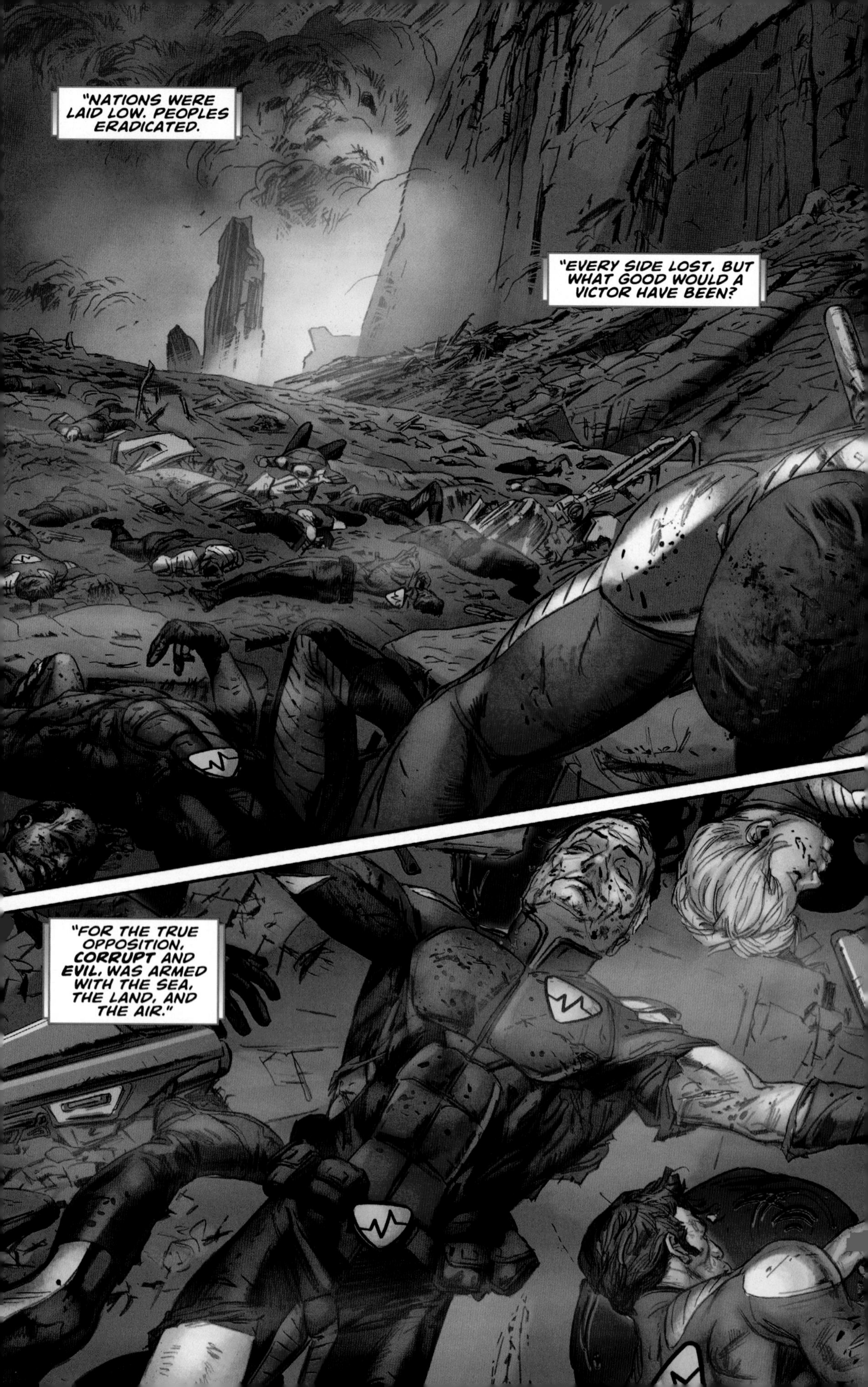
"NATIONS WERE LAID LOW. PEOPLES ERADICATED.
"EVERY SIDE LOST. BUT WHAT GOOD WOULD A VICTOR HAVE BEEN?
"FOR THE TRUE OPPOSITION, **CORRUPT** AND **EVIL**, WAS ARMED WITH THE SEA, THE LAND, AND THE AIR."

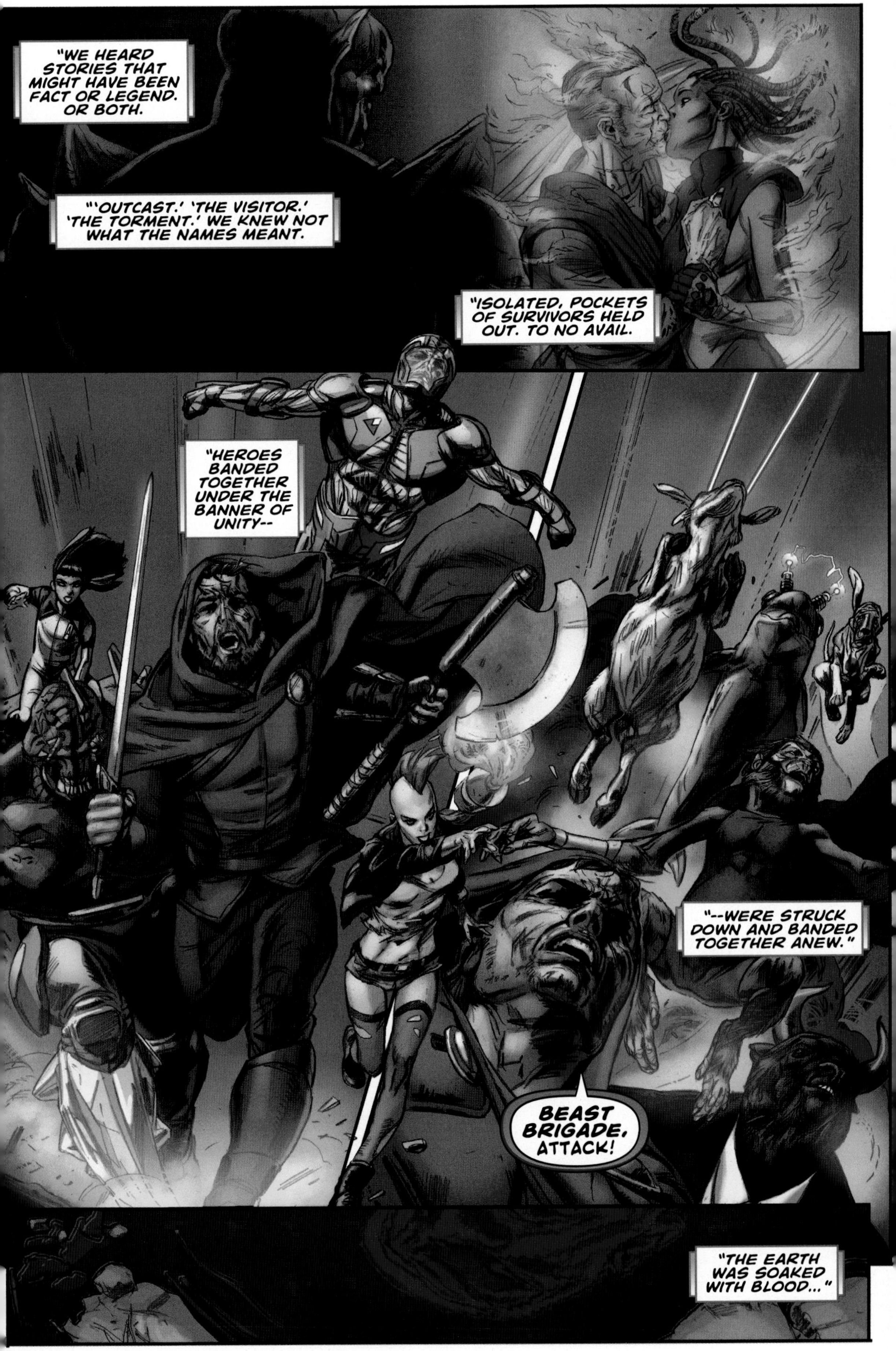
"WE HEARD STORIES THAT MIGHT HAVE BEEN FACT OR LEGEND. OR BOTH.
"'OUTCAST.' 'THE VISITOR.' 'THE TORMENT.' WE KNEW NOT WHAT THE NAMES MEANT.
"ISOLATED, POCKETS OF SURVIVORS HELD OUT. TO NO AVAIL.
"HEROES BANDED TOGETHER UNDER THE BANNER OF UNITY--
"--WERE STRUCK DOWN AND BANDED TOGETHER ANEW."
BEAST BRIGADE, ATTACK!
"THE EARTH WAS SOAKED WITH BLOOD..."

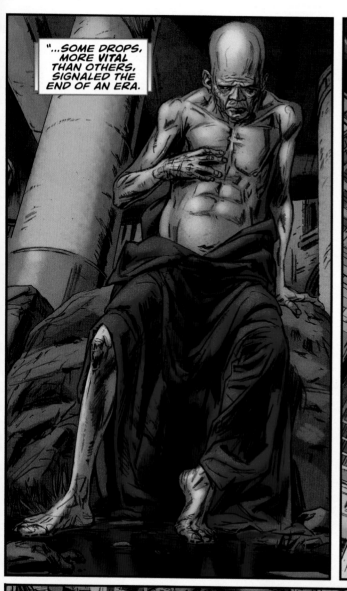

"...SOME DROPS, MORE VITAL THAN OTHERS, SIGNALED THE END OF AN ERA.

"DID WE DESERVE THE TUMULT?

"IN ALL OF HISTORY, WHY WERE WE THE ONES TO WATCH THE WORLD FALL?

"TO SEE ALL THAT WAS BUILT RECLAIMED BY THE GROUND WHENCE IT CAME?"

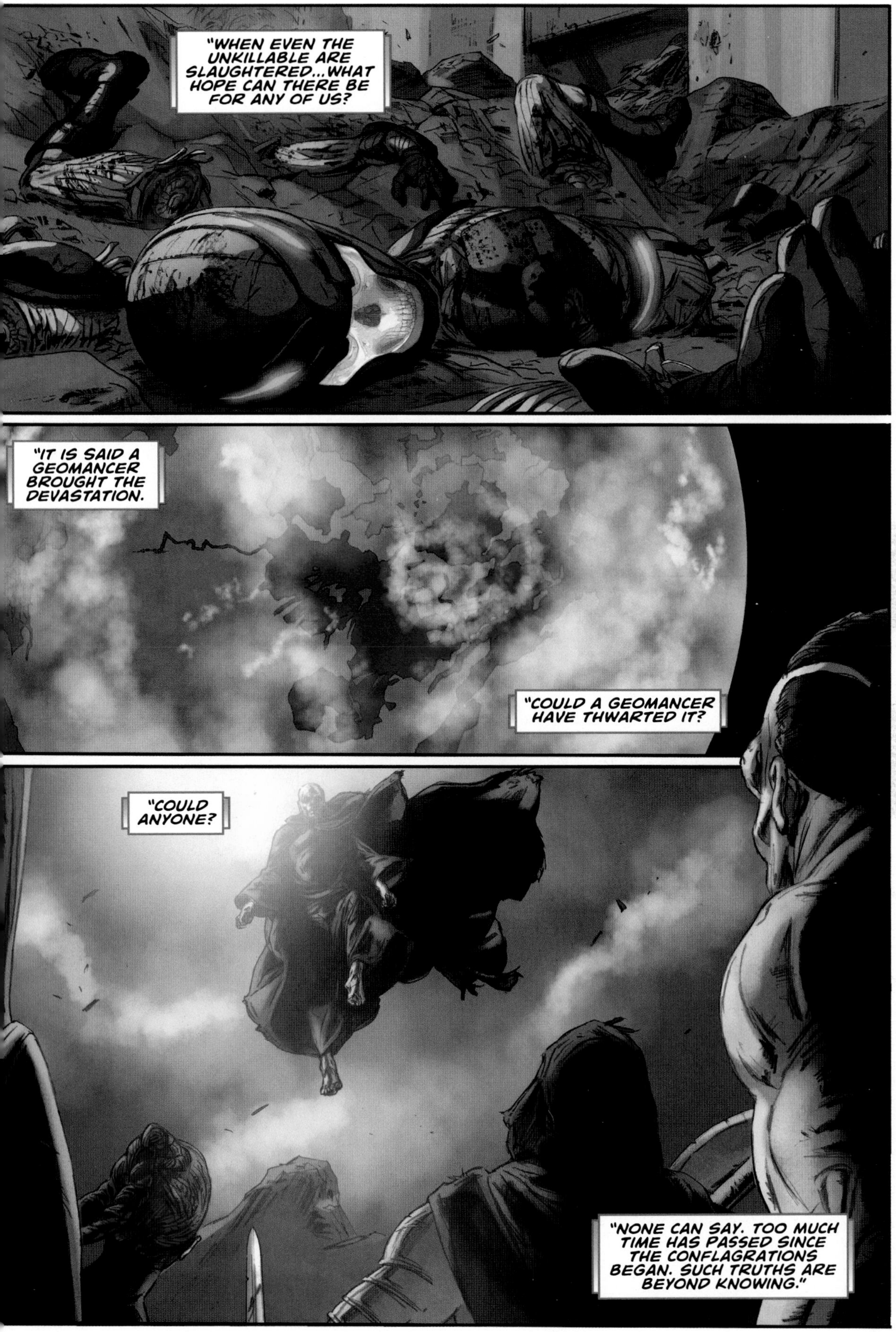
"WHEN EVEN THE UNKILLABLE ARE SLAUGHTERED...WHAT HOPE CAN THERE BE FOR ANY OF US?
"IT IS SAID A GEOMANCER BROUGHT THE DEVASTATION.
"COULD A GEOMANCER HAVE THWARTED IT?
"COULD ANYONE?
"NONE CAN SAY. TOO MUCH TIME HAS PASSED SINCE THE CONFLAGRATIONS BEGAN. SUCH TRUTHS ARE BEYOND KNOWING."

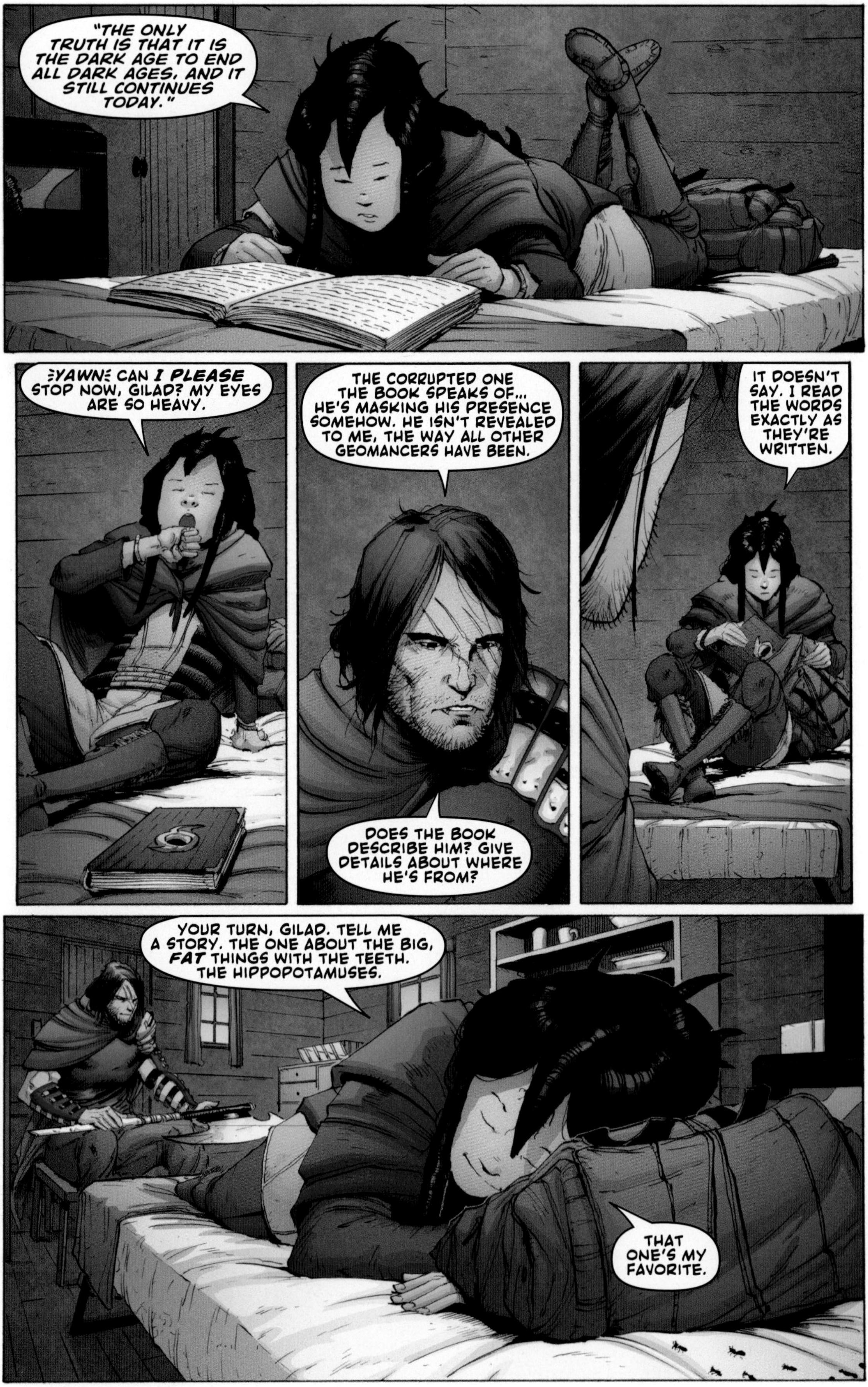
"THE ONLY TRUTH IS THAT IT IS THE DARK AGE TO END ALL DARK AGES, AND IT STILL CONTINUES TODAY."
≡YAWN≡ CAN I PLEASE STOP NOW, GILAD? MY EYES ARE SO HEAVY.
THE CORRUPTED ONE THE BOOK SPEAKS OF... HE'S MASKING HIS PRESENCE SOMEHOW. HE ISN'T REVEALED TO ME, THE WAY ALL OTHER GEOMANCERS HAVE BEEN.
DOES THE BOOK DESCRIBE HIM? GIVE DETAILS ABOUT WHERE HE'S FROM?
IT DOESN'T SAY. I READ THE WORDS EXACTLY AS THEY'RE WRITTEN.
YOUR TURN, GILAD. TELL ME A STORY. THE ONE ABOUT THE BIG, FAT THINGS WITH THE TEETH. THE HIPPOPOTAMUSES.
THAT ONE'S MY FAVORITE.

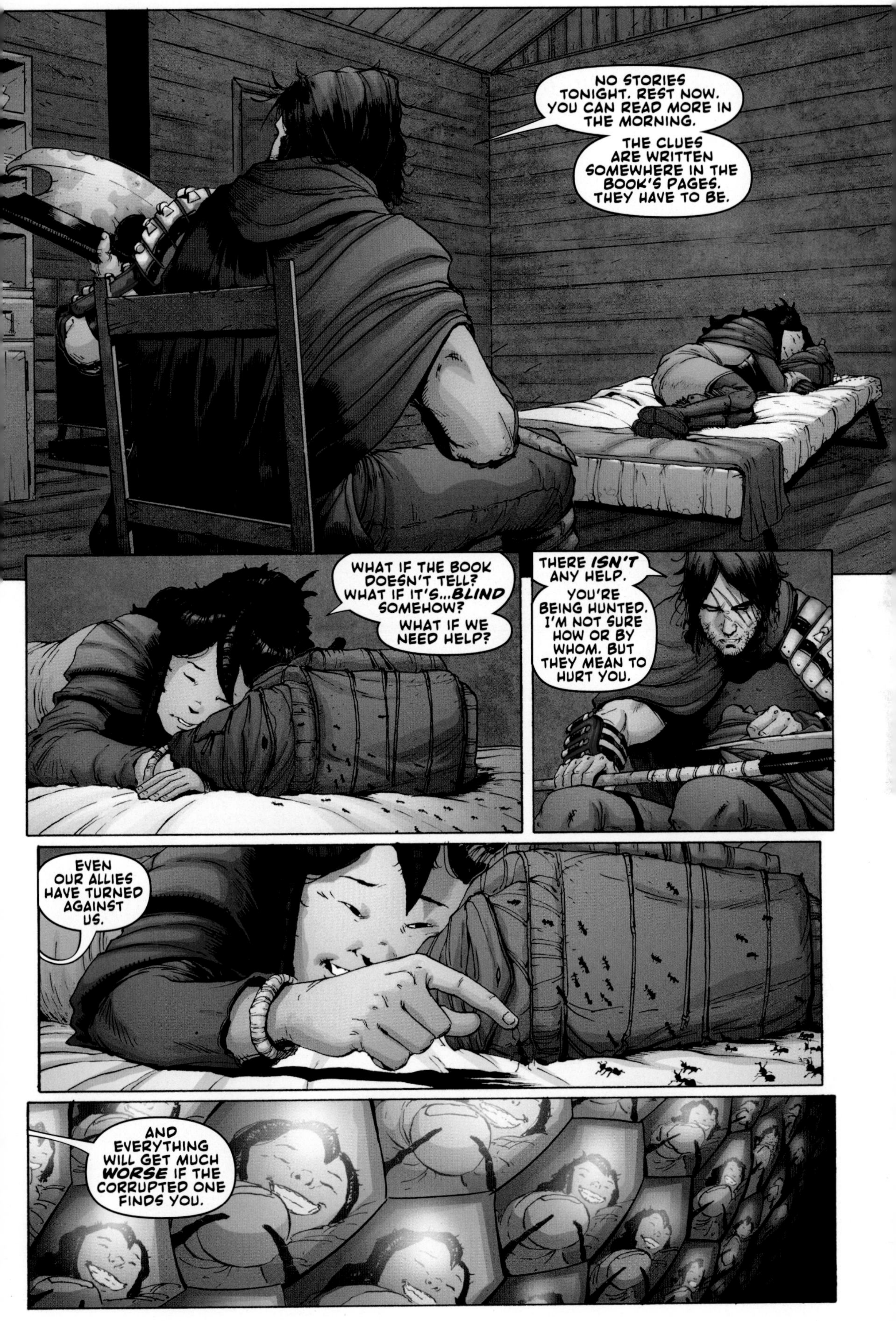
NO STORIES TONIGHT. REST NOW. YOU CAN READ MORE IN THE MORNING.
THE CLUES ARE WRITTEN SOMEWHERE IN THE BOOK'S PAGES. THEY HAVE TO BE.
WHAT IF THE BOOK DOESN'T TELL? WHAT IF IT'S...*BLIND* SOMEHOW?
WHAT IF WE NEED HELP?
THERE *ISN'T* ANY HELP.
YOU'RE BEING HUNTED. I'M NOT SURE HOW OR BY WHOM. BUT THEY MEAN TO HURT YOU.
EVEN OUR ALLIES HAVE TURNED AGAINST US.
AND EVERYTHING WILL GET MUCH *WORSE* IF THE CORRUPTED ONE FINDS YOU.

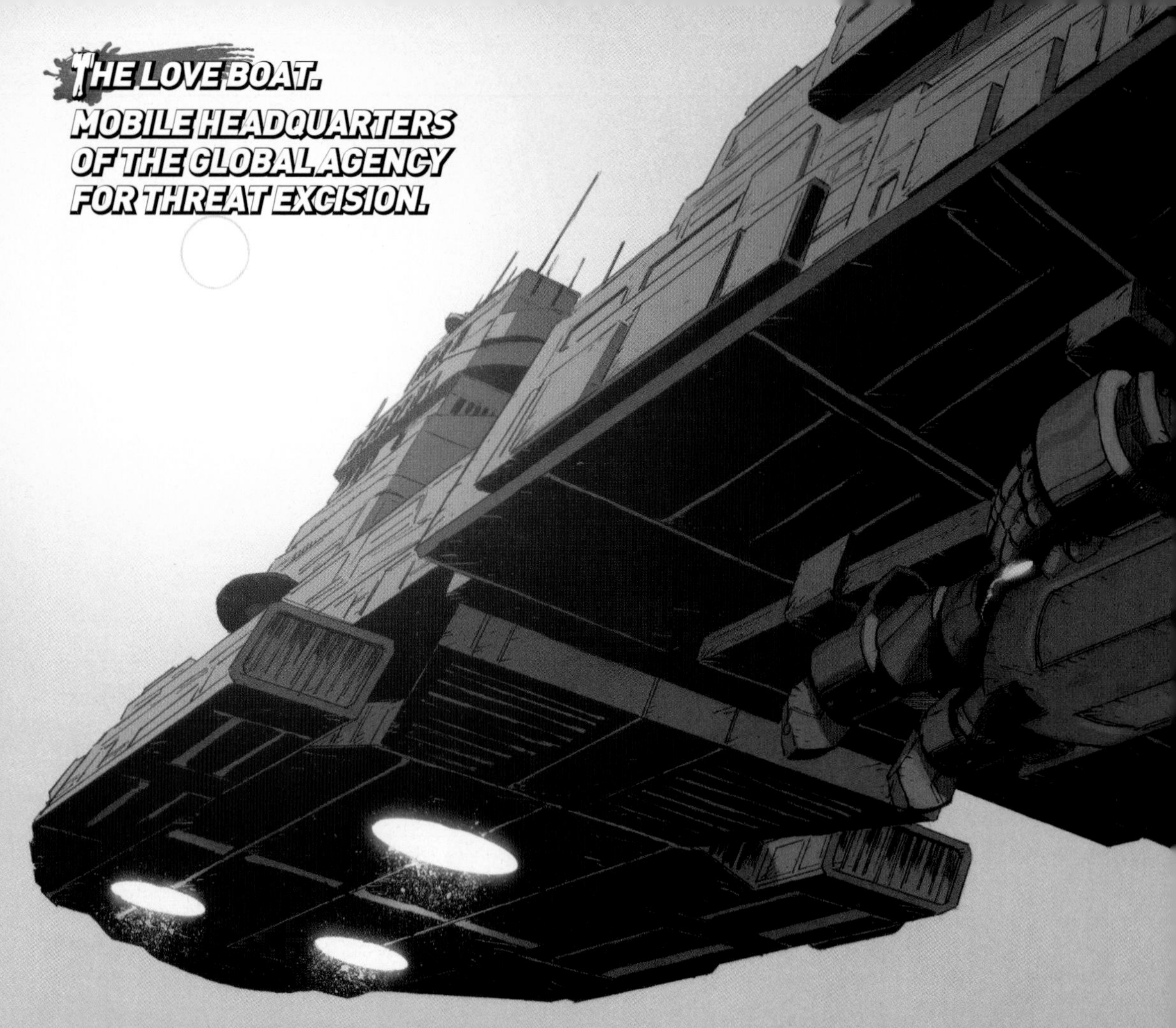
THE LOVE BOAT.
MOBILE HEADQUARTERS OF THE GLOBAL AGENCY FOR THREAT EXCISION.

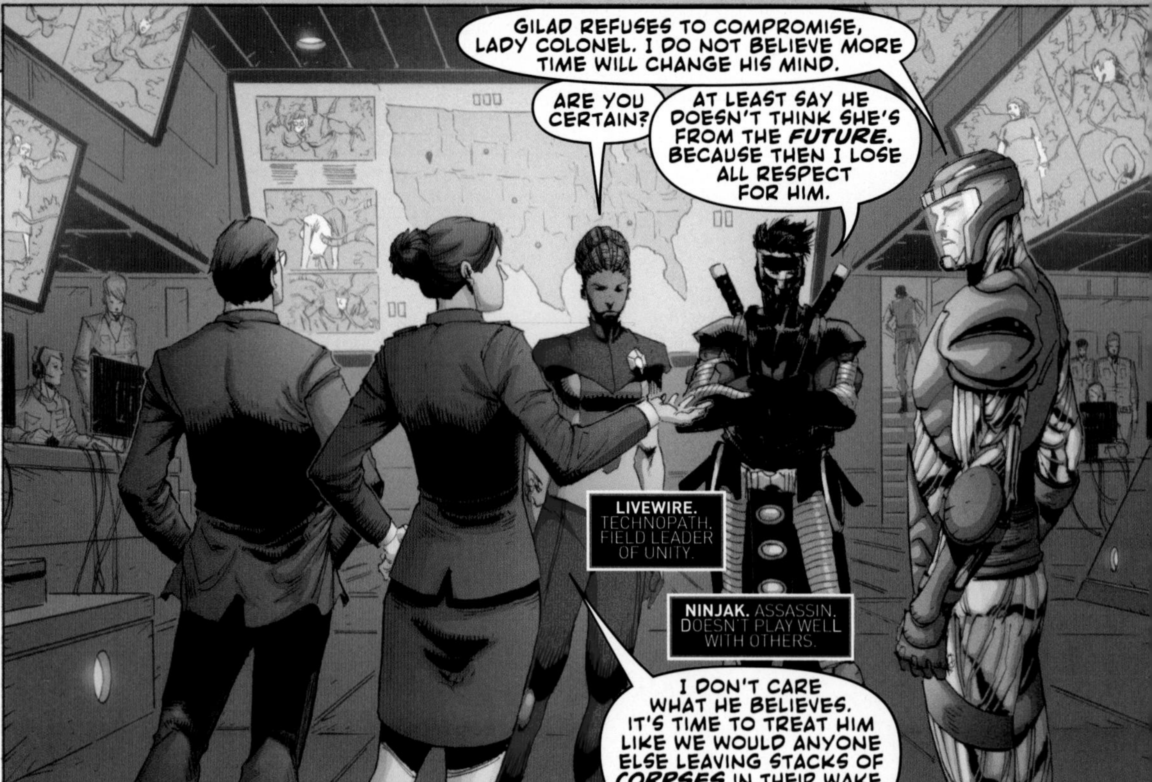
GILAD REFUSES TO COMPROMISE, LADY COLONEL. I DO NOT BELIEVE MORE TIME WILL CHANGE HIS MIND.
ARE YOU CERTAIN?
AT LEAST SAY HE DOESN'T THINK SHE'S FROM THE FUTURE. BECAUSE THEN I LOSE ALL RESPECT FOR HIM.
LIVEWIRE. TECHNOPATH. FIELD LEADER OF UNITY.
NINJAK. ASSASSIN. DOESN'T PLAY WELL WITH OTHERS.
I DON'T CARE WHAT HE BELIEVES. IT'S TIME TO TREAT HIM LIKE WE WOULD ANYONE ELSE LEAVING STACKS OF CORPSES IN THEIR WAKE.

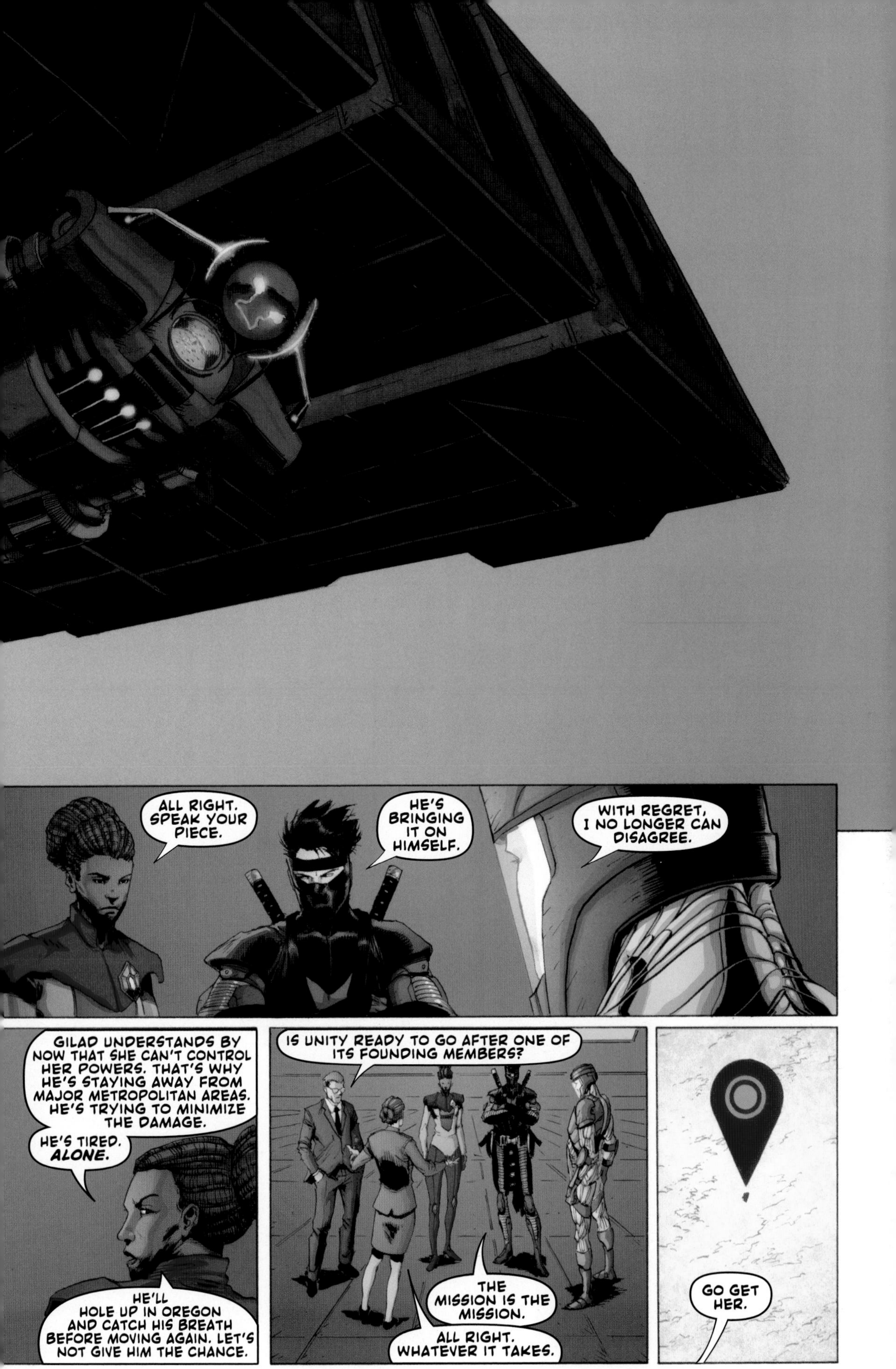

ALL RIGHT. SPEAK YOUR PIECE.
HE'S BRINGING IT ON HIMSELF.
WITH REGRET, I NO LONGER CAN DISAGREE.
GILAD UNDERSTANDS BY NOW THAT SHE CAN'T CONTROL HER POWERS. THAT'S WHY HE'S STAYING AWAY FROM MAJOR METROPOLITAN AREAS. HE'S TRYING TO MINIMIZE THE DAMAGE.
HE'S TIRED. *ALONE.*
HE'LL HOLE UP IN OREGON AND CATCH HIS BREATH BEFORE MOVING AGAIN. LET'S NOT GIVE HIM THE CHANCE.
IS UNITY READY TO GO AFTER ONE OF ITS FOUNDING MEMBERS?
THE MISSION IS THE MISSION.
ALL RIGHT. WHATEVER IT TAKES.
GO GET HER.

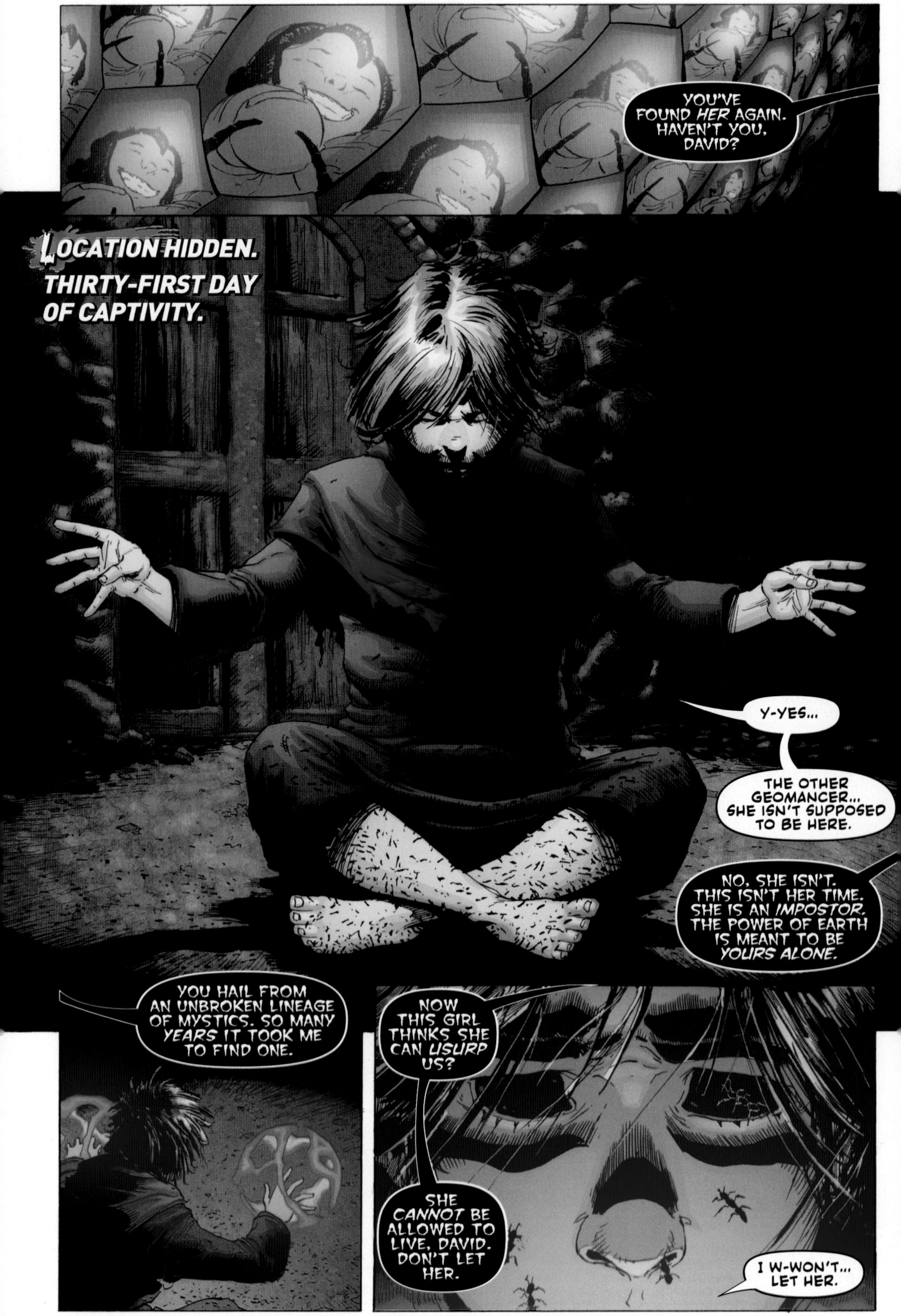
YOU'VE FOUND HER AGAIN. HAVEN'T YOU, DAVID?
LOCATION HIDDEN. THIRTY-FIRST DAY OF CAPTIVITY.
Y-YES...
THE OTHER GEOMANCER... SHE ISN'T SUPPOSED TO BE HERE.
NO, SHE ISN'T. THIS ISN'T HER TIME. SHE IS AN IMPOSTOR. THE POWER OF EARTH IS MEANT TO BE YOURS ALONE.
YOU HAIL FROM AN UNBROKEN LINEAGE OF MYSTICS. SO MANY YEARS IT TOOK ME TO FIND ONE.
NOW THIS GIRL THINKS SHE CAN USURP US?
SHE CANNOT BE ALLOWED TO LIVE, DAVID. DON'T LET HER.
I W-WON'T... LET HER.

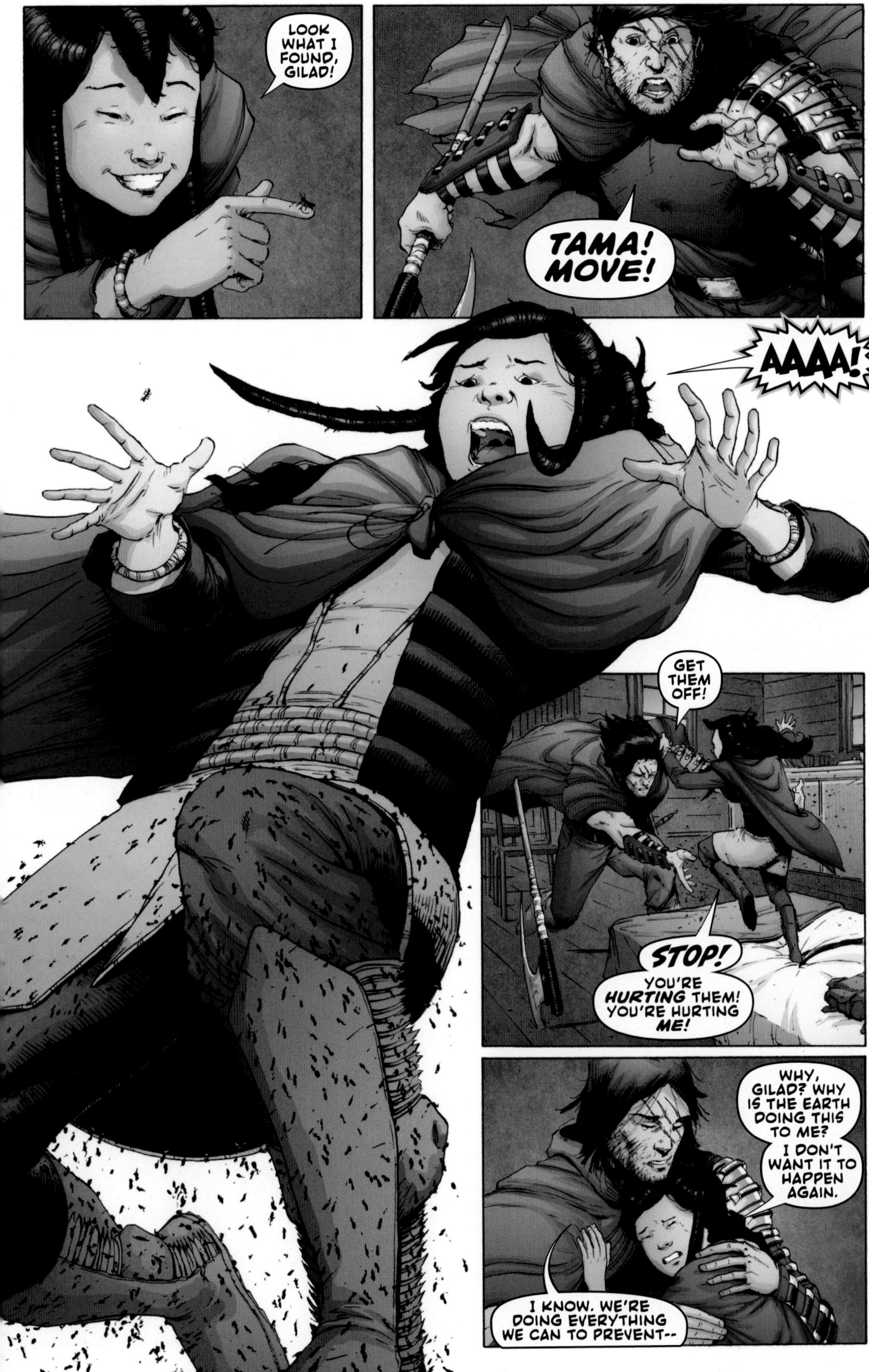
LOOK WHAT I FOUND, GILAD!
TAMA! MOVE!
AAAA!
GET THEM OFF!
STOP! YOU'RE HURTING THEM! YOU'RE HURTING ME!
WHY, GILAD? WHY IS THE EARTH DOING THIS TO ME?
I DON'T WANT IT TO HAPPEN AGAIN.
I KNOW. WE'RE DOING EVERYTHING WE CAN TO PREVENT--

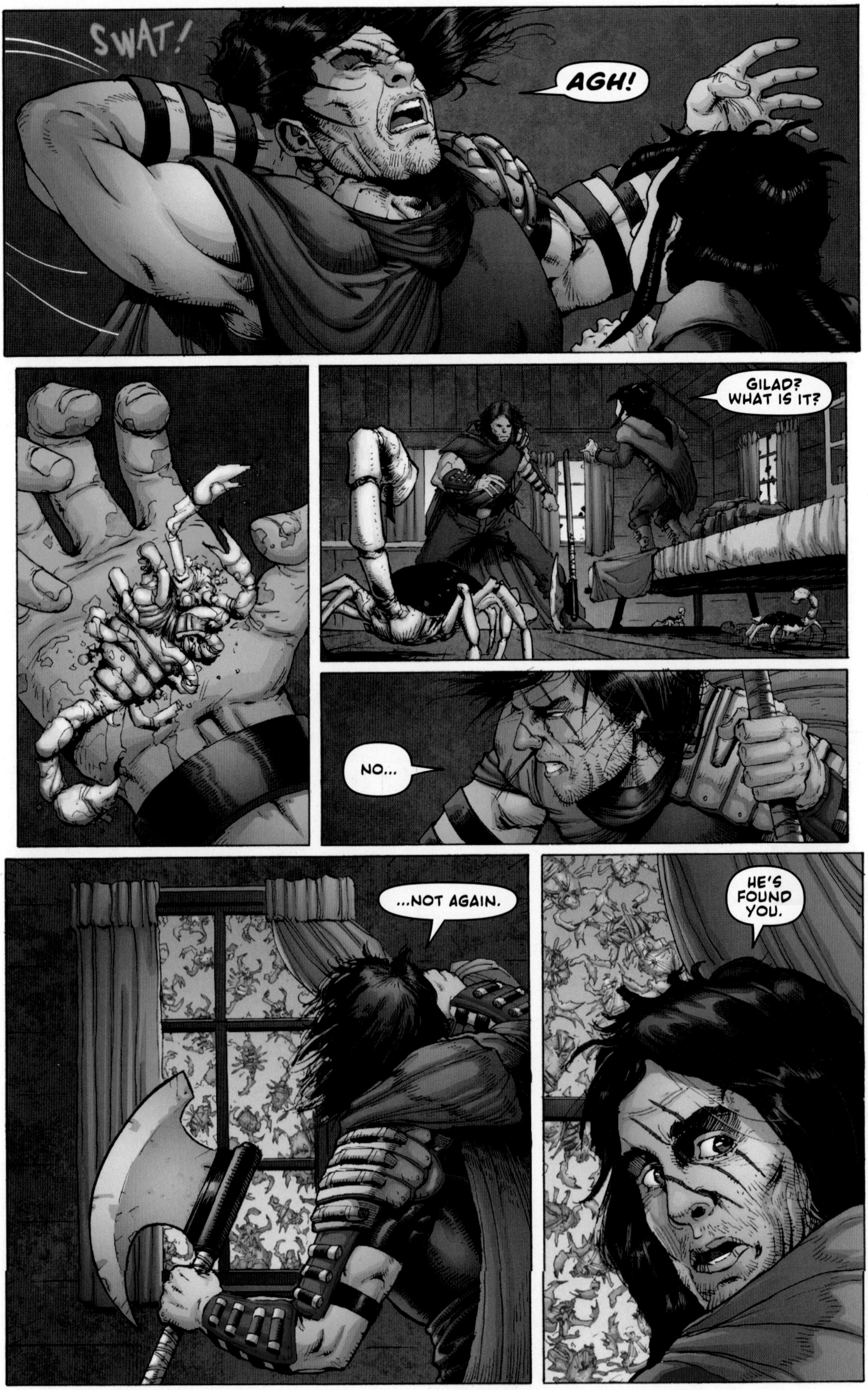
SWAT!
AGH!
GILAD? WHAT IS IT?
NO...
...NOT AGAIN.
HE'S FOUND YOU.

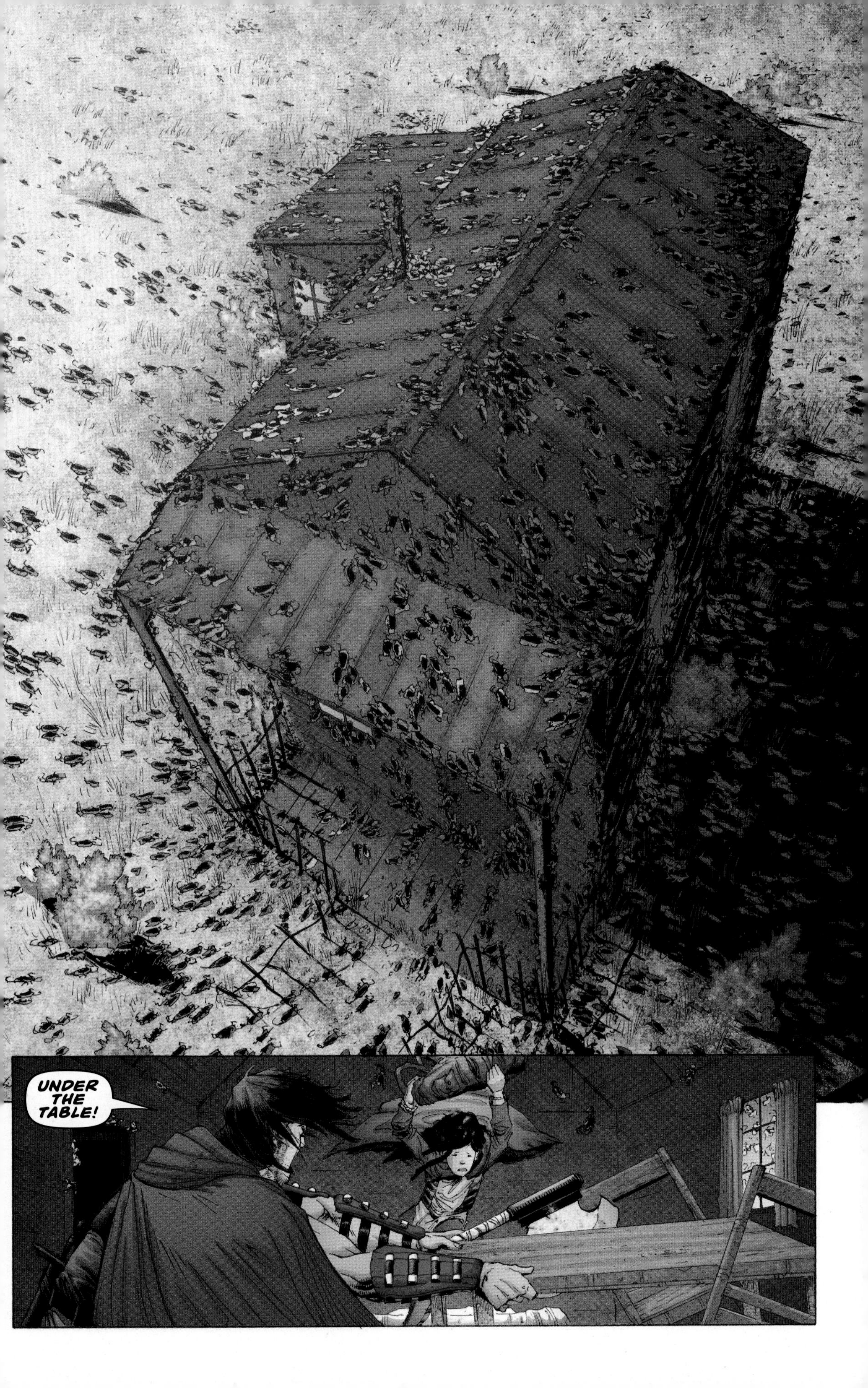
UNDER THE TABLE!

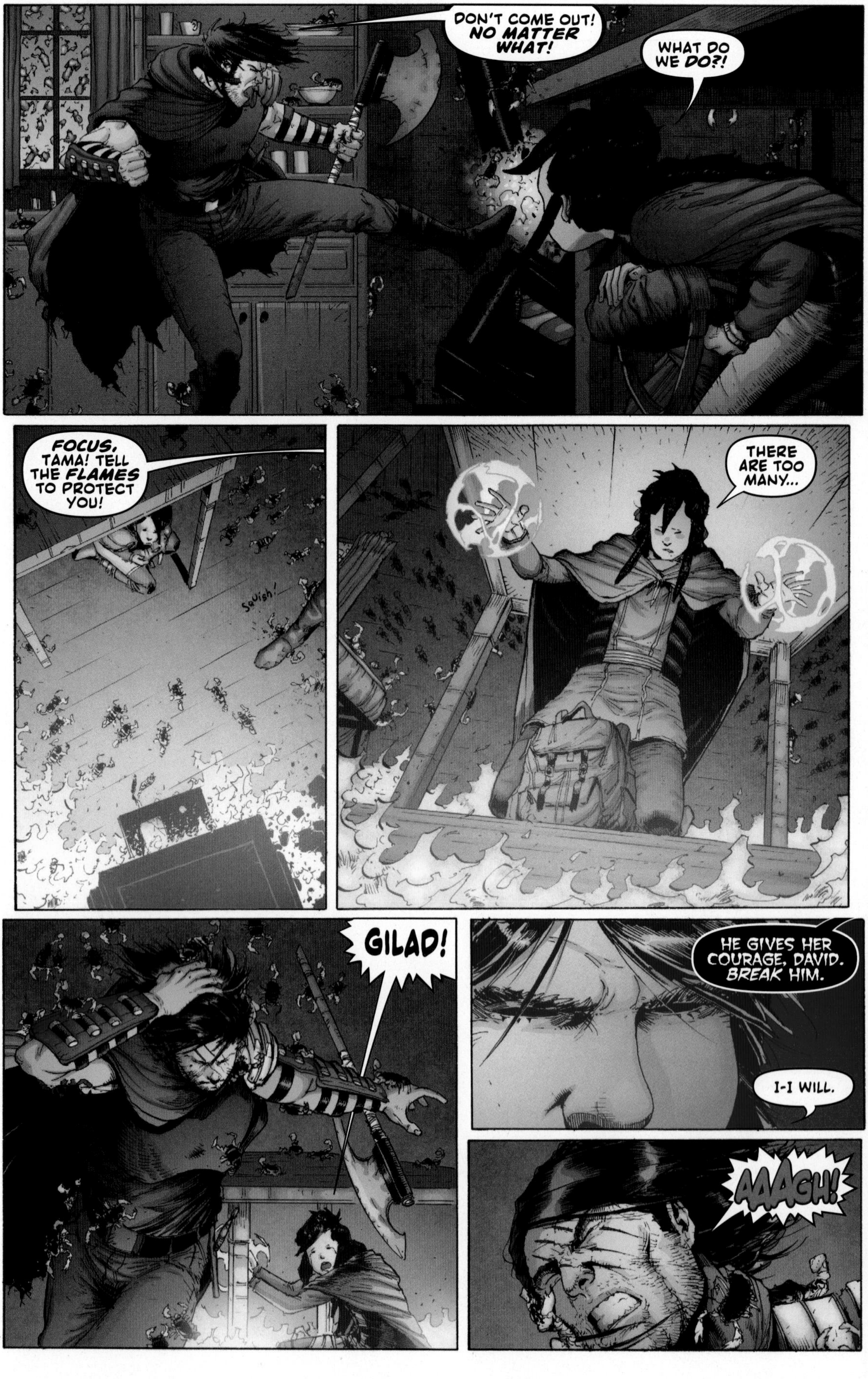
DON'T COME OUT! NO MATTER WHAT!
WHAT DO WE DO?!
FOCUS, TAMA! TELL THE FLAMES TO PROTECT YOU!
SQUISH!
THERE ARE TOO MANY...
GILAD!
HE GIVES HER COURAGE, DAVID. BREAK HIM.
I-I WILL.
AAAGH!

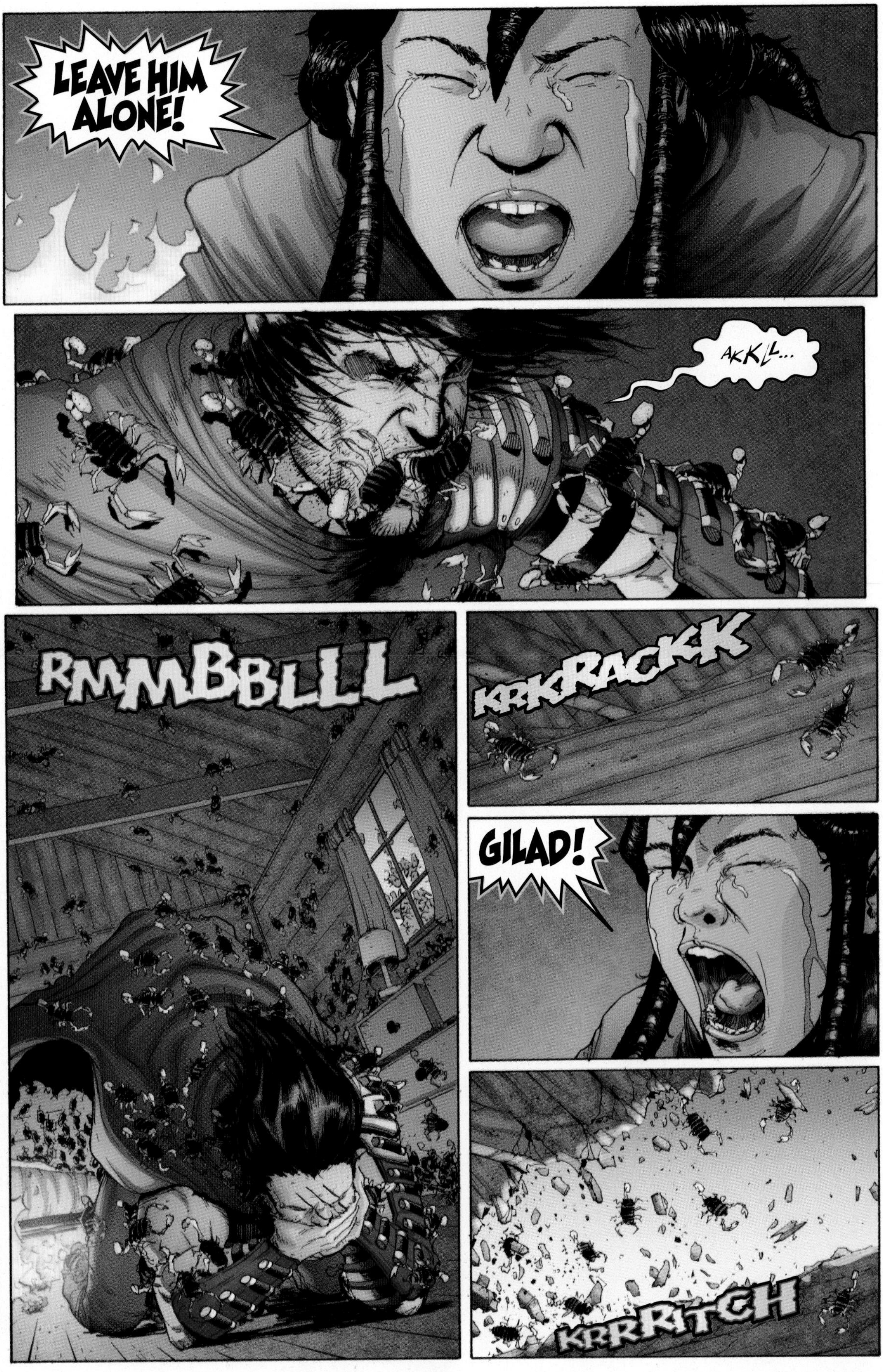
LEAVE HIM ALONE!
AKKLL...
RMMBBLLL
KRKRACKK
GILAD!
KRRRITCH

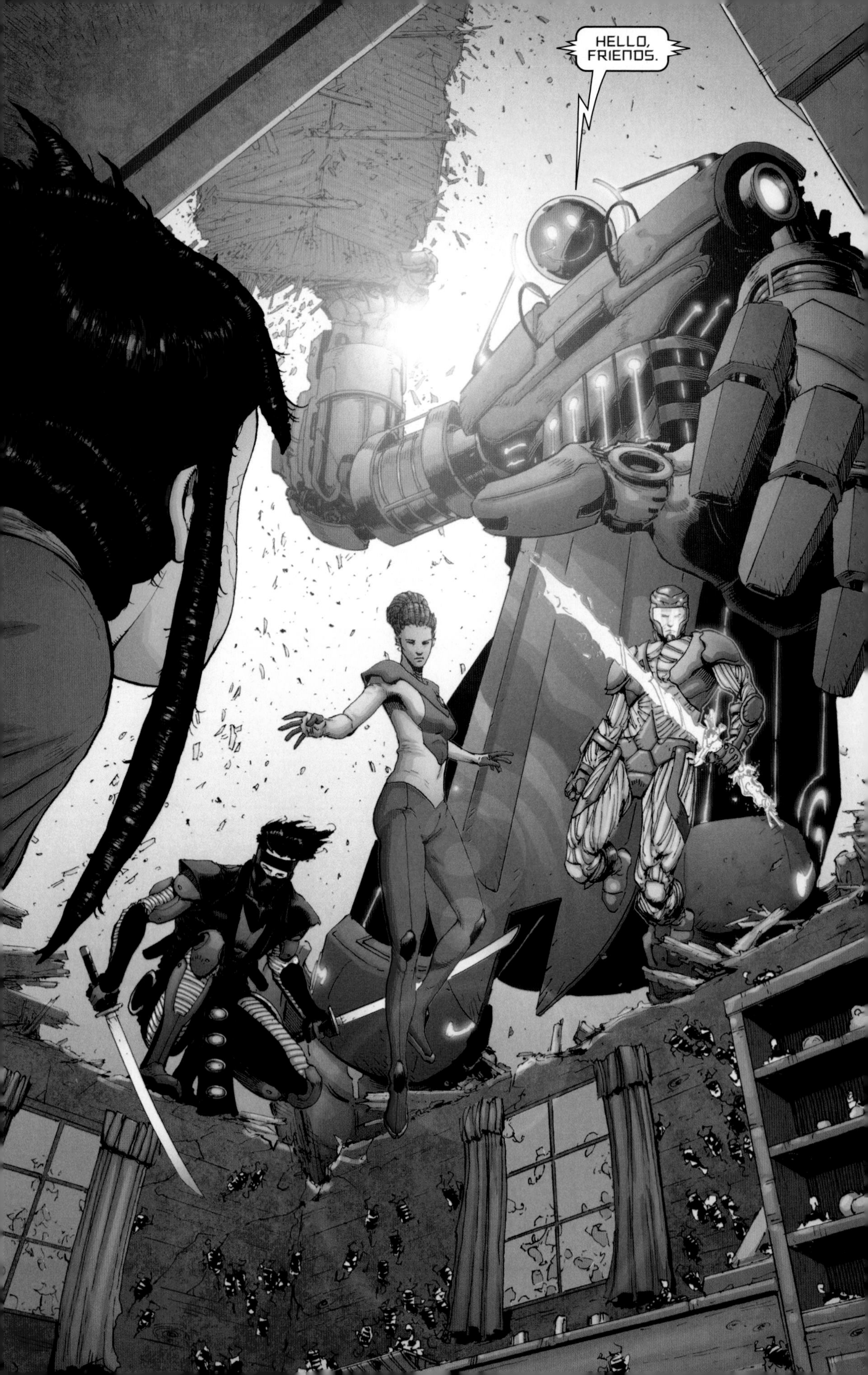
HELLO, FRIENDS.

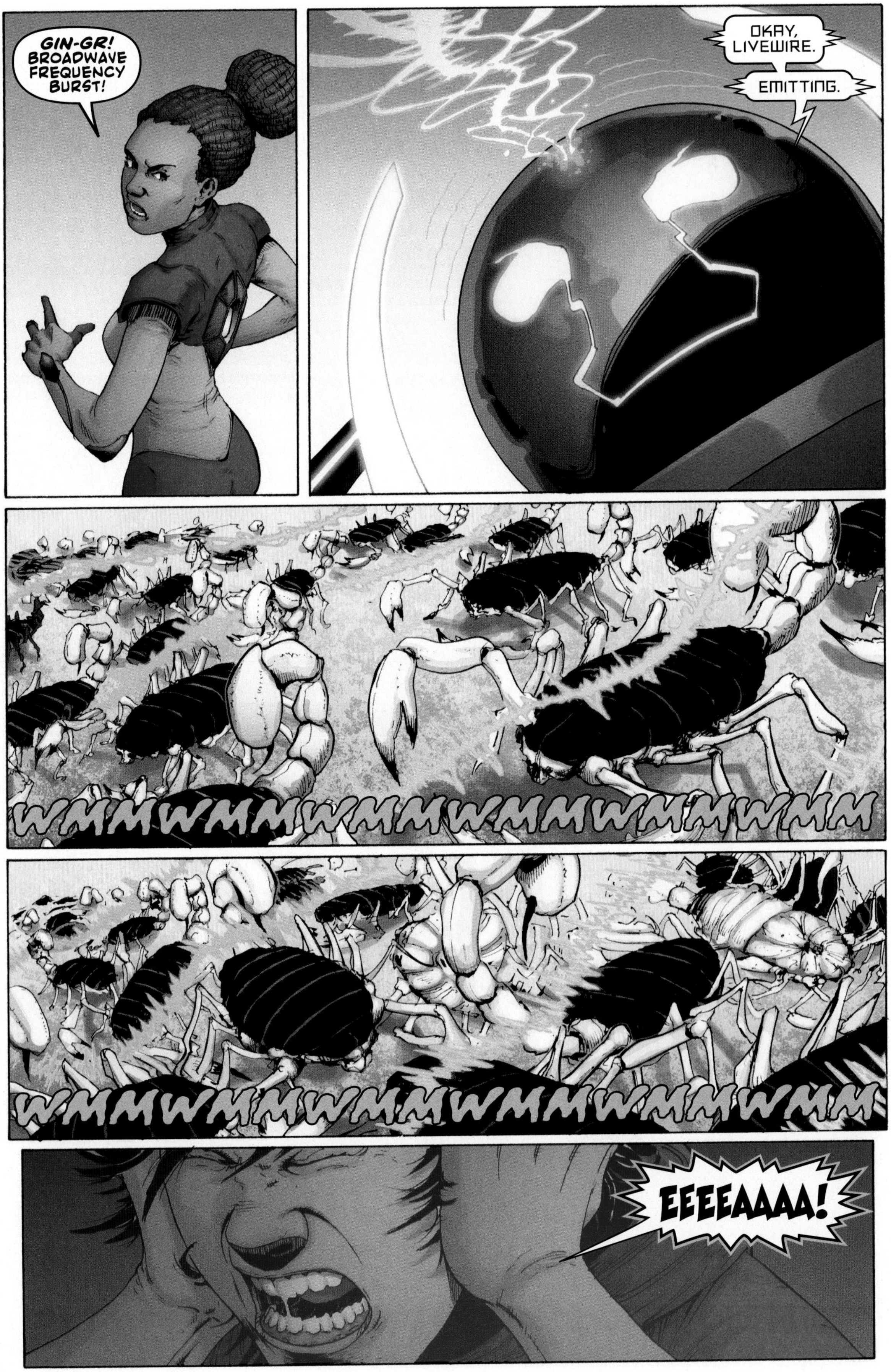
GIN-GR! BROADWAVE FREQUENCY BURST!
OKAY, LIVEWIRE.
EMITTING.
WMMWMMWMMWMMWMMWMM
WMMWMMWMMWMMWMMWMM
EEEEAAAA!

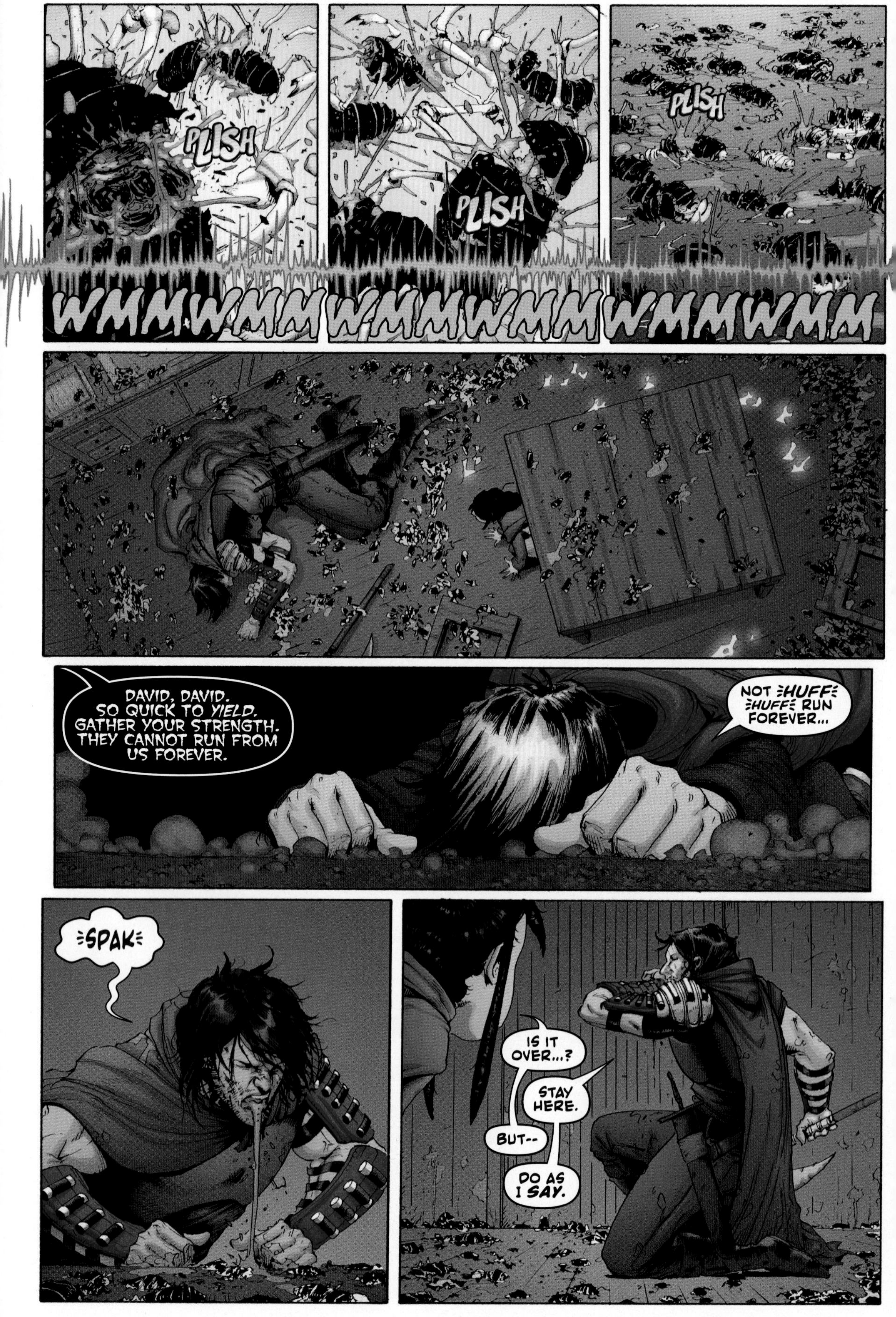
PLISH
PLISH
PLISH
WMMWMMWMMWMMWMMWMM
DAVID, DAVID. SO QUICK TO YIELD. GATHER YOUR STRENGTH. THEY CANNOT RUN FROM US FOREVER.
NOT HUFF HUFF RUN FOREVER...
SPAK
IS IT OVER...?
STAY HERE.
BUT--
DO AS I SAY.

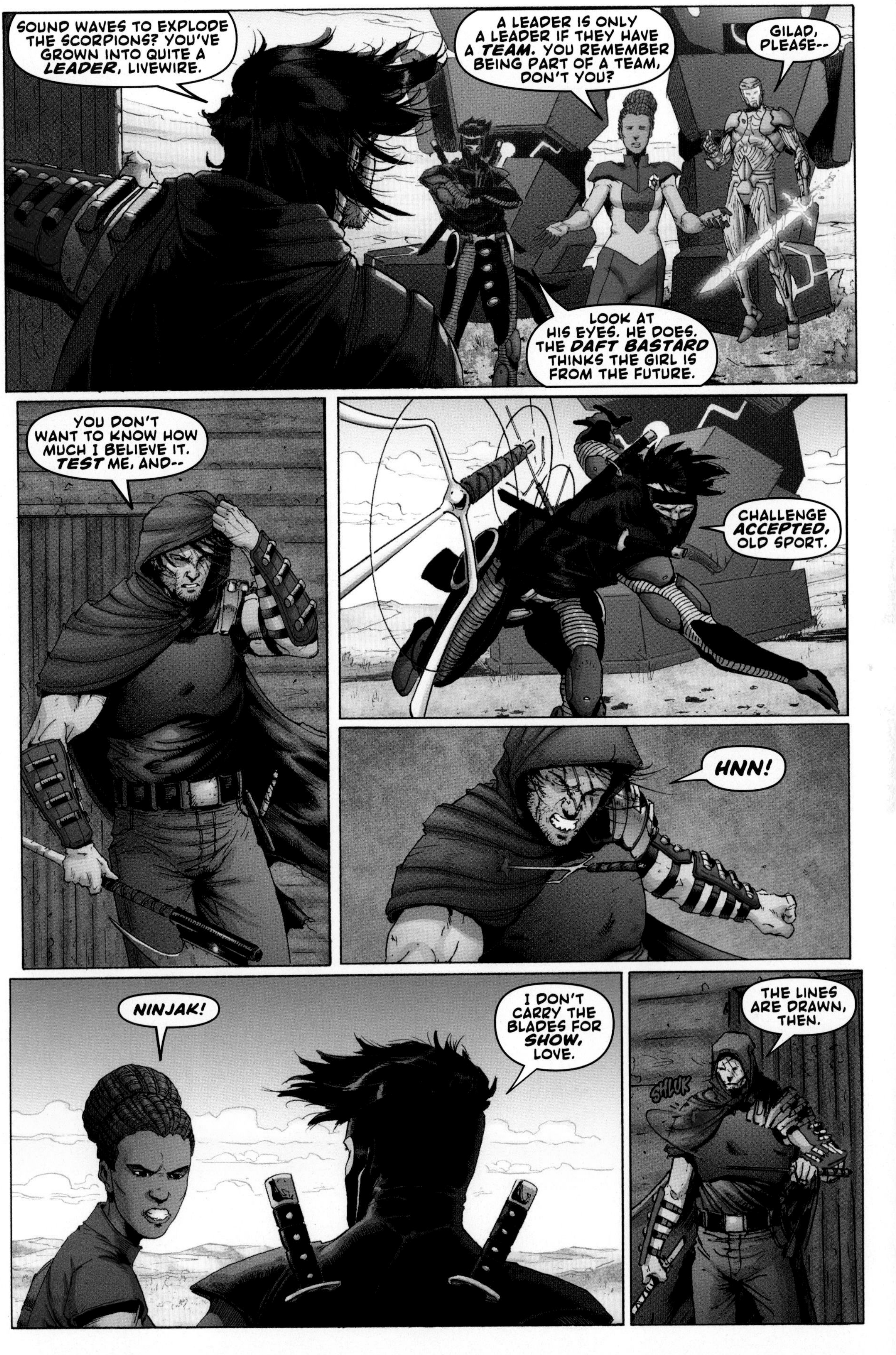
SOUND WAVES TO EXPLODE THE SCORPIONS? YOU'VE GROWN INTO QUITE A LEADER, LIVEWIRE.
A LEADER IS ONLY A LEADER IF THEY HAVE A TEAM. YOU REMEMBER BEING PART OF A TEAM, DON'T YOU?
GILAD, PLEASE--
LOOK AT HIS EYES. HE DOES. THE DAFT BASTARD THINKS THE GIRL IS FROM THE FUTURE.
YOU DON'T WANT TO KNOW HOW MUCH I BELIEVE IT. TEST ME, AND--
CHALLENGE ACCEPTED, OLD SPORT.
HNN!
NINJAK!
I DON'T CARRY THE BLADES FOR SHOW, LOVE.
THE LINES ARE DRAWN, THEN.
SHLUK

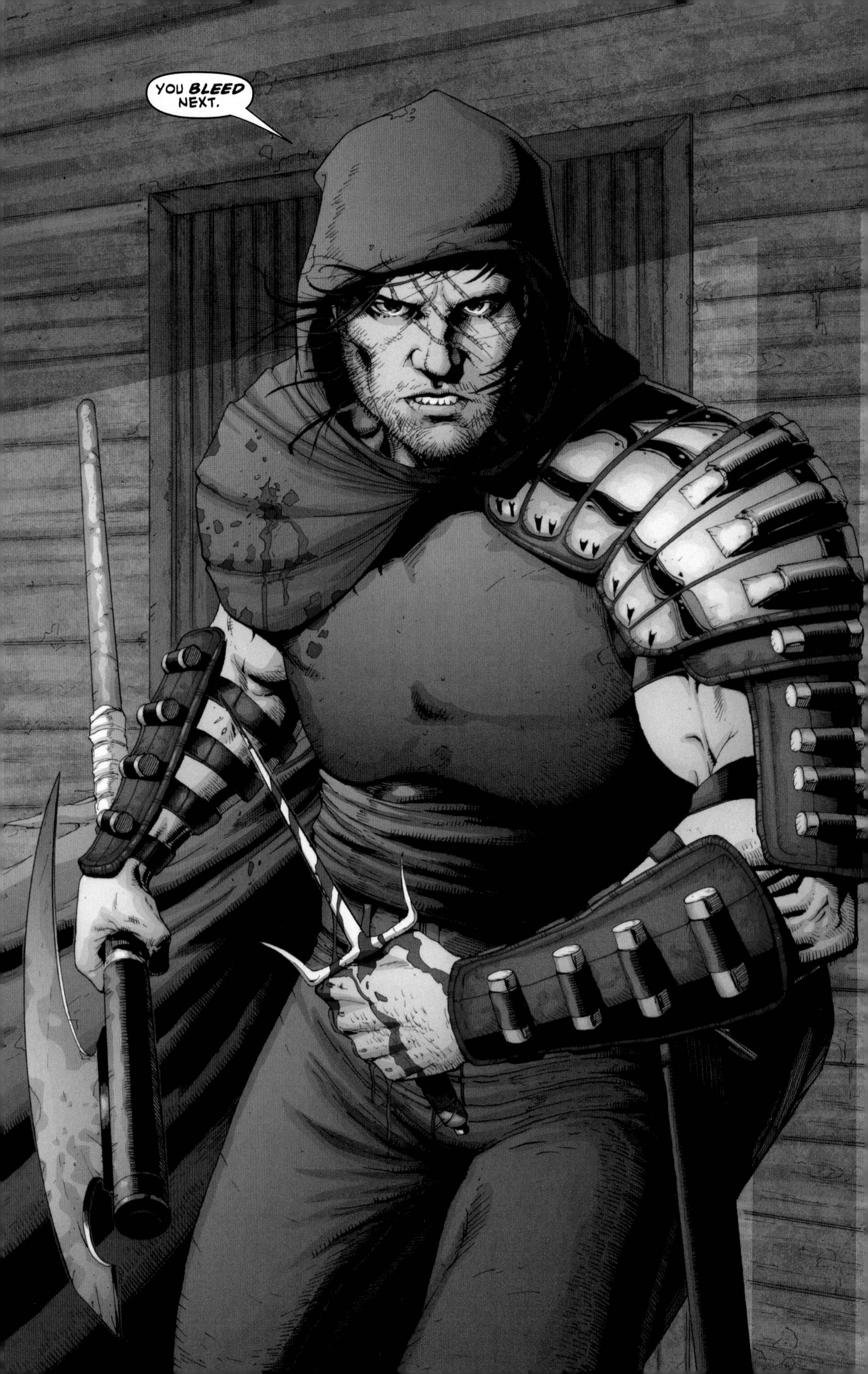
YOU BLEED NEXT.

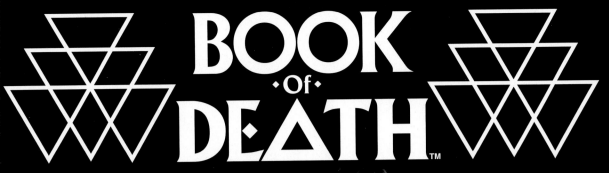

ROBERT VENDITTI
ROBERT GILL
DOUG BRAITHWAITE
DAVID BARON
BRIAN REBER

VALIANT

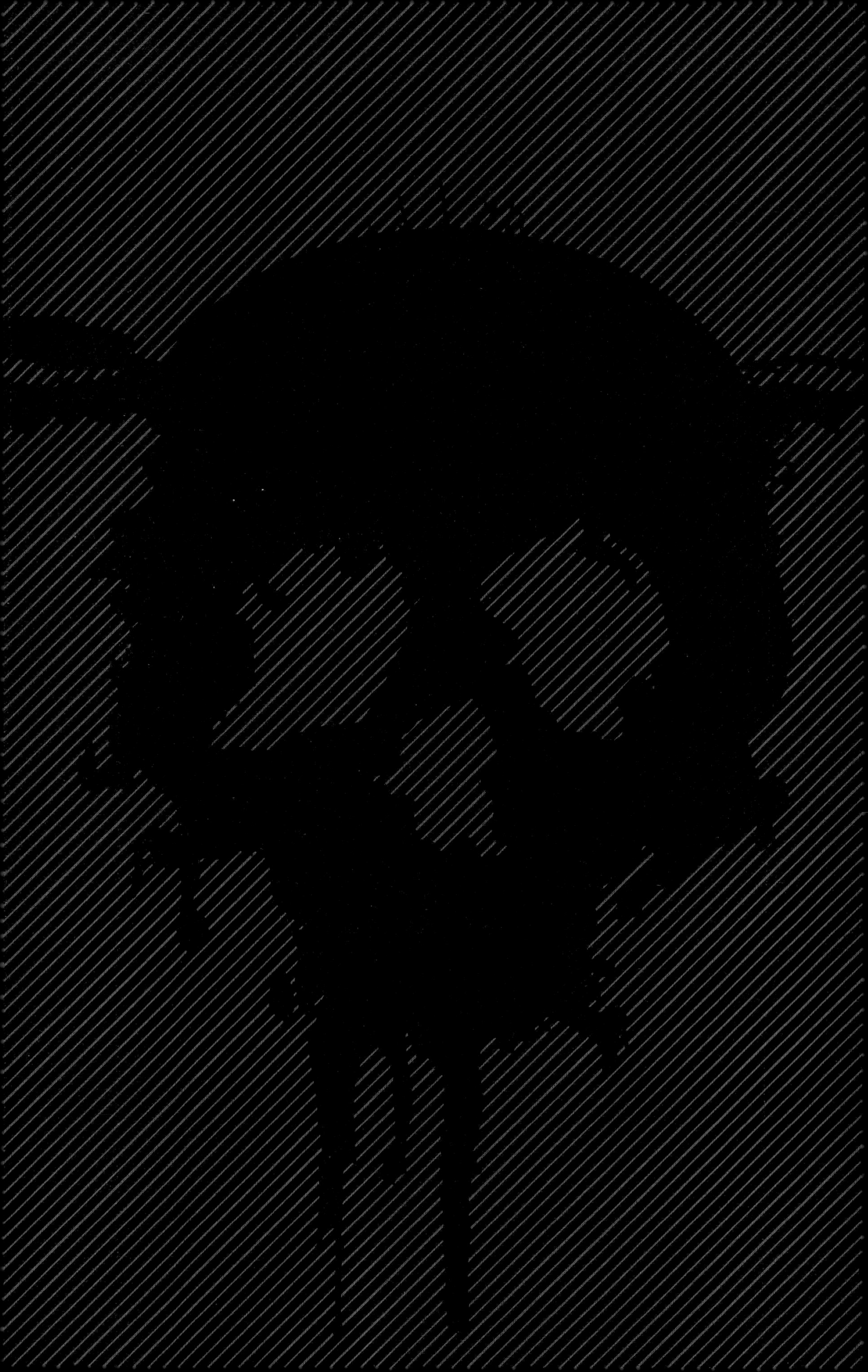

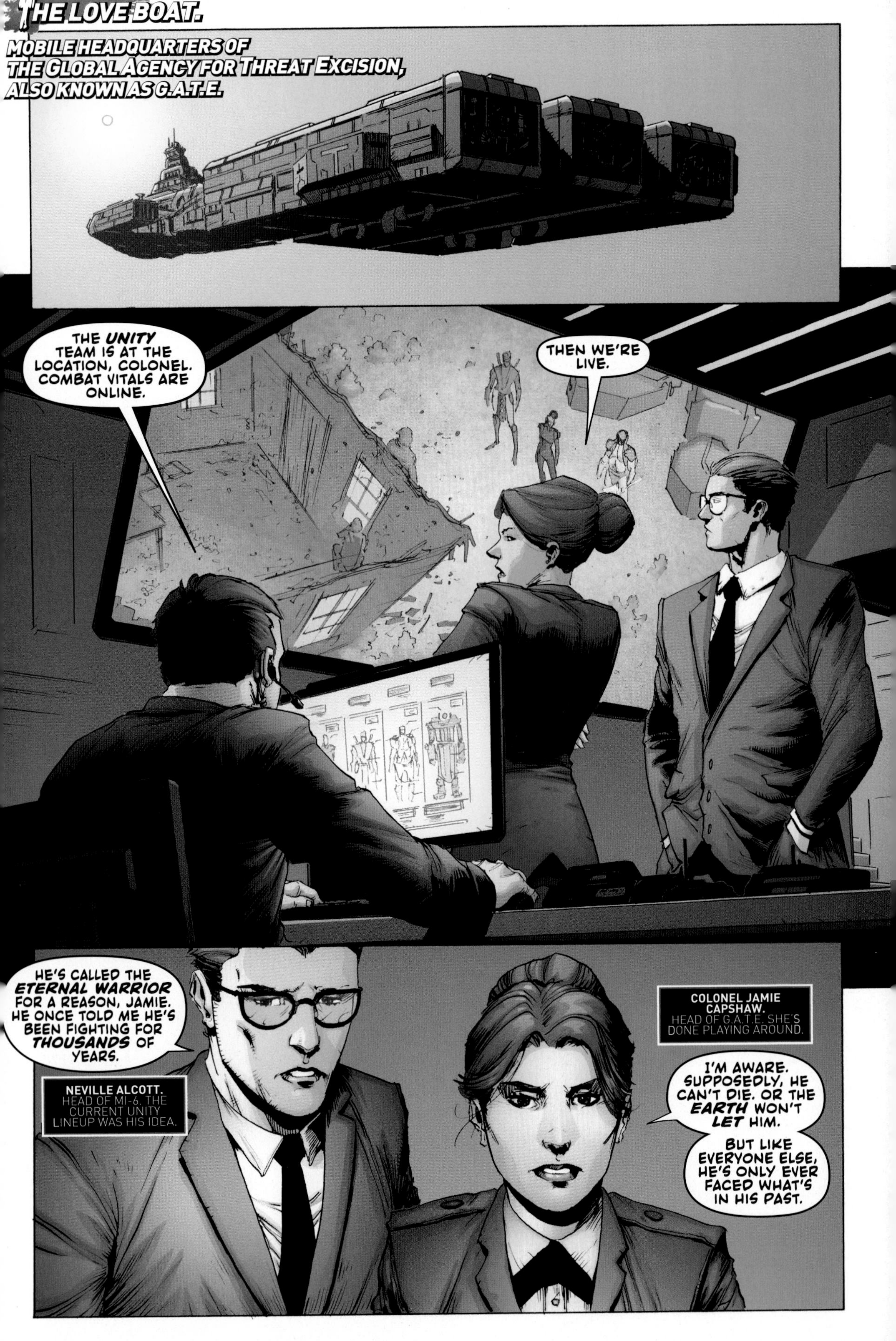
THE LOVE BOAT.
MOBILE HEADQUARTERS OF THE GLOBAL AGENCY FOR THREAT EXCISION, ALSO KNOWN AS G.A.T.E.
THE UNITY TEAM IS AT THE LOCATION, COLONEL. COMBAT VITALS ARE ONLINE.
THEN WE'RE LIVE.
HE'S CALLED THE ETERNAL WARRIOR FOR A REASON, JAMIE. HE ONCE TOLD ME HE'S BEEN FIGHTING FOR THOUSANDS OF YEARS.
NEVILLE ALCOTT. HEAD OF MI-6. THE CURRENT UNITY LINEUP WAS HIS IDEA.
COLONEL JAMIE CAPSHAW. HEAD OF G.A.T.E. SHE'S DONE PLAYING AROUND.
I'M AWARE. SUPPOSEDLY, HE CAN'T DIE. OR THE EARTH WON'T LET HIM.
BUT LIKE EVERYONE ELSE, HE'S ONLY EVER FACED WHAT'S IN HIS PAST.

"HE'S NEVER GONE AGAINST ANYTHING LIKE WHAT'S IN FRONT OF HIM NOW."
DON'T DO THIS, GILAD.
LIVEWIRE. TECHNOPATH. EXPERIENCED ENOUGH TO KNOW FIGHTING IS THE LAST OPTION.
ENOUGH FOOLISHNESS. PUT DOWN YOUR WEAPONS.
X-O MANOWAR. FIFTH-CENTURY VISIGOTH IN SENTIENT ALIEN ARMOR. FIGHTING IS USUALLY HIS ONLY OPTION.
YOU DON'T, I'VE GOT PLENTY MORE BLADES I CAN STICK YOU WITH, OLD SPORT.
NINJAK. ASSASSIN. HOLDS AN UNDEFEATED RECORD IN FIGHTS TO THE DEATH.

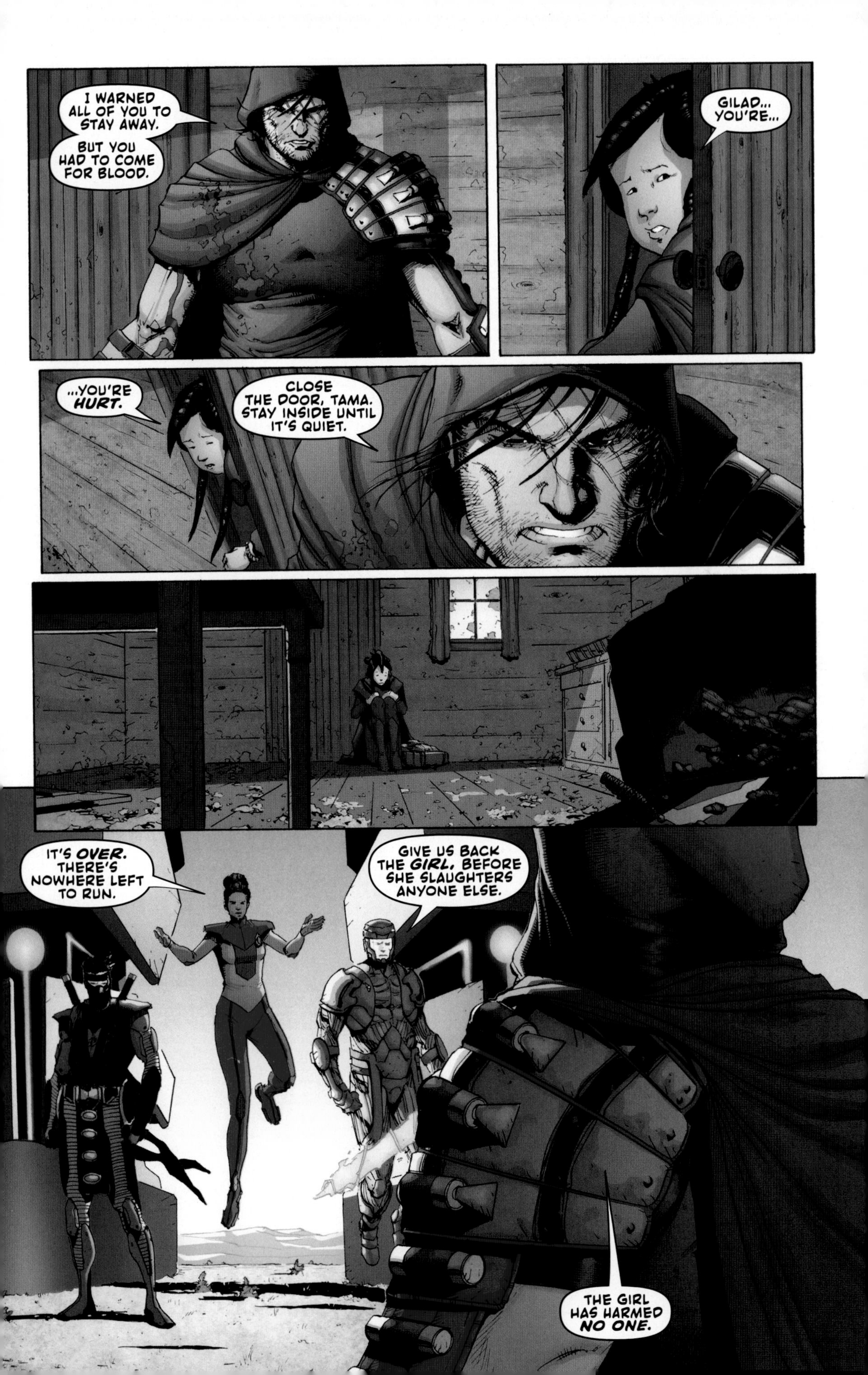
I WARNED ALL OF YOU TO STAY AWAY.
BUT YOU HAD TO COME FOR BLOOD.
GILAD... YOU'RE...
...YOU'RE **HURT**.
CLOSE THE DOOR, TAMA. STAY INSIDE UNTIL IT'S QUIET.
IT'S **OVER**. THERE'S NOWHERE LEFT TO RUN.
GIVE US BACK THE **GIRL**, BEFORE SHE SLAUGHTERS ANYONE ELSE.
THE GIRL HAS HARMED **NO ONE**.

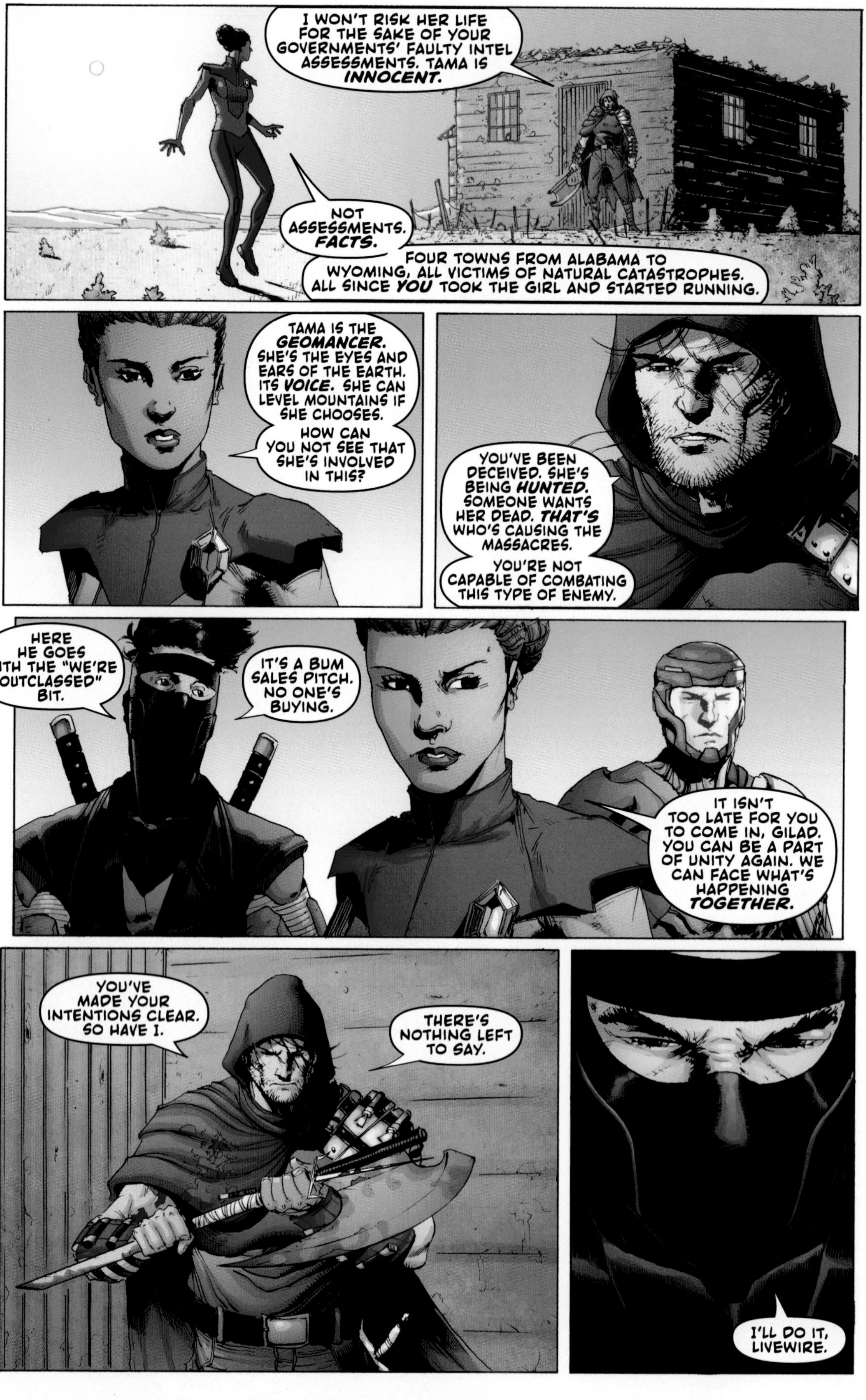
I WON'T RISK HER LIFE FOR THE SAKE OF YOUR GOVERNMENTS' FAULTY INTEL ASSESSMENTS. TAMA IS INNOCENT.
NOT ASSESSMENTS. FACTS.
FOUR TOWNS FROM ALABAMA TO WYOMING, ALL VICTIMS OF NATURAL CATASTROPHES. ALL SINCE YOU TOOK THE GIRL AND STARTED RUNNING.
TAMA IS THE GEOMANCER. SHE'S THE EYES AND EARS OF THE EARTH. ITS VOICE. SHE CAN LEVEL MOUNTAINS IF SHE CHOOSES.
HOW CAN YOU NOT SEE THAT SHE'S INVOLVED IN THIS?
YOU'VE BEEN DECEIVED. SHE'S BEING HUNTED. SOMEONE WANTS HER DEAD. THAT'S WHO'S CAUSING THE MASSACRES.
YOU'RE NOT CAPABLE OF COMBATING THIS TYPE OF ENEMY.
HERE HE GOES WITH THE "WE'RE OUTCLASSED" BIT.
IT'S A BUM SALES PITCH. NO ONE'S BUYING.
IT ISN'T TOO LATE FOR YOU TO COME IN, GILAD. YOU CAN BE A PART OF UNITY AGAIN. WE CAN FACE WHAT'S HAPPENING TOGETHER.
YOU'VE MADE YOUR INTENTIONS CLEAR. SO HAVE I.
THERE'S NOTHING LEFT TO SAY.
I'LL DO IT, LIVEWIRE.

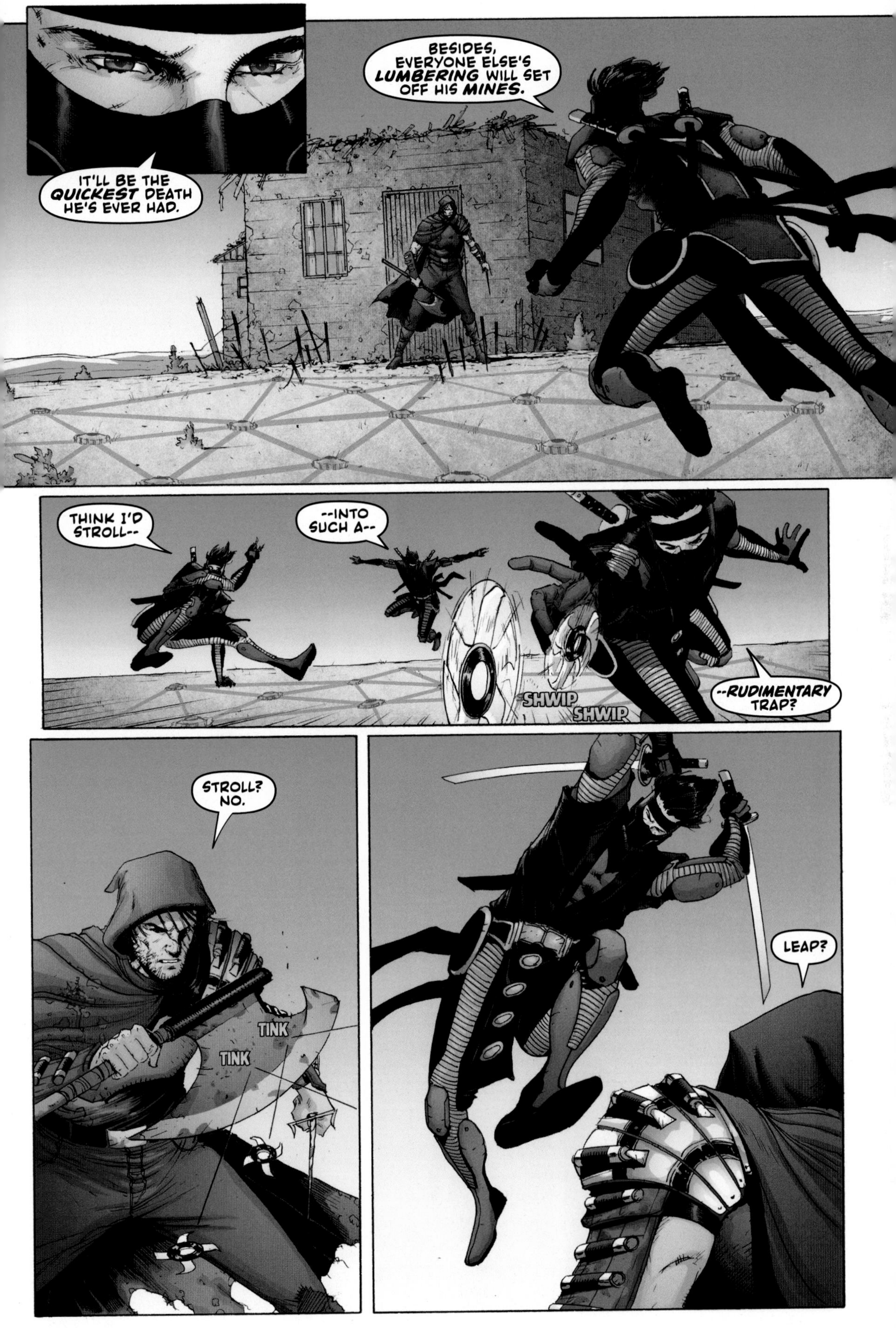

IT'LL BE THE QUICKEST DEATH HE'S EVER HAD.
BESIDES, EVERYONE ELSE'S LUMBERING WILL SET OFF HIS MINES.
THINK I'D STROLL--
--INTO SUCH A--
SHWIP
SHWIP
--RUDIMENTARY TRAP?
STROLL? NO.
TINK
TINK
LEAP?

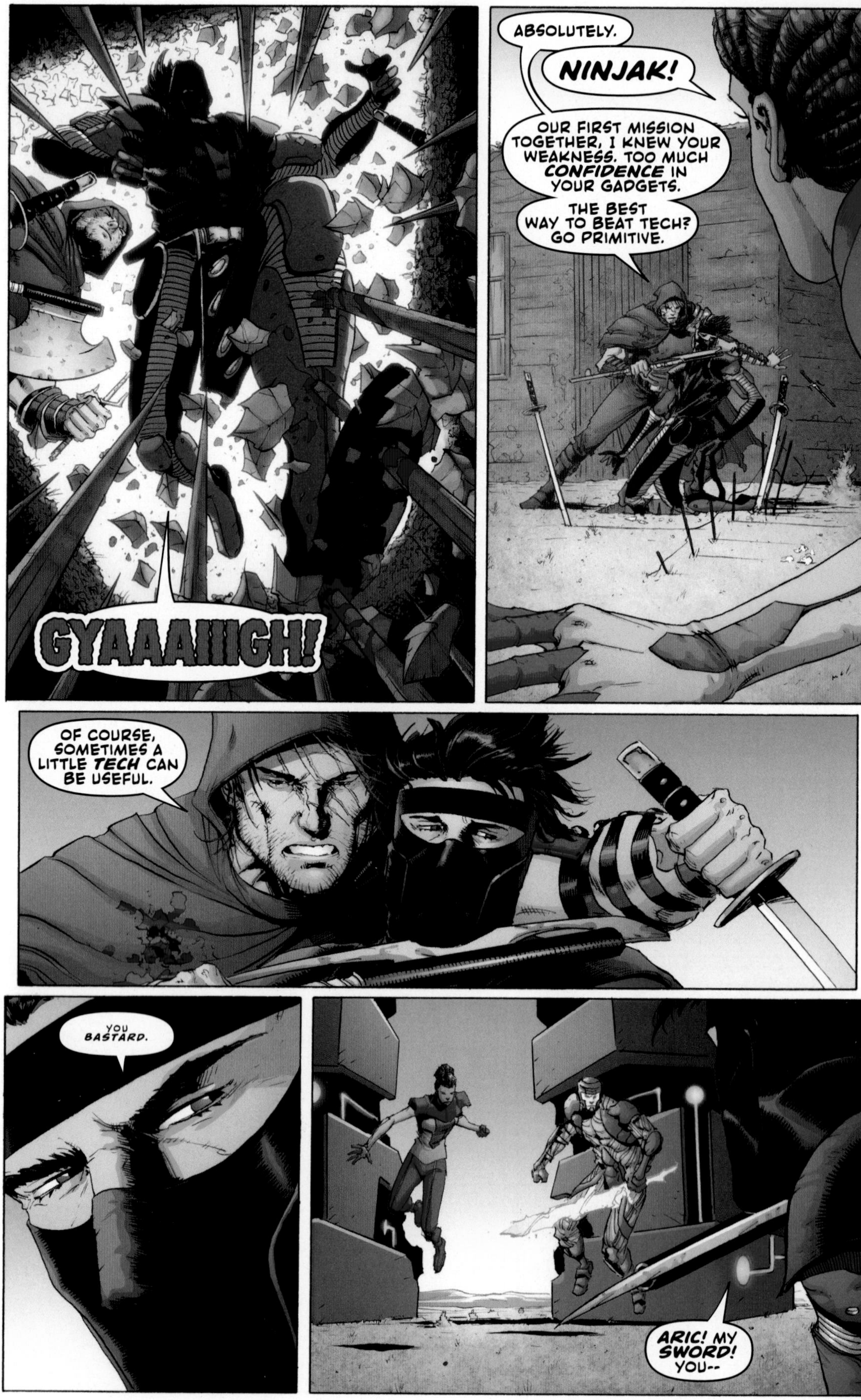
GYAAAIIIGH!
ABSOLUTELY.
NINJAK!
OUR FIRST MISSION TOGETHER, I KNEW YOUR WEAKNESS. TOO MUCH CONFIDENCE IN YOUR GADGETS.
THE BEST WAY TO BEAT TECH? GO PRIMITIVE.
OF COURSE, SOMETIMES A LITTLE TECH CAN BE USEFUL.
YOU BASTARD.
ARIC! MY SWORD! YOU--

SHUT UP, OLD SPORT.

KRAK

NINJAK IS UNCONSCIOUS.

GILAD...IS ATTACKING US?

GIN-GR. BENEVOLENT DEATH ROBOT. UNITY'S HOME AWAY FROM HOME.

HE HAS LOST HIS SENSES!

PAFF PAFF

PAFF PAFF

ALWAYS THE OX, ARIC.

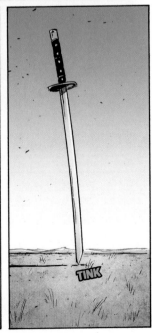

TINK

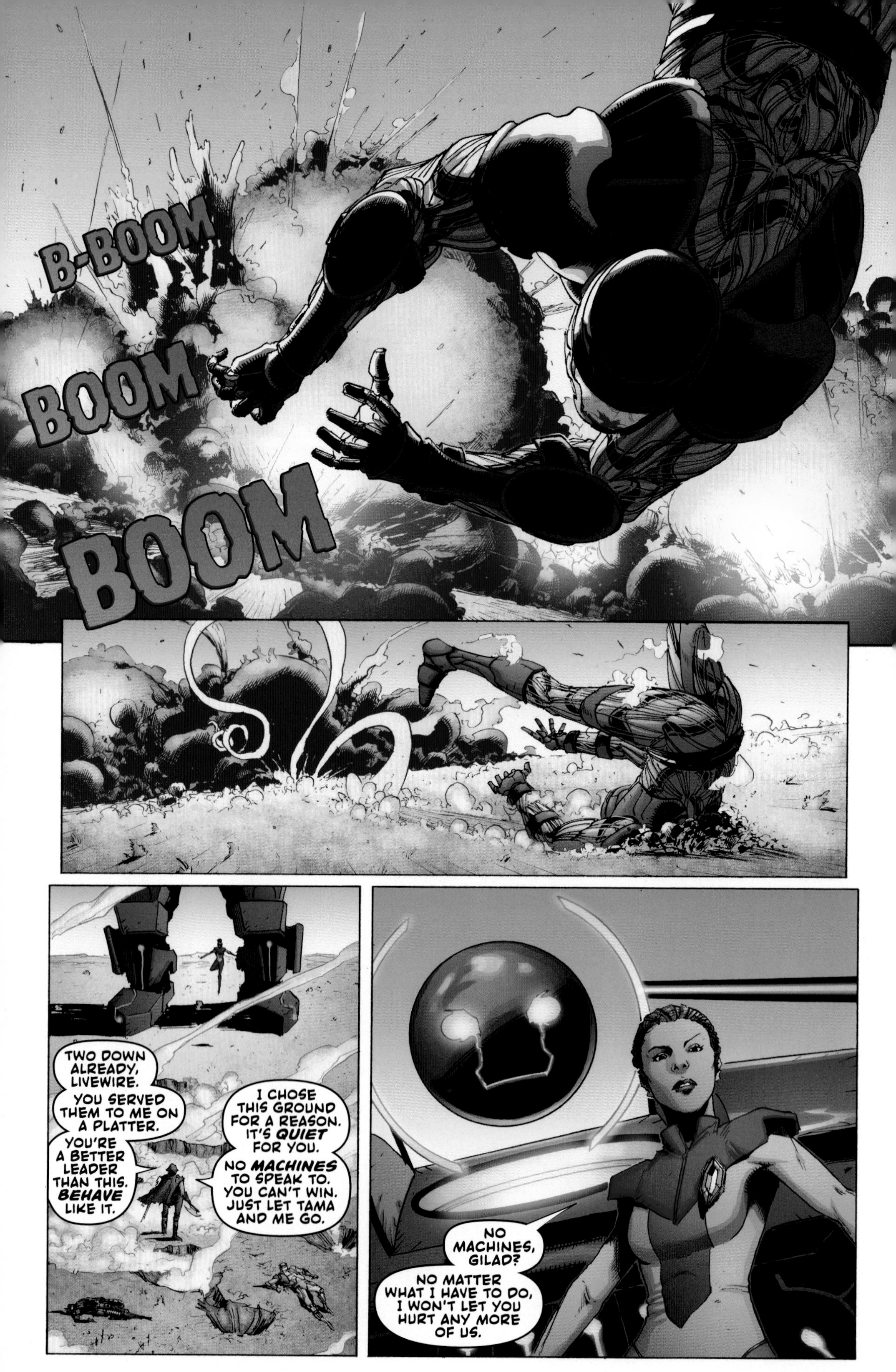
B-BOOM
BOOM
BOOM
TWO DOWN ALREADY, LIVEWIRE.
YOU SERVED THEM TO ME ON A PLATTER.
YOU'RE A BETTER LEADER THAN THIS. BEHAVE LIKE IT.
I CHOSE THIS GROUND FOR A REASON. IT'S QUIET FOR YOU.
NO MACHINES TO SPEAK TO. YOU CAN'T WIN. JUST LET TAMA AND ME GO.
NO MACHINES, GILAD?
NO MATTER WHAT I HAVE TO DO, I WON'T LET YOU HURT ANY MORE OF US.

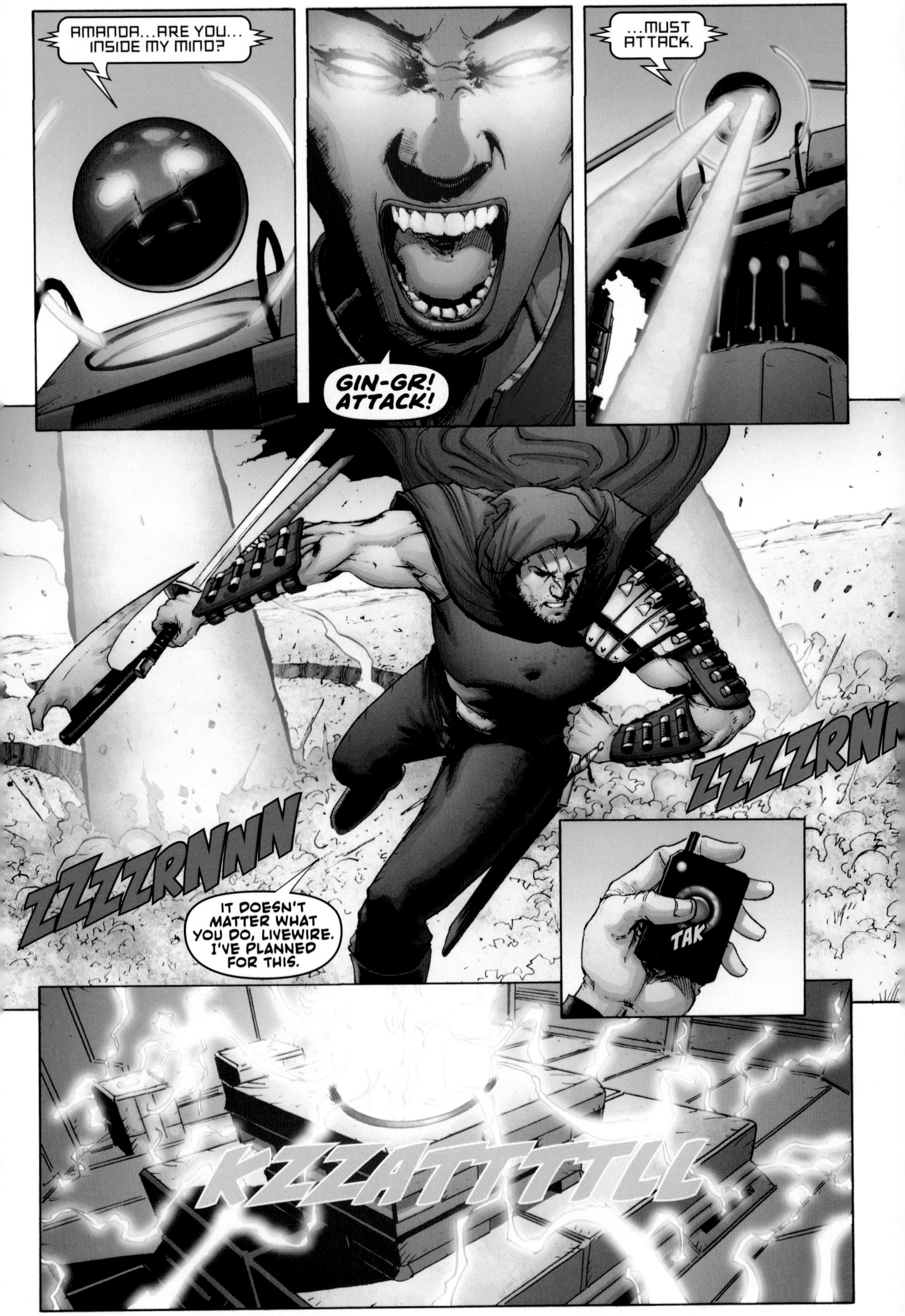
AMANDA...ARE YOU... INSIDE MY MIND?
GIN-GR! ATTACK!
...MUST ATTACK.
ZZZZZRNNN
IT DOESN'T MATTER WHAT YOU DO, LIVEWIRE. I'VE PLANNED FOR THIS.
TAK
KZZATTTTLL

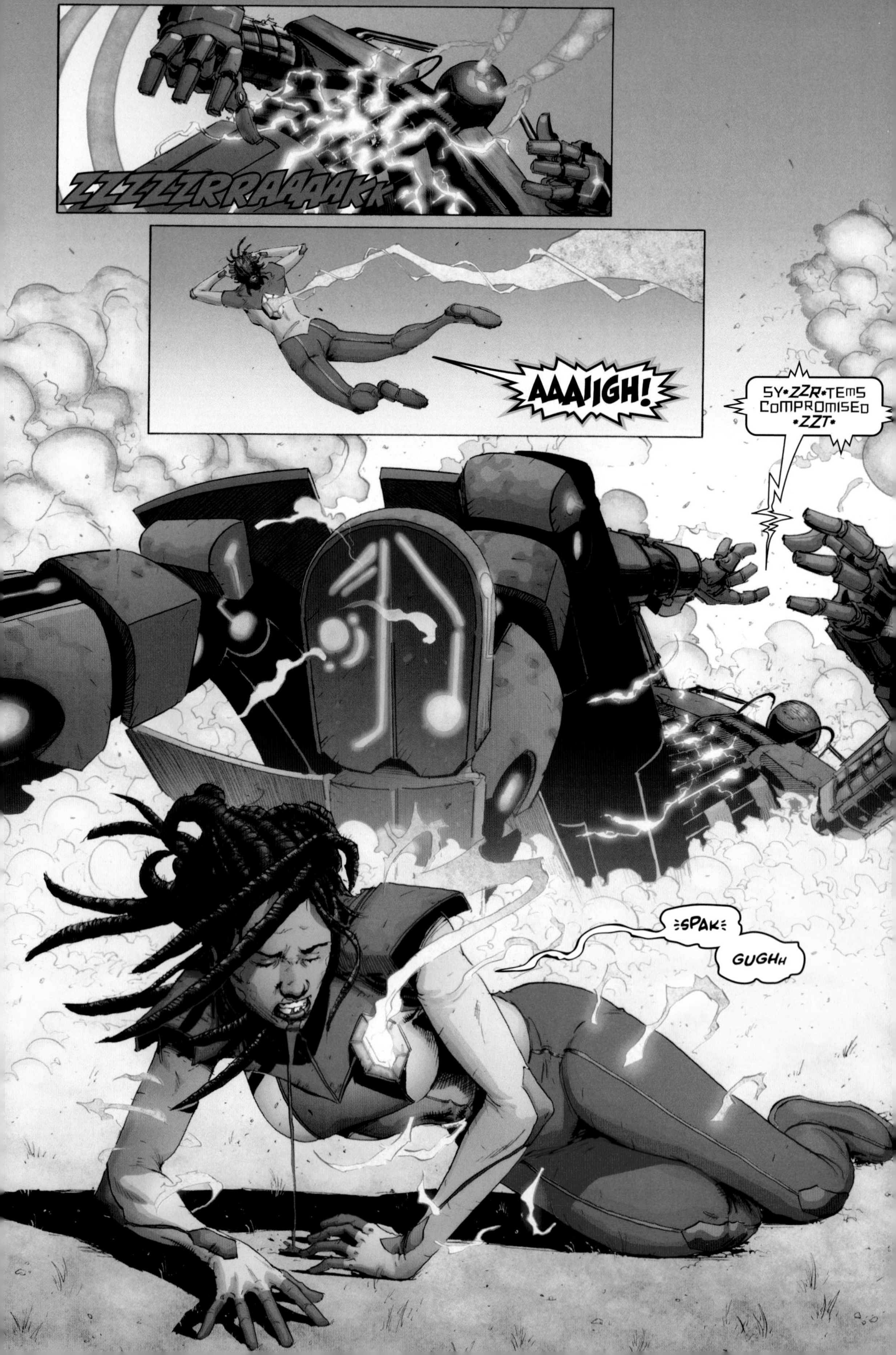

ZZZZZRRAAAAKK
AAAIIGH!
SY•ZZR•TEMS COMPROMISED •ZZT•
SPAK
GUGHH

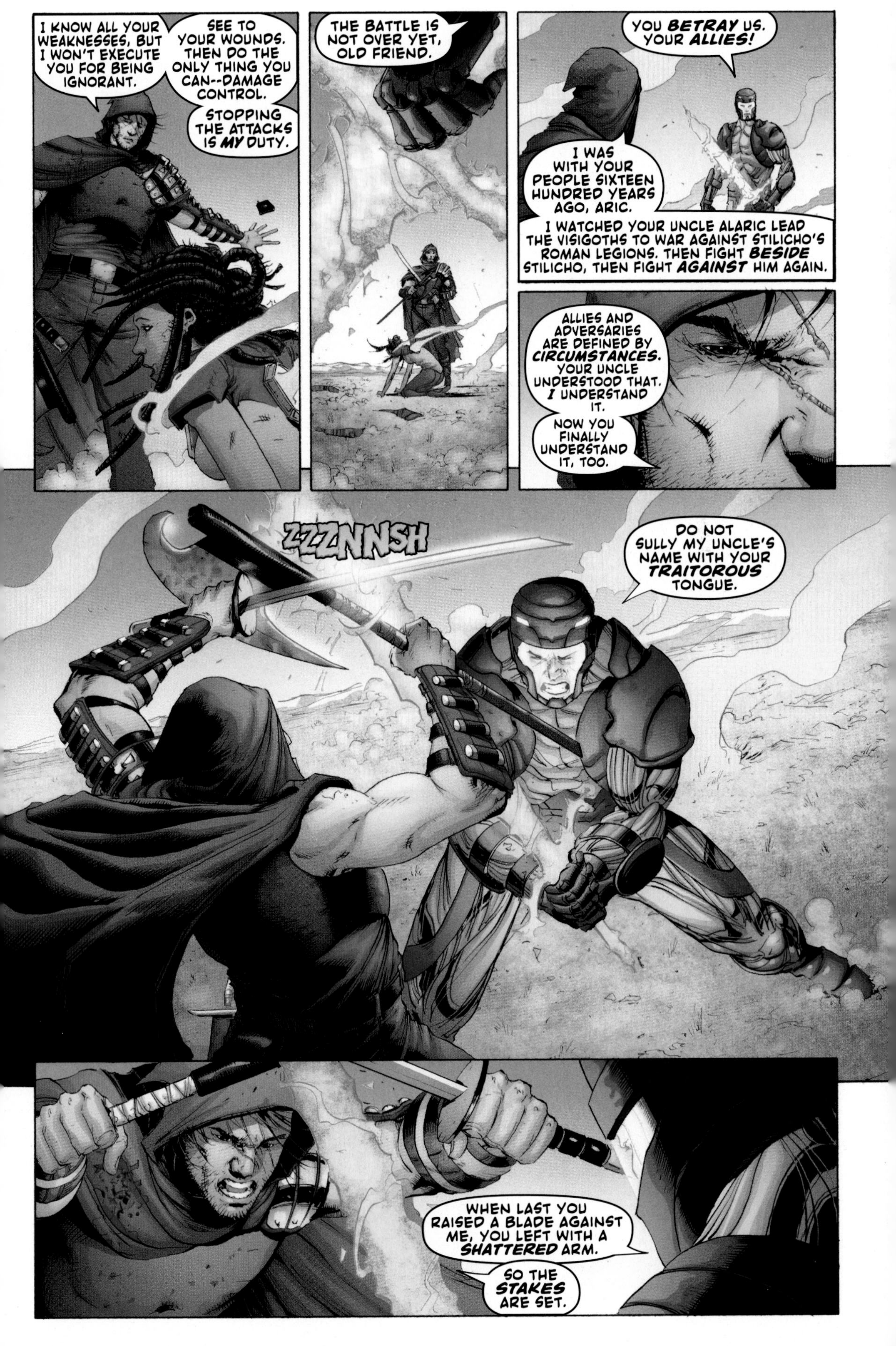
I KNOW ALL YOUR WEAKNESSES, BUT I WON'T EXECUTE YOU FOR BEING IGNORANT.
SEE TO YOUR WOUNDS. THEN DO THE ONLY THING YOU CAN--DAMAGE CONTROL.
STOPPING THE ATTACKS IS MY DUTY.
THE BATTLE IS NOT OVER YET, OLD FRIEND.
YOU BETRAY US. YOUR ALLIES!
I WAS WITH YOUR PEOPLE SIXTEEN HUNDRED YEARS AGO, ARIC.
I WATCHED YOUR UNCLE ALARIC LEAD THE VISIGOTHS TO WAR AGAINST STILICHO'S ROMAN LEGIONS. THEN FIGHT BESIDE STILICHO, THEN FIGHT AGAINST HIM AGAIN.
ALLIES AND ADVERSARIES ARE DEFINED BY CIRCUMSTANCES. YOUR UNCLE UNDERSTOOD THAT. I UNDERSTAND IT.
NOW YOU FINALLY UNDERSTAND IT, TOO.
ZZZNNNSH
DO NOT SULLY MY UNCLE'S NAME WITH YOUR TRAITOROUS TONGUE.
WHEN LAST YOU RAISED A BLADE AGAINST ME, YOU LEFT WITH A SHATTERED ARM.
SO THE STAKES ARE SET.

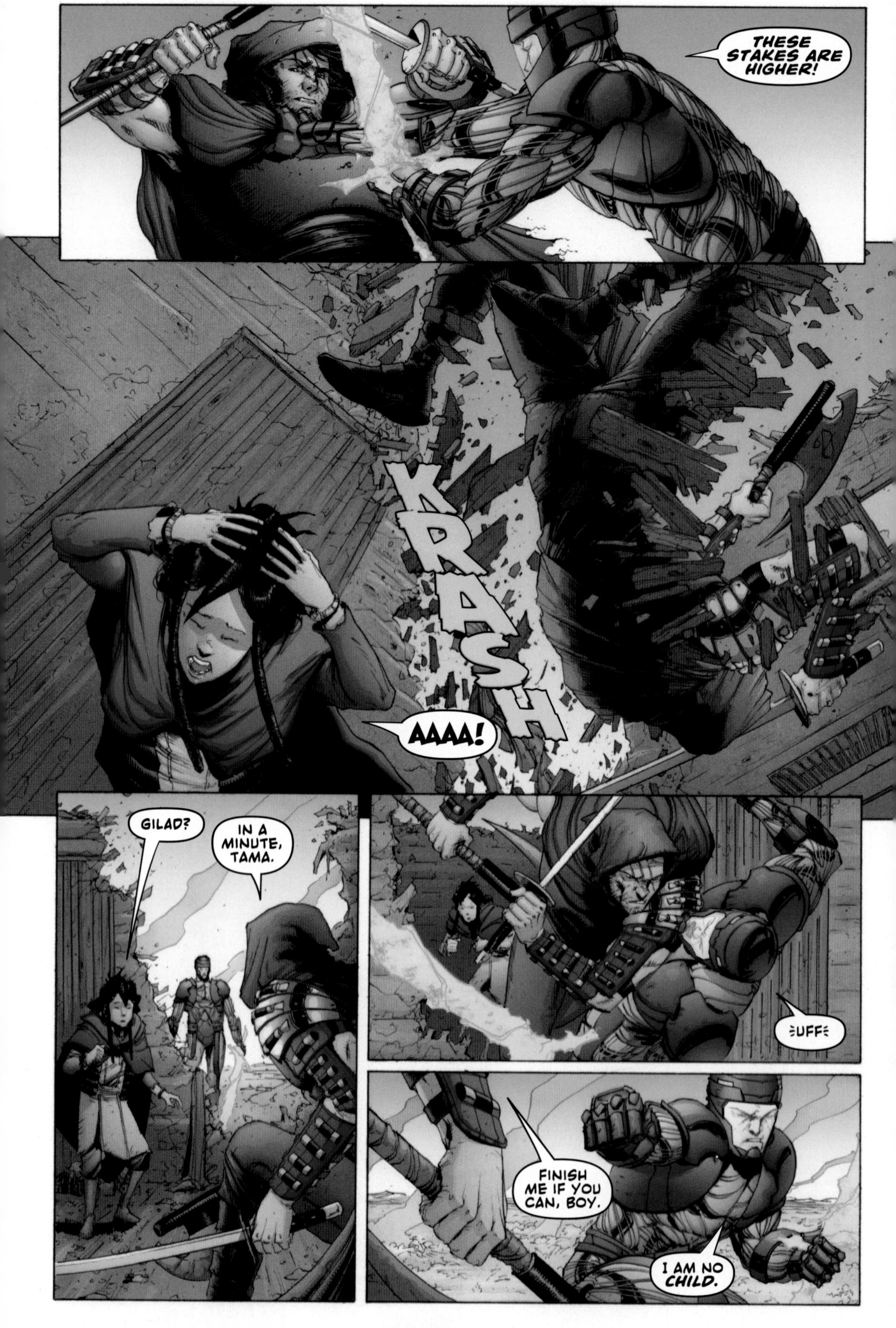
THESE STAKES ARE HIGHER!
KRASH
AAAA!
GILAD?
IN A MINUTE, TAMA.
UFF
FINISH ME IF YOU CAN, BOY.
I AM NO CHILD.

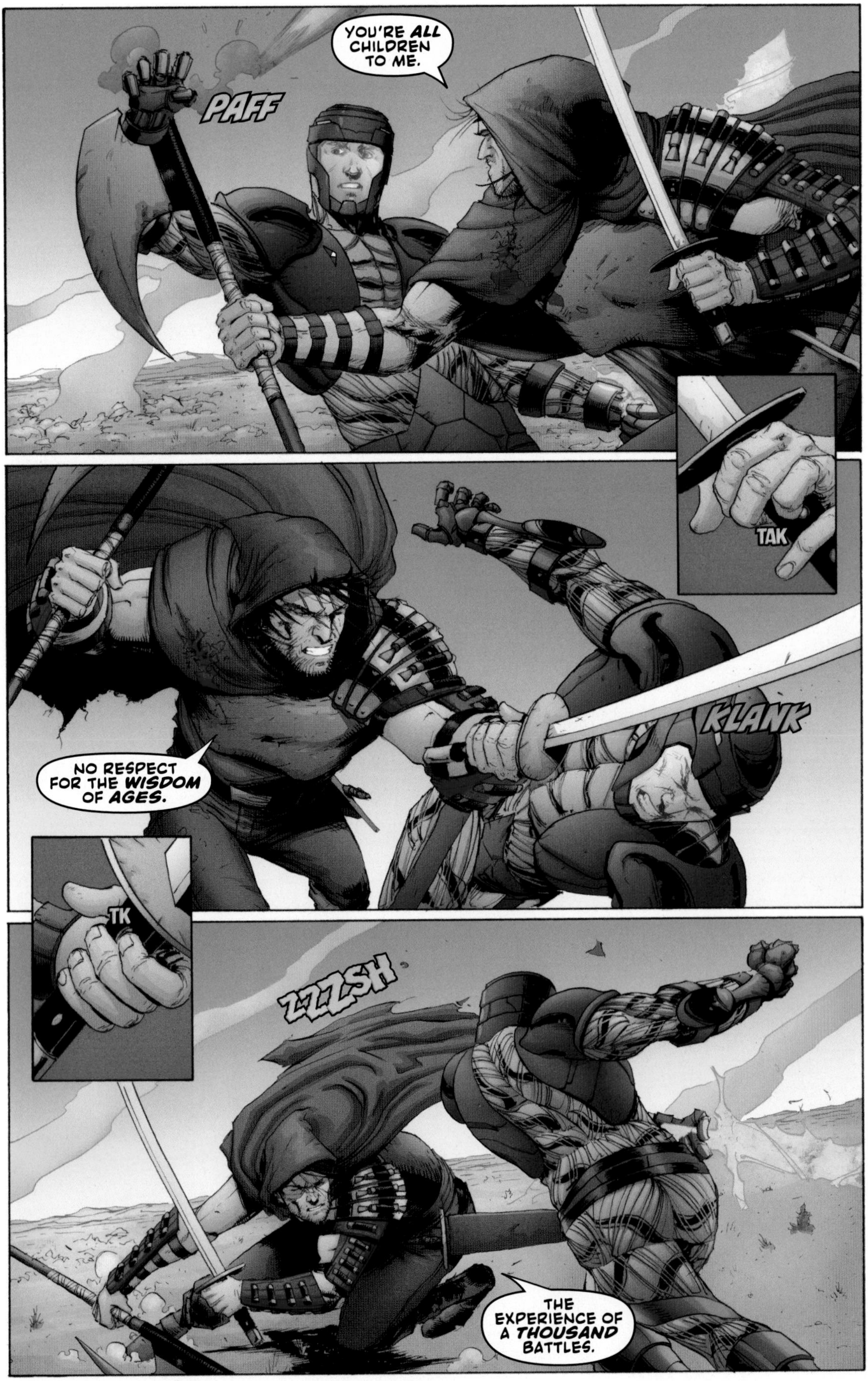
YOU'RE ALL CHILDREN TO ME.
PAFF
TAK
KLANK
NO RESPECT FOR THE WISDOM OF AGES.
TK
ZZZSH
THE EXPERIENCE OF A THOUSAND BATTLES.

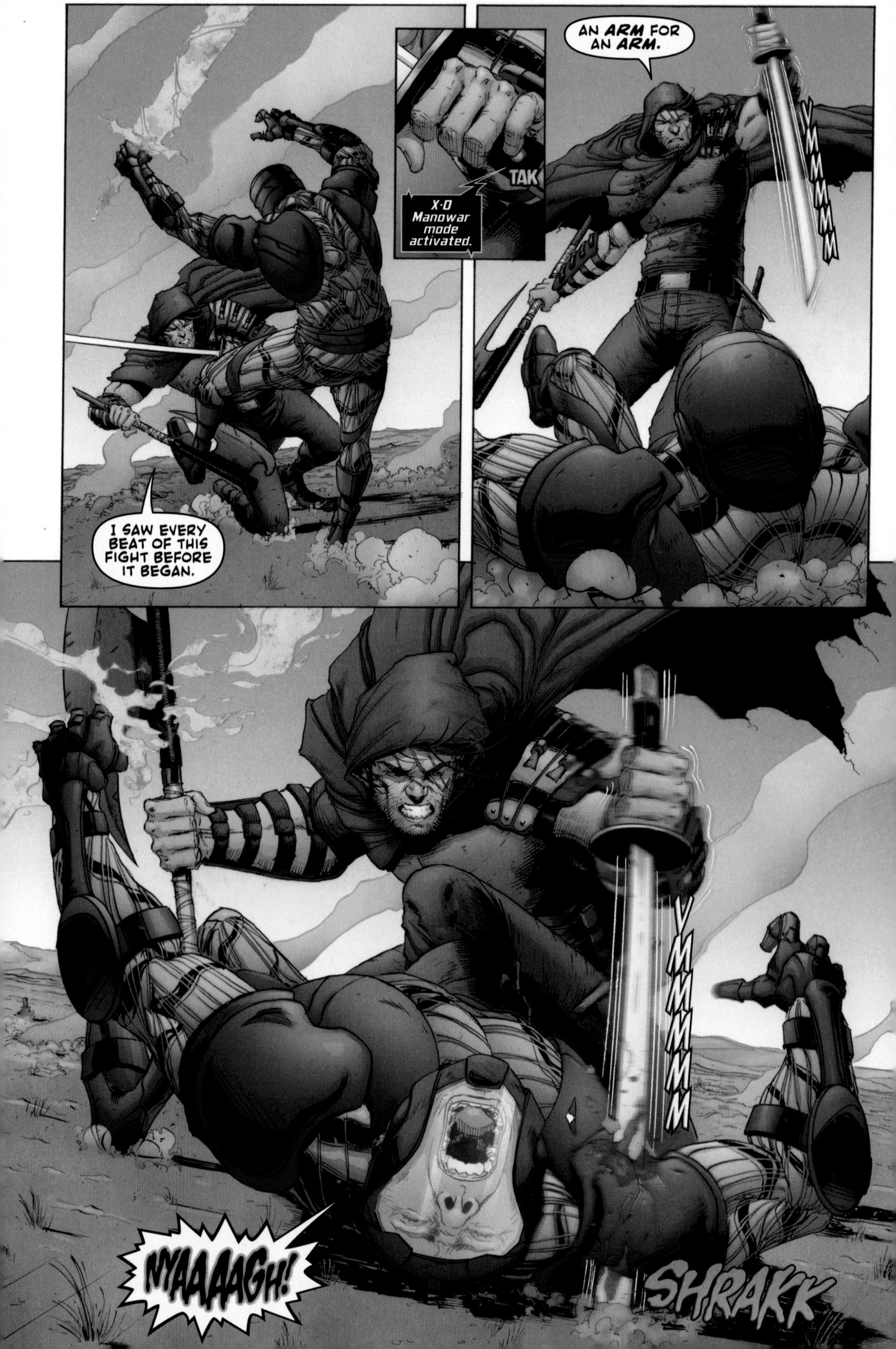
TAK
X-O Manowar mode activated.
I SAW EVERY BEAT OF THIS FIGHT BEFORE IT BEGAN.
AN ARM FOR AN ARM.
VMMMMM
VMMMMMM
NYAAAAGH!
SHRAKK

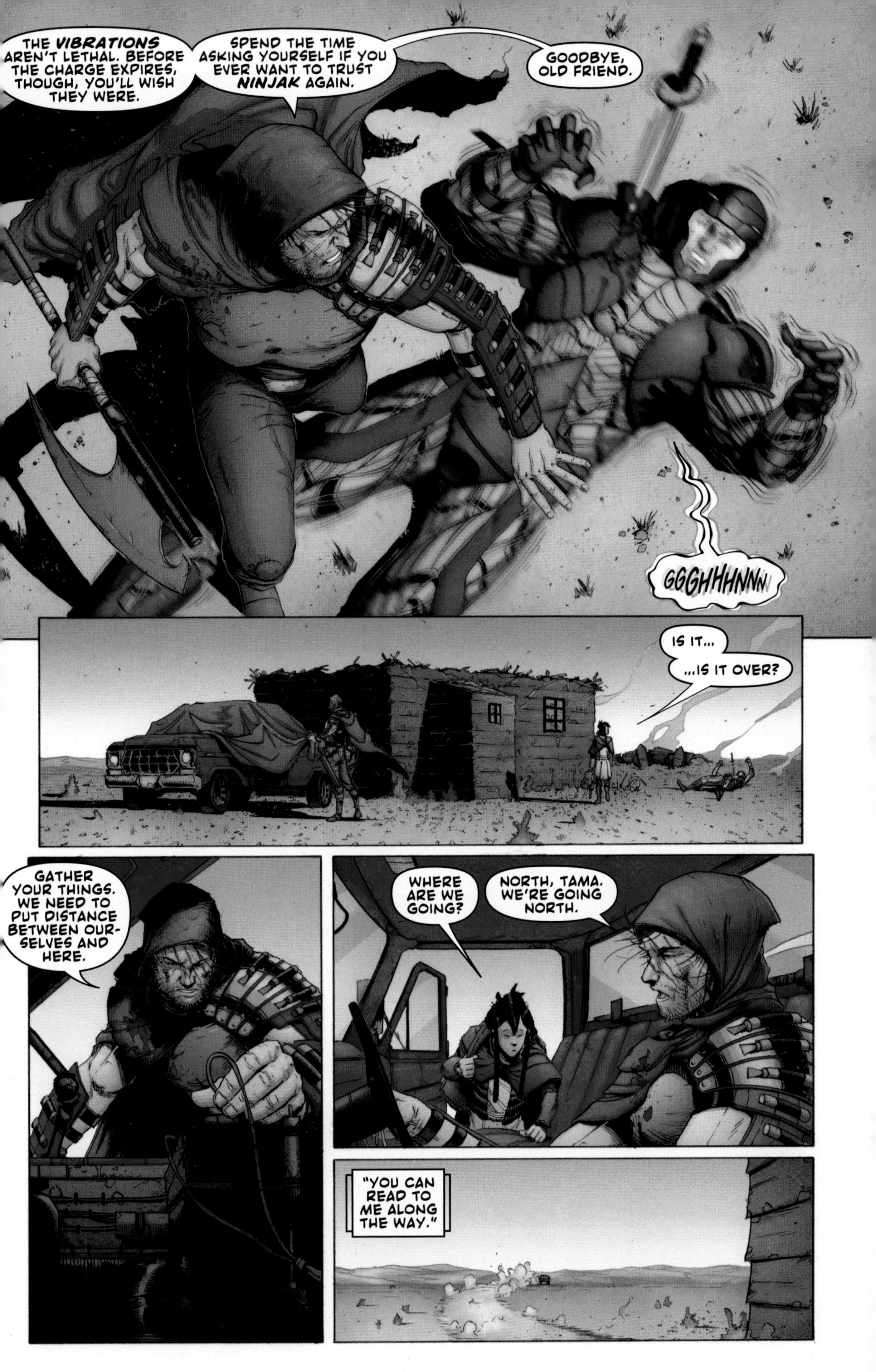
THE VIBRATIONS AREN'T LETHAL. BEFORE THE CHARGE EXPIRES, THOUGH, YOU'LL WISH THEY WERE.
SPEND THE TIME ASKING YOURSELF IF YOU EVER WANT TO TRUST NINJAK AGAIN.
GOODBYE, OLD FRIEND.
GGGHHHNNN
IS IT...
...IS IT OVER?
GATHER YOUR THINGS. WE NEED TO PUT DISTANCE BETWEEN OUR-SELVES AND HERE.
WHERE ARE WE GOING?
NORTH, TAMA. WE'RE GOING NORTH.
"YOU CAN READ TO ME ALONG THE WAY."

C-COLD...

...CAN I P-PLEASE SEE MY MOM?

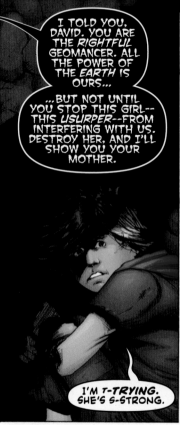

I TOLD YOU, DAVID. YOU ARE THE *RIGHTFUL* GEOMANCER. ALL THE POWER OF THE *EARTH* IS OURS...

...BUT NOT UNTIL YOU STOP THIS GIRL-- THIS *USURPER*--FROM INTERFERING WITH US. DESTROY HER, AND I'LL SHOW YOU YOUR MOTHER.

I'M T-TRYING. SHE'S S-STRONG.

LISTEN TO MY VOICE, DAVID. YOU BELIEVE THAT I WANT TO *HELP* YOU. DON'T YOU?

Y-YES...

...MASTER.

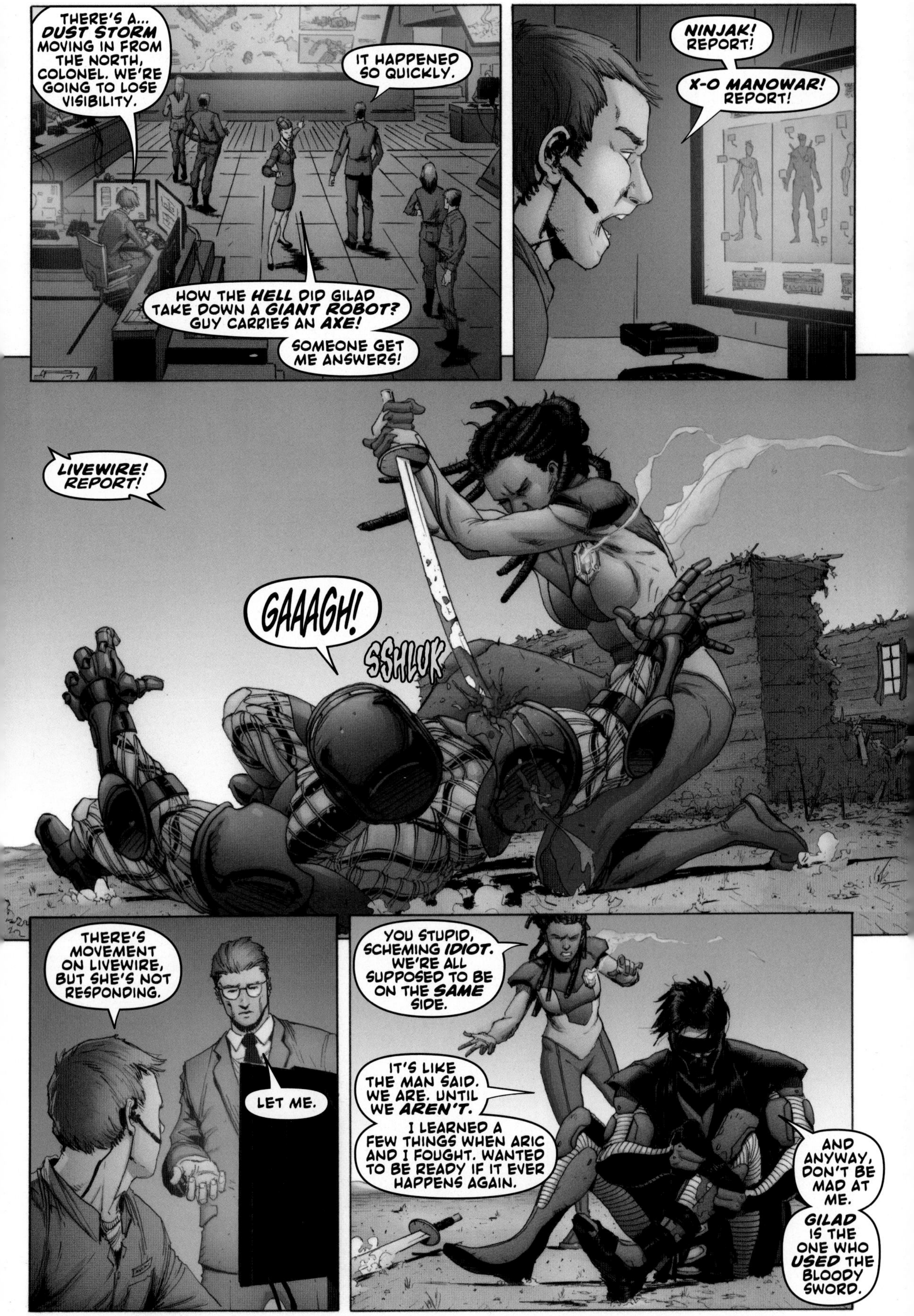
THERE'S A... DUST STORM MOVING IN FROM THE NORTH, COLONEL. WE'RE GOING TO LOSE VISIBILITY.
IT HAPPENED SO QUICKLY.
HOW THE HELL DID GILAD TAKE DOWN A GIANT ROBOT? GUY CARRIES AN AXE!
SOMEONE GET ME ANSWERS!
NINJAK! REPORT!
X-O MANOWAR! REPORT!
LIVEWIRE! REPORT!
GAAAGH!
SSHLUK
THERE'S MOVEMENT ON LIVEWIRE, BUT SHE'S NOT RESPONDING.
LET ME.
YOU STUPID, SCHEMING IDIOT. WE'RE ALL SUPPOSED TO BE ON THE SAME SIDE.
IT'S LIKE THE MAN SAID. WE ARE. UNTIL WE AREN'T.
I LEARNED A FEW THINGS WHEN ARIC AND I FOUGHT. WANTED TO BE READY IF IT EVER HAPPENS AGAIN.
AND ANYWAY, DON'T BE MAD AT ME.
GILAD IS THE ONE WHO USED THE BLOODY SWORD.

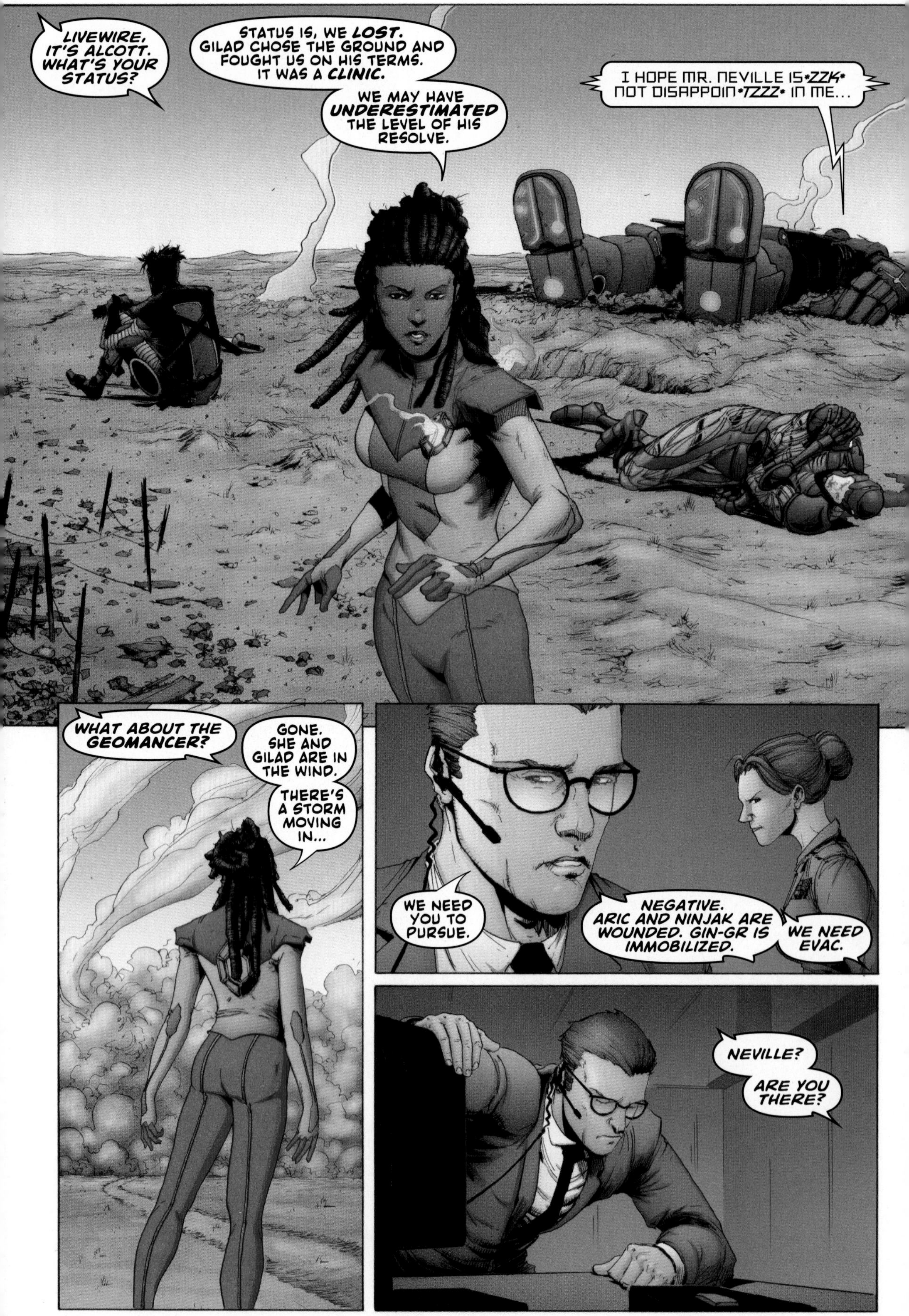
LIVEWIRE, IT'S ALCOTT. WHAT'S YOUR STATUS?
STATUS IS, WE LOST. GILAD CHOSE THE GROUND AND FOUGHT US ON HIS TERMS. IT WAS A CLINIC.
WE MAY HAVE UNDERESTIMATED THE LEVEL OF HIS RESOLVE.
I HOPE MR. NEVILLE IS*ZZK* NOT DISAPPOIN*TZZZ* IN ME...
WHAT ABOUT THE GEOMANCER?
GONE. SHE AND GILAD ARE IN THE WIND.
THERE'S A STORM MOVING IN...
WE NEED YOU TO PURSUE.
NEGATIVE. ARIC AND NINJAK ARE WOUNDED. GIN-GR IS IMMOBILIZED.
WE NEED EVAC.
NEVILLE?
ARE YOU THERE?

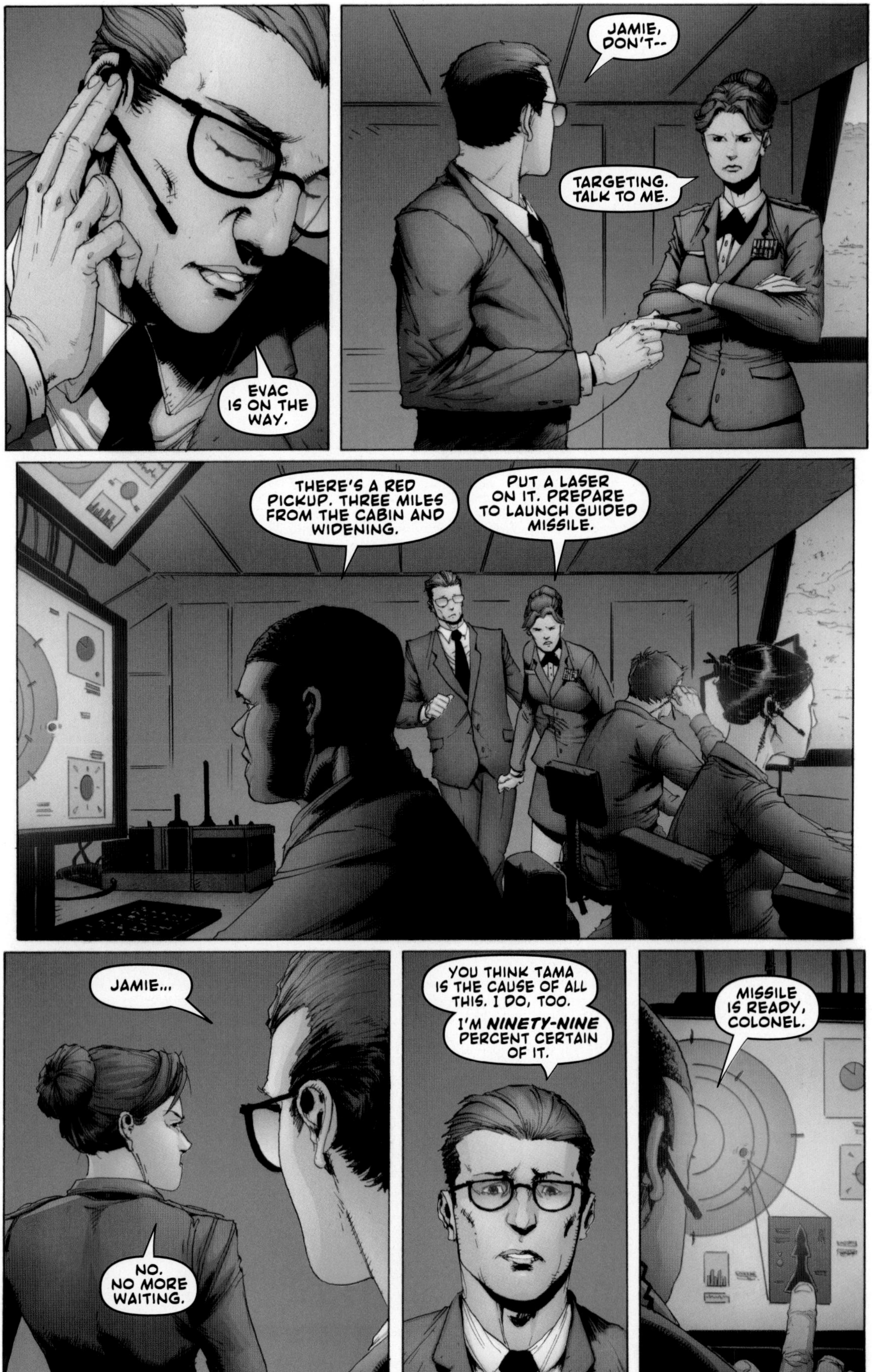
EVAC IS ON THE WAY.
JAMIE, DON'T--
TARGETING. TALK TO ME.
THERE'S A RED PICKUP. THREE MILES FROM THE CABIN AND WIDENING.
PUT A LASER ON IT. PREPARE TO LAUNCH GUIDED MISSILE.
JAMIE...
NO. NO MORE WAITING.
YOU THINK TAMA IS THE CAUSE OF ALL THIS. I DO, TOO.
I'M NINETY-NINE PERCENT CERTAIN OF IT.
MISSILE IS READY, COLONEL.

BUT IT'S THAT *ONE PERCENT* THAT WORRIES ME.

WHAT IF GILAD IS SPOT-ON? WHAT IF TAMA *ISN'T* THE CAUSE?

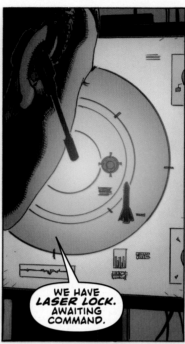

WE HAVE *LASER LOCK.* AWAITING COMMAND.

ONCE A MISSILE LEAVES *THE TUBE,* THERE'S NO CALLING IT BACK. THERE'S JUST THE AFTERMATH.

COLONEL!

WE'VE *LOST* LOCK!

THEY *DISAPPEARED* IN THE DUST STORM!

YOU TURN OUT TO BE WRONG, I'LL KILL YOU MYSELF.

SO WHAT NOW?

UNITY IS THE BEST WE'VE GOT.

WE GET THEM PATCHED UP AND BACK IN THE FIELD.

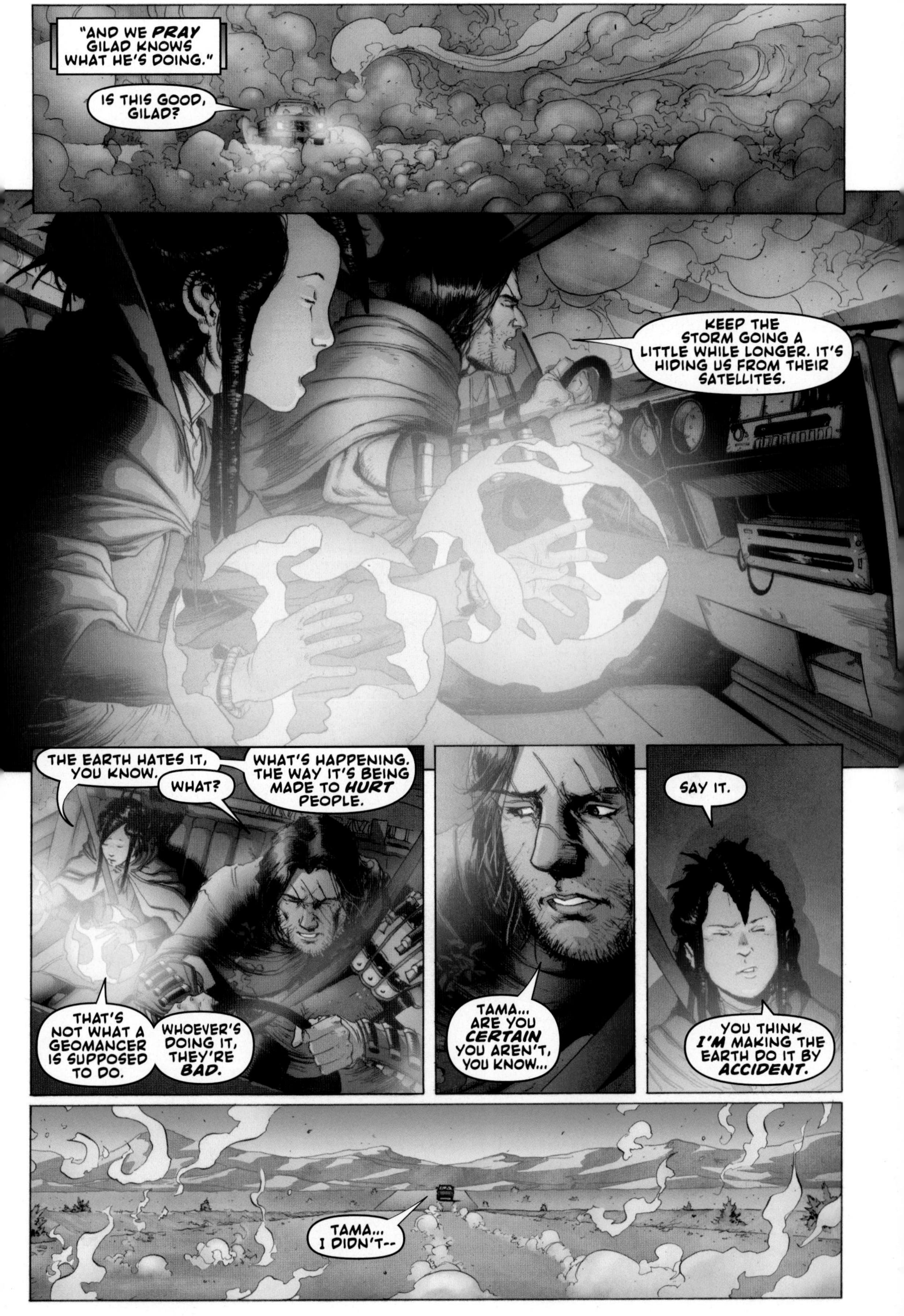
"AND WE *PRAY* GILAD KNOWS WHAT HE'S DOING."
IS THIS GOOD, GILAD?
KEEP THE STORM GOING A LITTLE WHILE LONGER. IT'S HIDING US FROM THEIR SATELLITES.
THE EARTH HATES IT, YOU KNOW.
WHAT?
WHAT'S HAPPENING. THE WAY IT'S BEING MADE TO *HURT* PEOPLE.
THAT'S NOT WHAT A GEOMANCER IS SUPPOSED TO DO.
WHOEVER'S DOING IT, THEY'RE *BAD*.
TAMA... ARE YOU *CERTAIN* YOU AREN'T, YOU KNOW...
SAY IT.
YOU THINK *I'M* MAKING THE EARTH DO IT BY *ACCIDENT*.
TAMA... I DIDN'T--

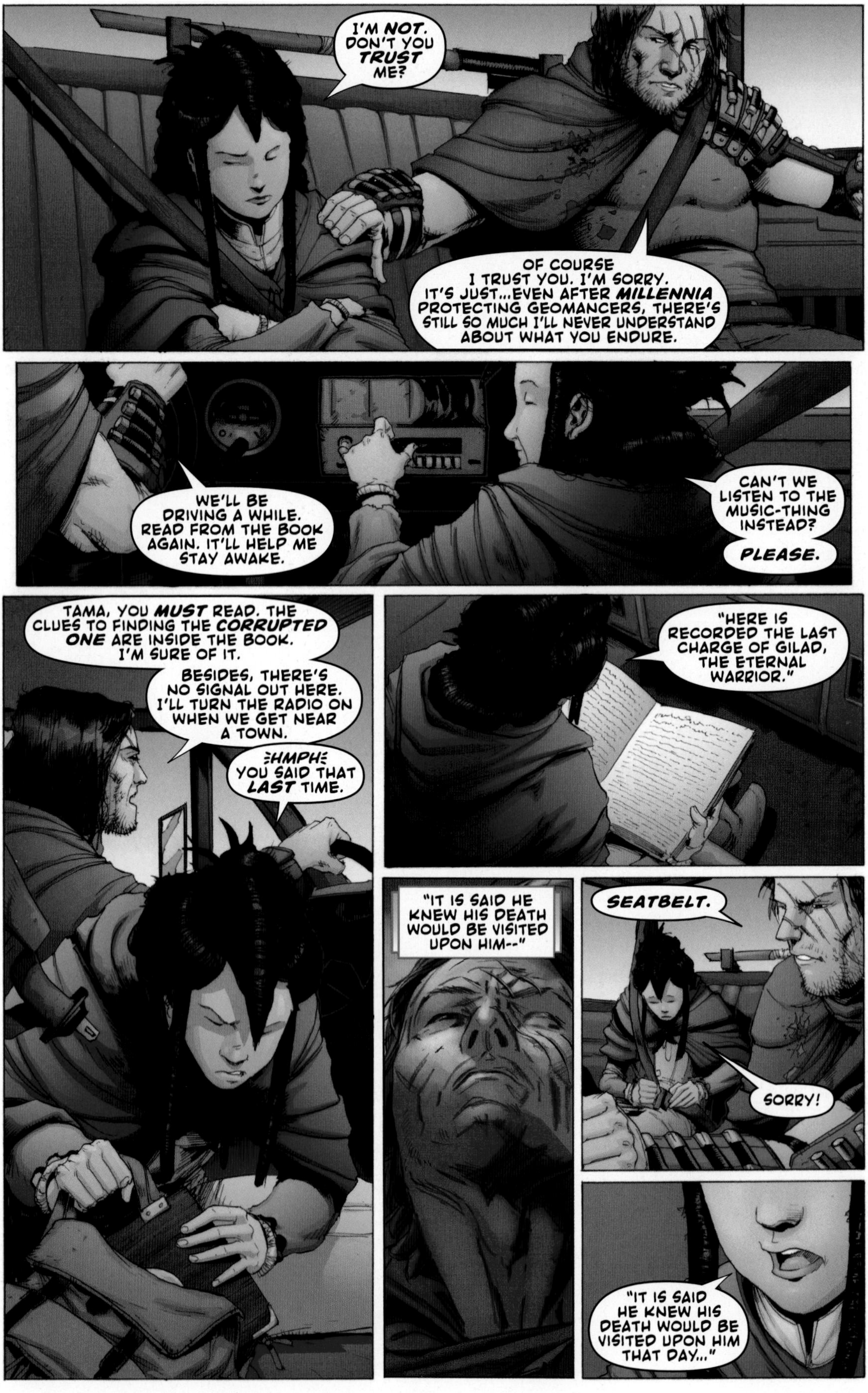
I'M NOT. DON'T YOU TRUST ME?
OF COURSE I TRUST YOU. I'M SORRY. IT'S JUST...EVEN AFTER MILLENNIA PROTECTING GEOMANCERS, THERE'S STILL SO MUCH I'LL NEVER UNDERSTAND ABOUT WHAT YOU ENDURE.
WE'LL BE DRIVING A WHILE. READ FROM THE BOOK AGAIN. IT'LL HELP ME STAY AWAKE.
CAN'T WE LISTEN TO THE MUSIC-THING INSTEAD?
PLEASE.
TAMA, YOU MUST READ. THE CLUES TO FINDING THE CORRUPTED ONE ARE INSIDE THE BOOK. I'M SURE OF IT.
BESIDES, THERE'S NO SIGNAL OUT HERE. I'LL TURN THE RADIO ON WHEN WE GET NEAR A TOWN.
HMPH
YOU SAID THAT LAST TIME.
"HERE IS RECORDED THE LAST CHARGE OF GILAD, THE ETERNAL WARRIOR."
"IT IS SAID HE KNEW HIS DEATH WOULD BE VISITED UPON HIM--"
SEATBELT.
SORRY!
"IT IS SAID HE KNEW HIS DEATH WOULD BE VISITED UPON HIM THAT DAY..."

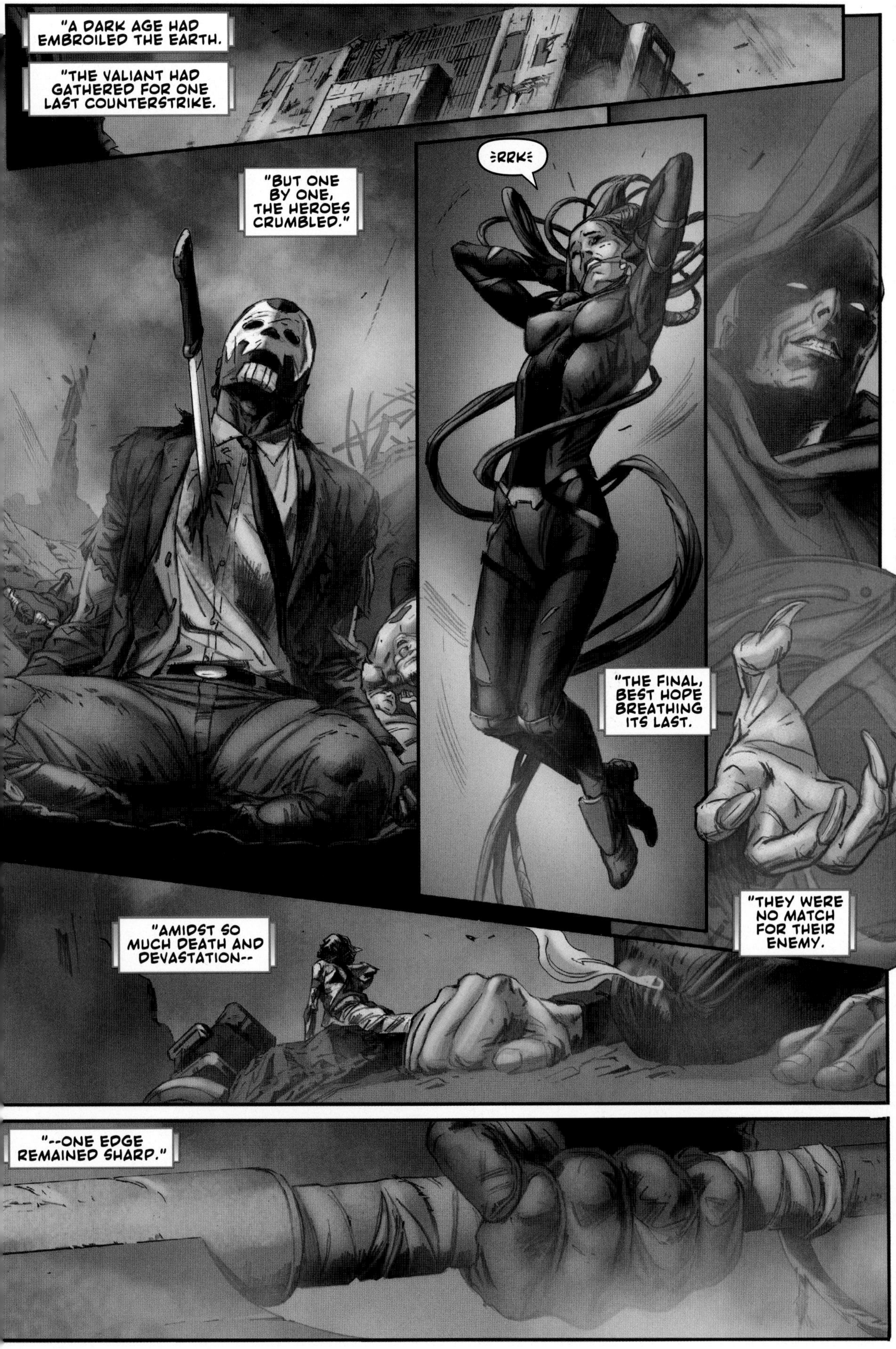
"A DARK AGE HAD EMBROILED THE EARTH.
"THE VALIANT HAD GATHERED FOR ONE LAST COUNTERSTRIKE.
"BUT ONE BY ONE, THE HEROES CRUMBLED."
RRK
"THE FINAL, BEST HOPE BREATHING ITS LAST.
"THEY WERE NO MATCH FOR THEIR ENEMY.
"AMIDST SO MUCH DEATH AND DEVASTATION--
"--ONE EDGE REMAINED SHARP."

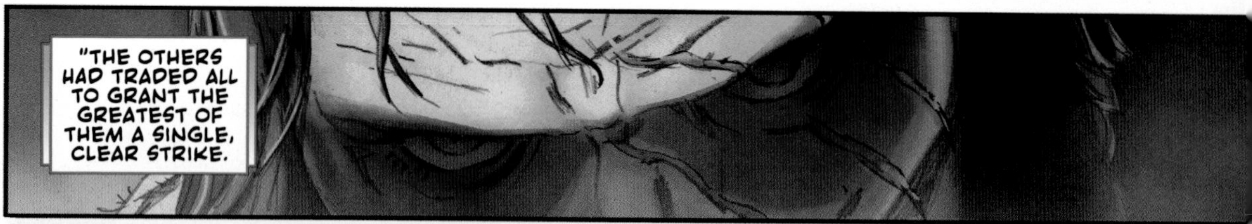
"THE OTHERS HAD TRADED ALL TO GRANT THE GREATEST OF THEM A SINGLE, CLEAR STRIKE.

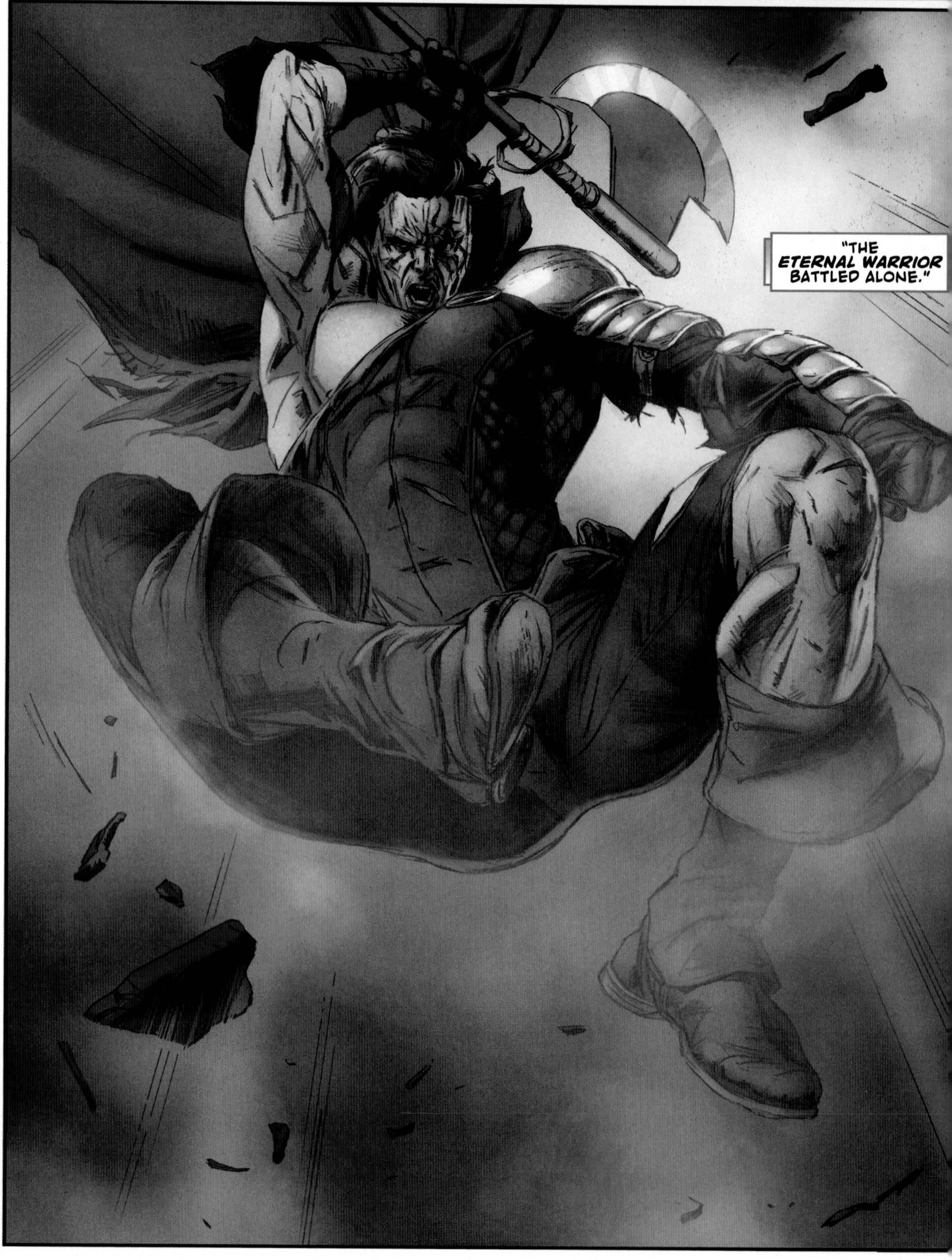
"THE *ETERNAL WARRIOR* BATTLED ALONE."

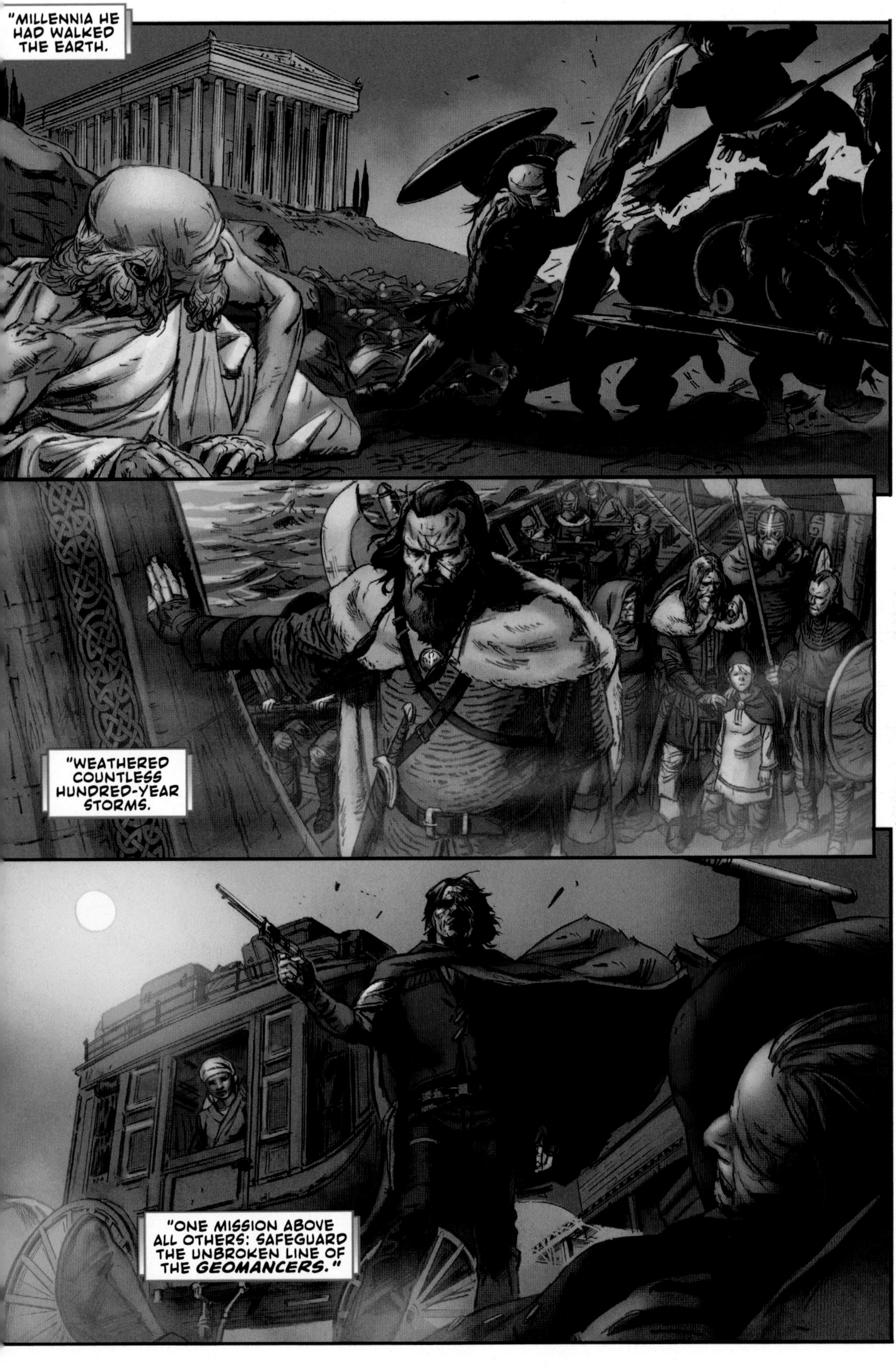
"MILLENNIA HE HAD WALKED THE EARTH.
"WEATHERED COUNTLESS HUNDRED-YEAR STORMS.
"ONE MISSION ABOVE ALL OTHERS: SAFEGUARD THE UNBROKEN LINE OF THE GEOMANCERS."

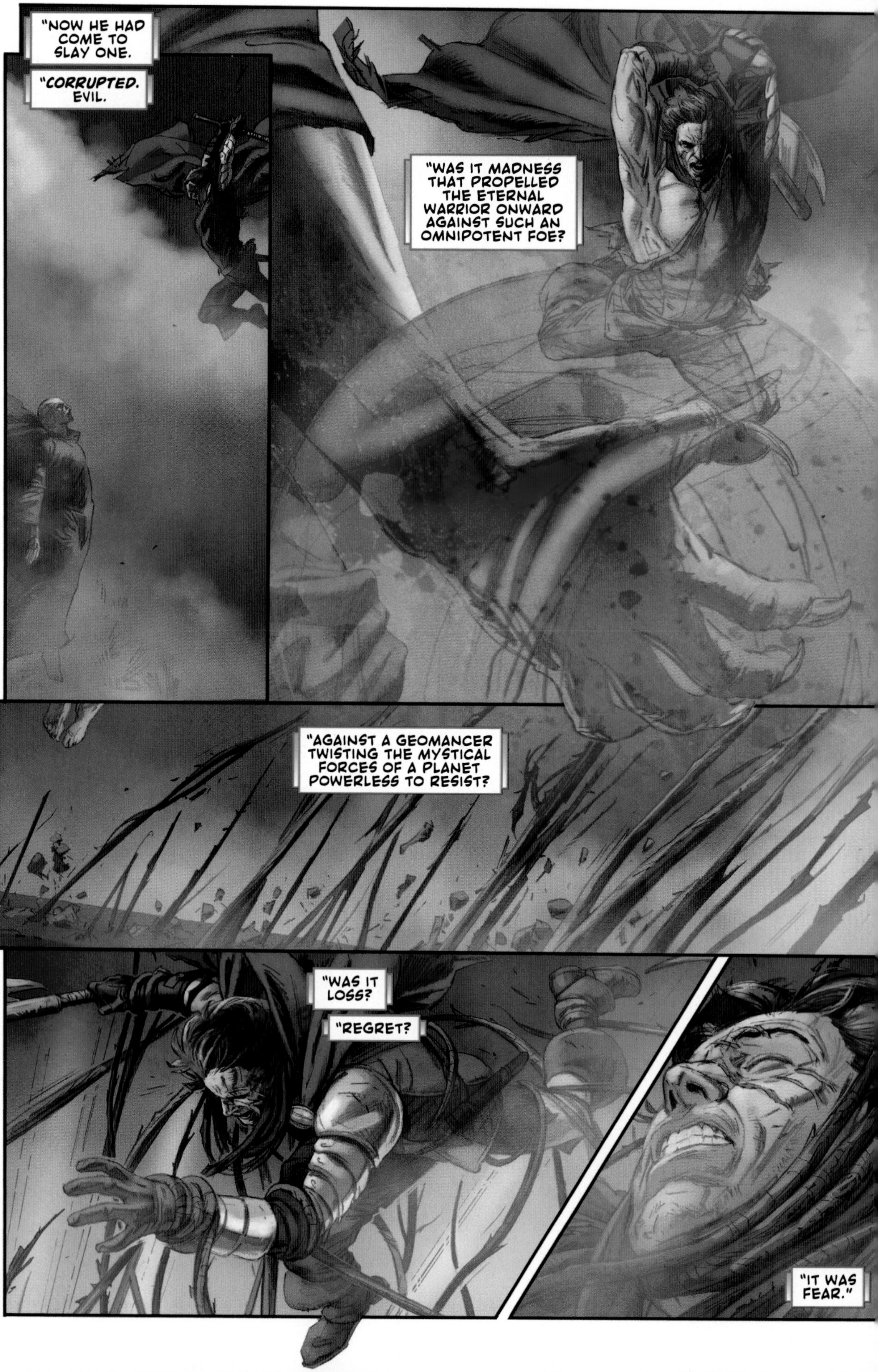

"NOW HE HAD COME TO SLAY ONE.
"CORRUPTED. EVIL.
"WAS IT MADNESS THAT PROPELLED THE ETERNAL WARRIOR ONWARD AGAINST SUCH AN OMNIPOTENT FOE?
"AGAINST A GEOMANCER TWISTING THE MYSTICAL FORCES OF A PLANET POWERLESS TO RESIST?
"WAS IT LOSS?
"REGRET?
"IT WAS FEAR."

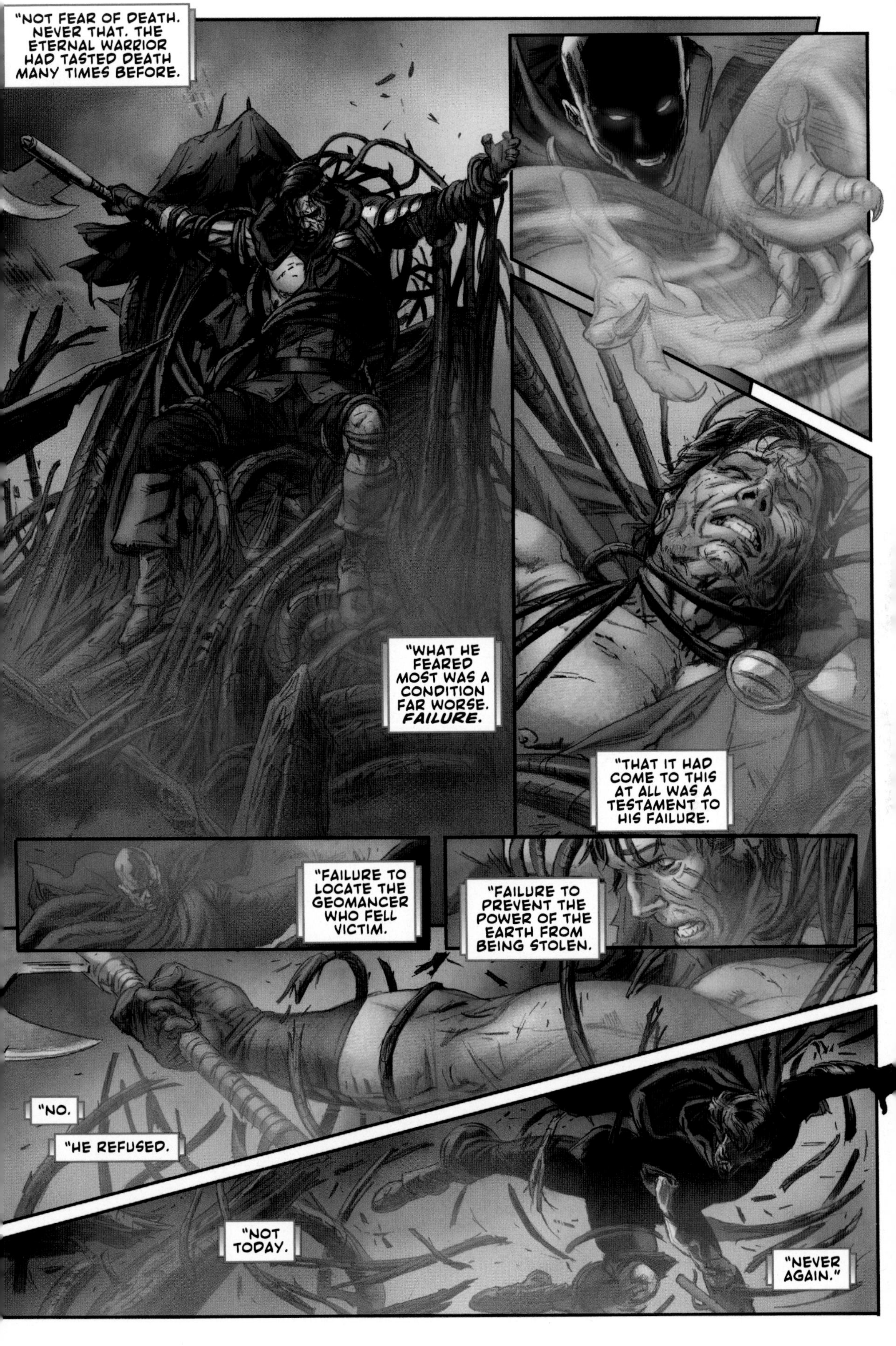
"NOT FEAR OF DEATH. NEVER THAT. THE ETERNAL WARRIOR HAD TASTED DEATH MANY TIMES BEFORE.
"WHAT HE FEARED MOST WAS A CONDITION FAR WORSE. *FAILURE.*
"THAT IT HAD COME TO THIS AT ALL WAS A TESTAMENT TO HIS FAILURE.
"FAILURE TO LOCATE THE GEOMANCER WHO FELL VICTIM.
"FAILURE TO PREVENT THE POWER OF THE EARTH FROM BEING STOLEN.
"NO.
"HE REFUSED.
"NOT TODAY.
"NEVER AGAIN."

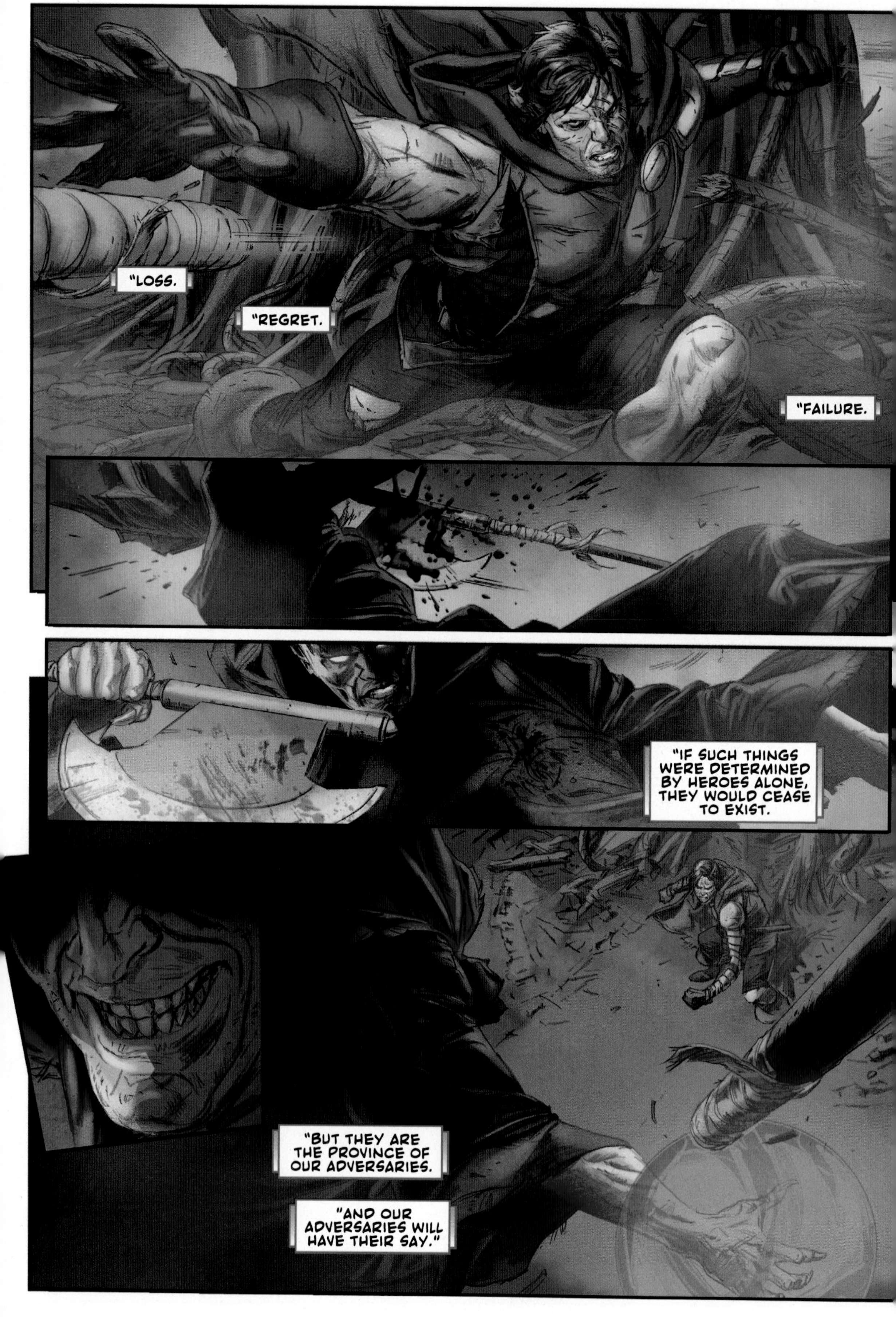
"LOSS.
"REGRET.
"FAILURE.
"IF SUCH THINGS WERE DETERMINED BY HEROES ALONE, THEY WOULD CEASE TO EXIST.
"BUT THEY ARE THE PROVINCE OF OUR ADVERSARIES.
"AND OUR ADVERSARIES WILL HAVE THEIR SAY."

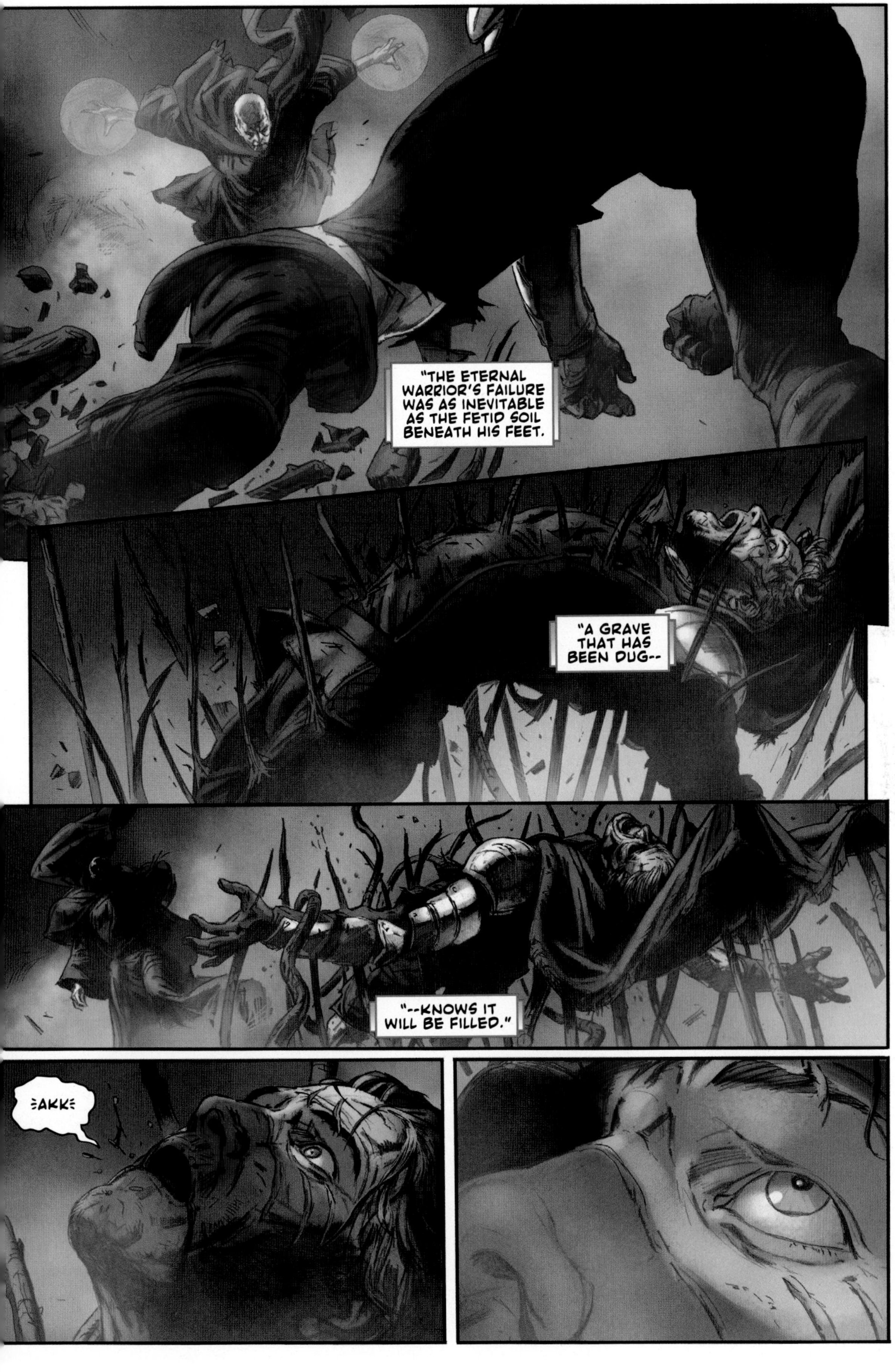
"THE ETERNAL WARRIOR'S FAILURE WAS AS INEVITABLE AS THE FETID SOIL BENEATH HIS FEET.
"A GRAVE THAT HAS BEEN DUG--
"--KNOWS IT WILL BE FILLED."
AKK

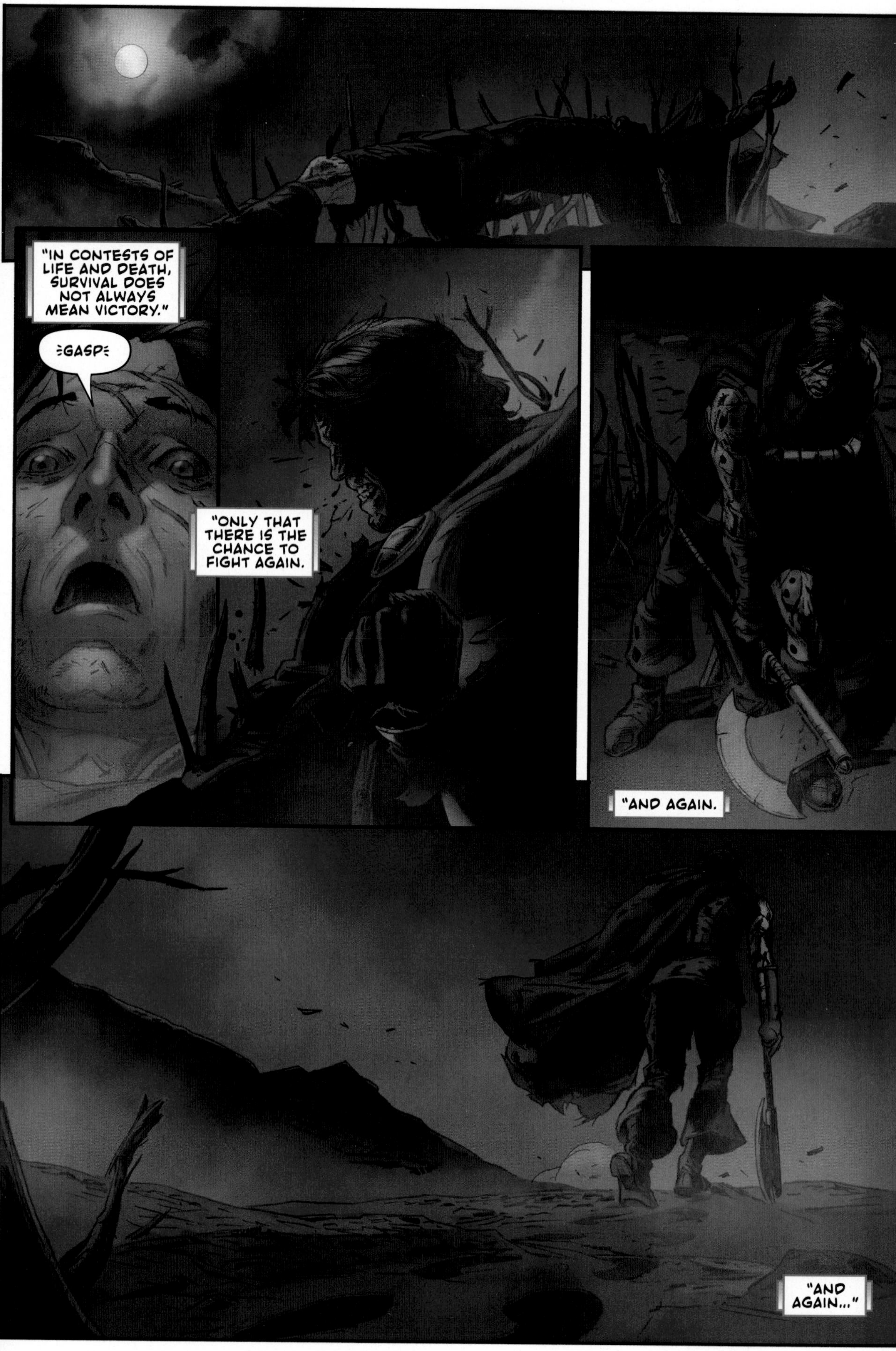
"IN CONTESTS OF LIFE AND DEATH, SURVIVAL DOES NOT ALWAYS MEAN VICTORY."
GASP
"ONLY THAT THERE IS THE CHANCE TO FIGHT AGAIN.
"AND AGAIN.
"AND AGAIN..."

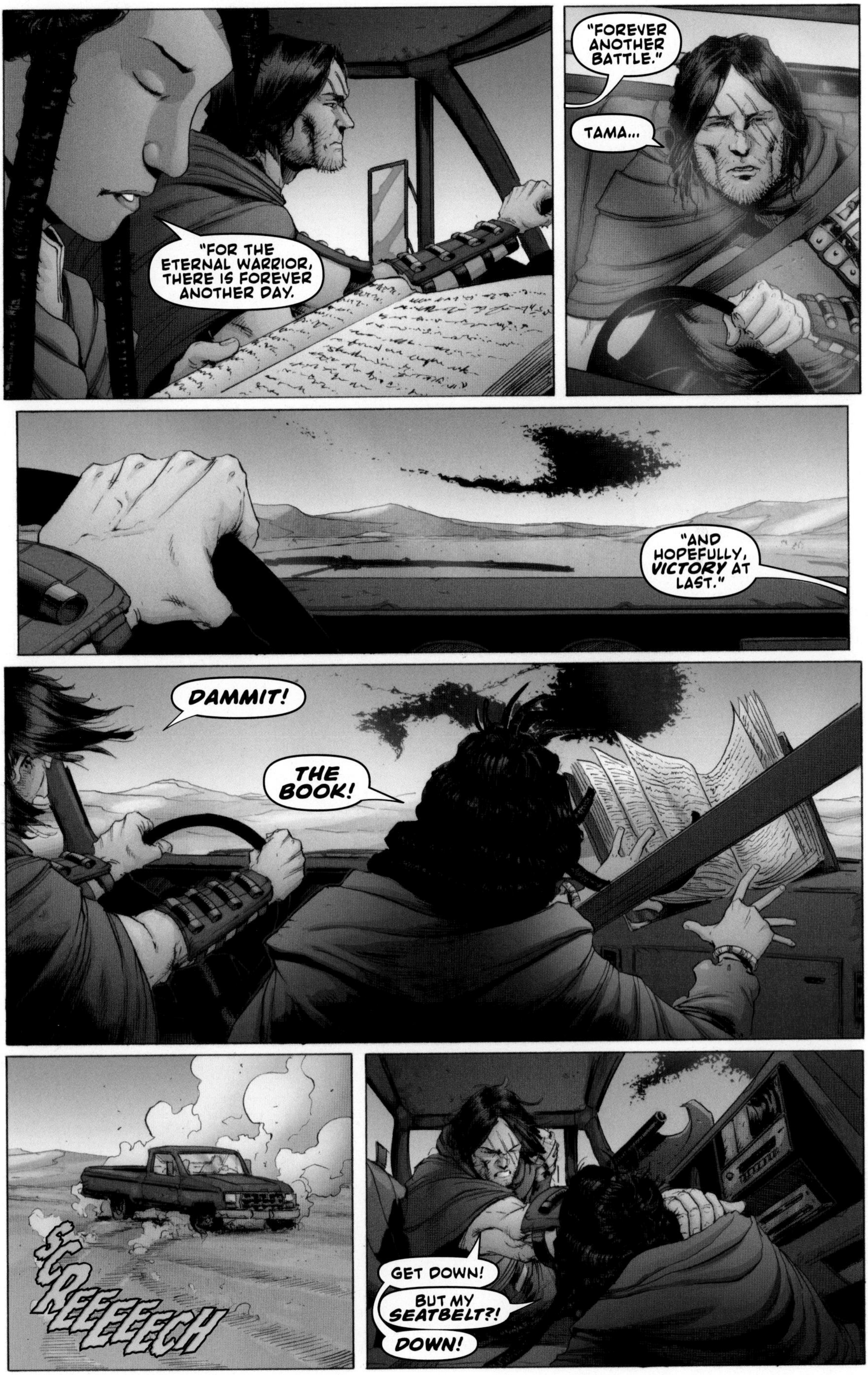
"FOR THE ETERNAL WARRIOR, THERE IS FOREVER ANOTHER DAY.
"FOREVER ANOTHER BATTLE."
TAMA...
"AND HOPEFULLY, VICTORY AT LAST."
DAMMIT!
THE BOOK!
SCREEEEECH
GET DOWN!
BUT MY SEATBELT?!
DOWN!

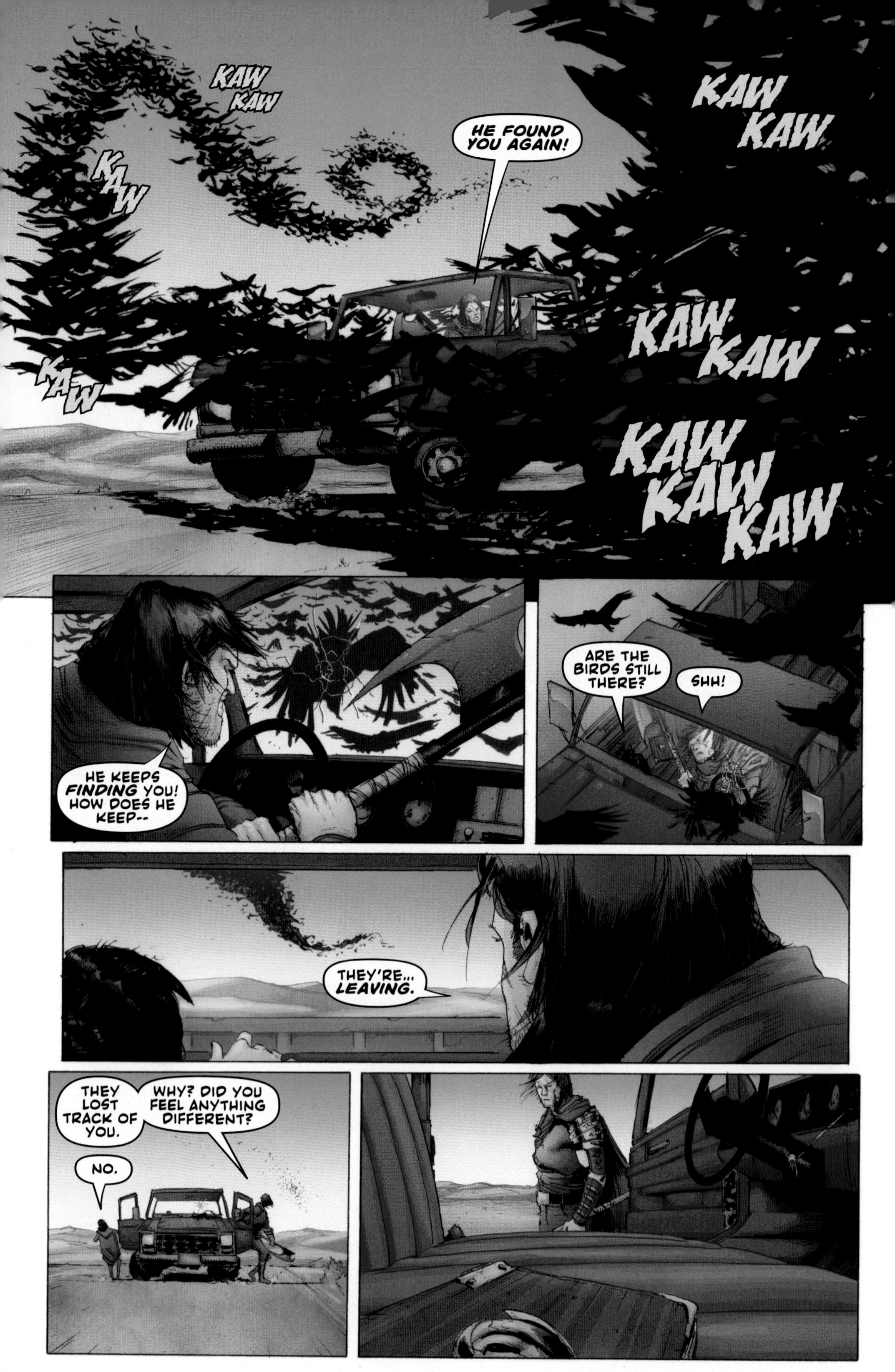
KAW KAW
KAW
KAW
HE FOUND YOU AGAIN!
KAW KAW
KAW KAW
KAW KAW KAW
HE KEEPS FINDING YOU! HOW DOES HE KEEP--
ARE THE BIRDS STILL THERE?
SHH!
THEY'RE... LEAVING.
THEY LOST TRACK OF YOU.
WHY? DID YOU FEEL ANYTHING DIFFERENT?
NO.

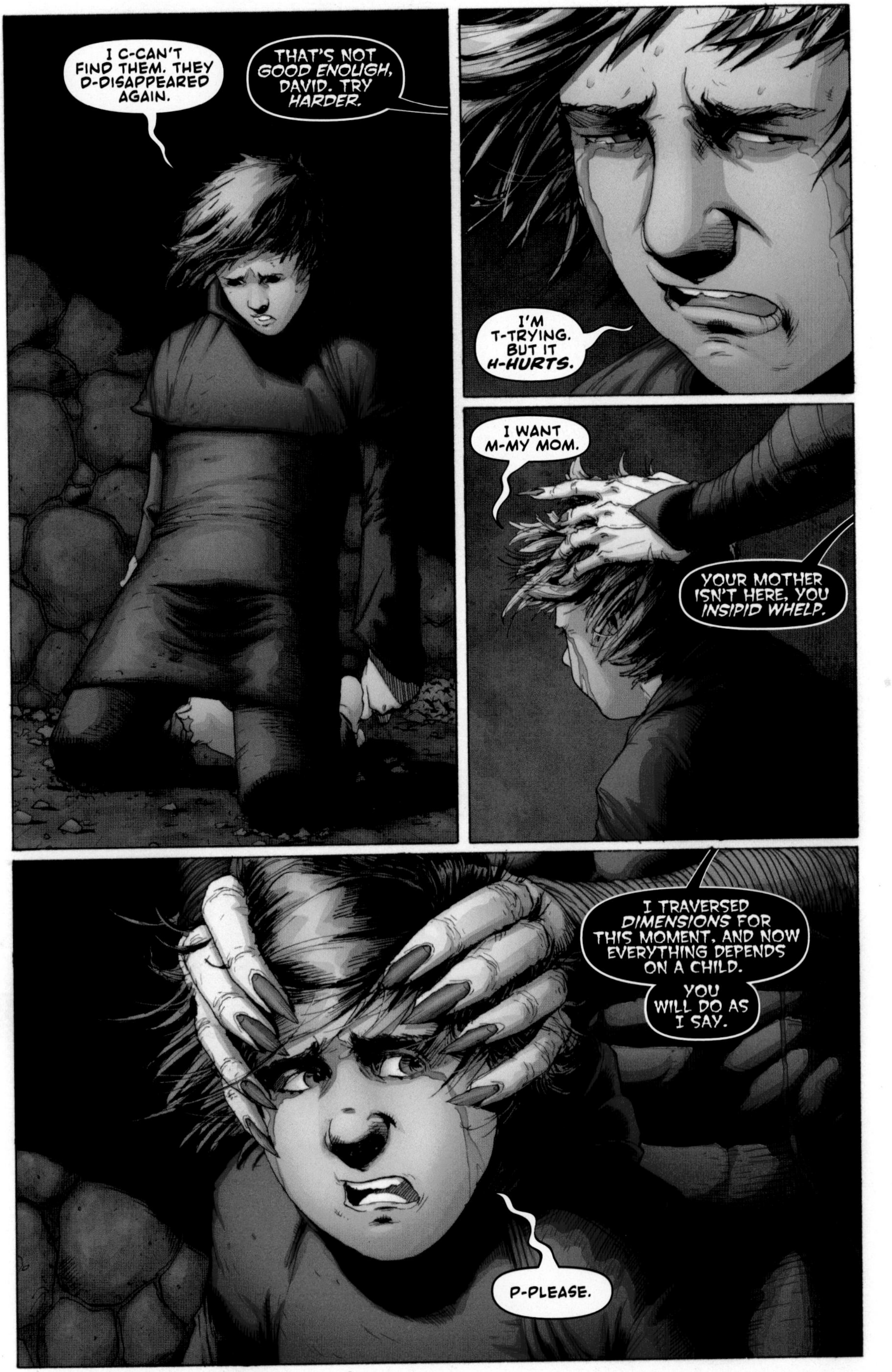
I C-CAN'T FIND THEM. THEY D-DISAPPEARED AGAIN.
THAT'S NOT GOOD ENOUGH, DAVID. TRY HARDER.
I'M T-TRYING. BUT IT H-HURTS.
I WANT M-MY MOM.
YOUR MOTHER ISN'T HERE, YOU INSIPID WHELP.
I TRAVERSED DIMENSIONS FOR THIS MOMENT, AND NOW EVERYTHING DEPENDS ON A CHILD.
YOU WILL DO AS I SAY.
P-PLEASE.

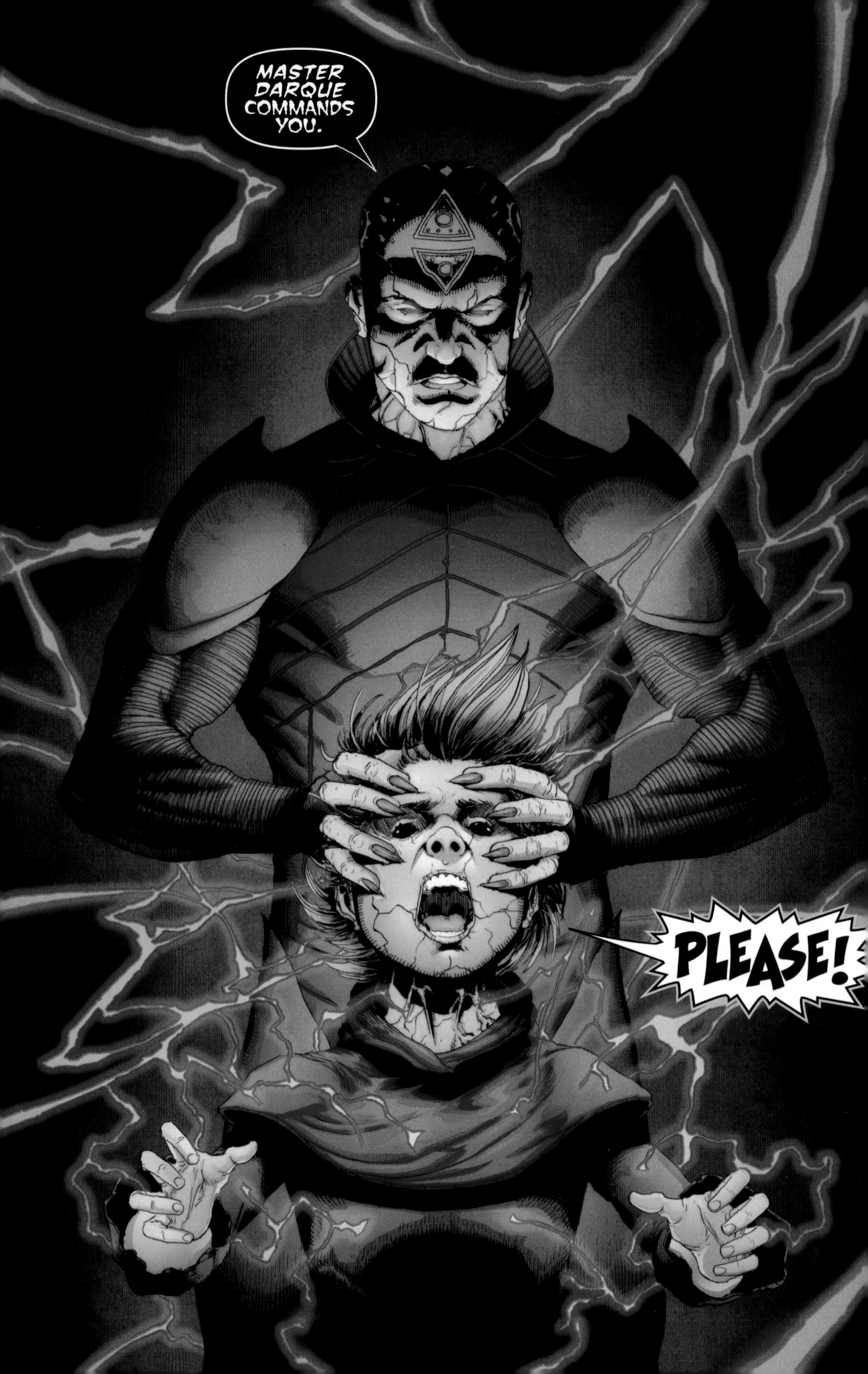
MASTER DARQUE COMMANDS YOU.
PLEASE!

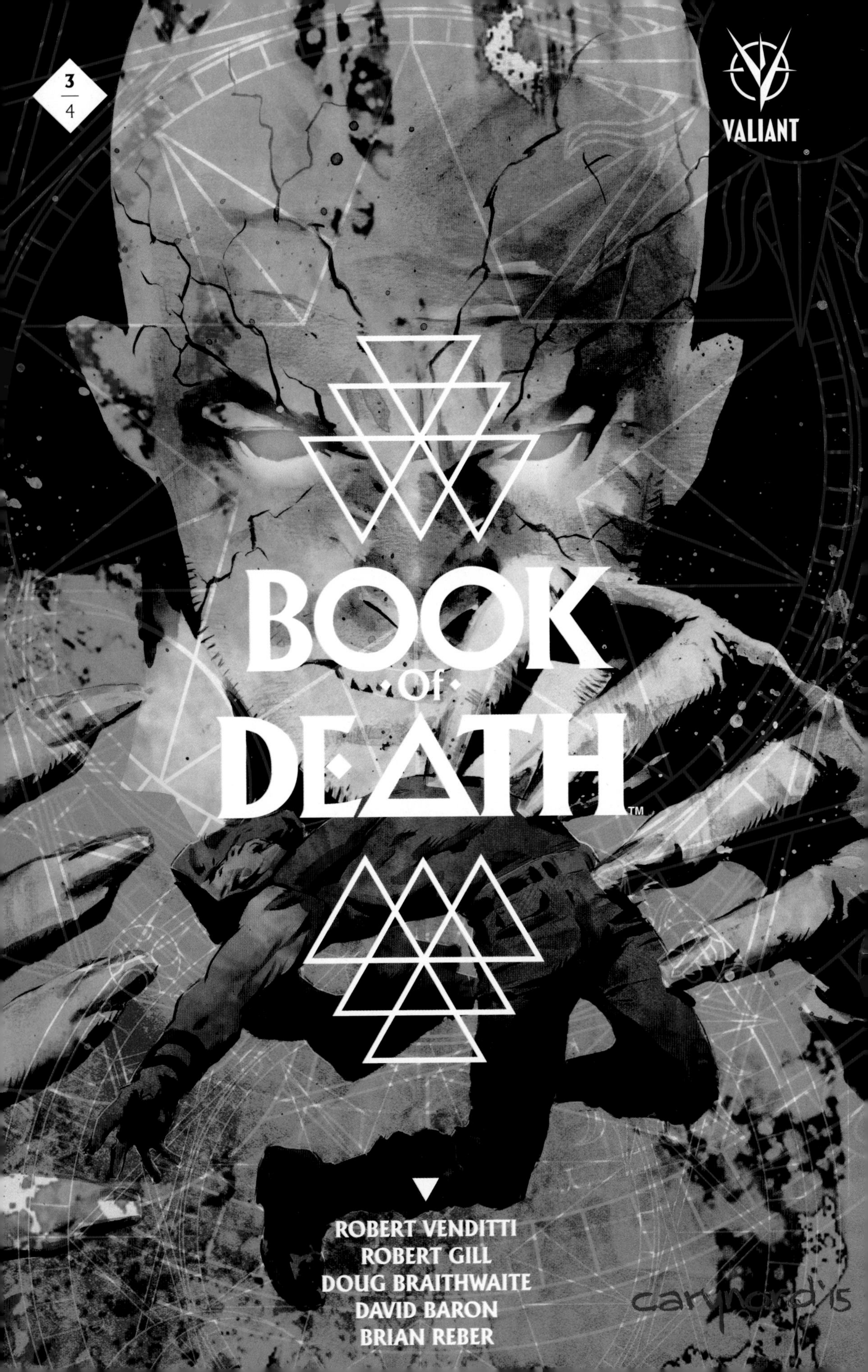
3
4
VALIANT
BOOK
of
DEATH
ROBERT VENDITTI
ROBERT GILL
DOUG BRAITHWAITE
DAVID BARON
BRIAN REBER
carynord '15

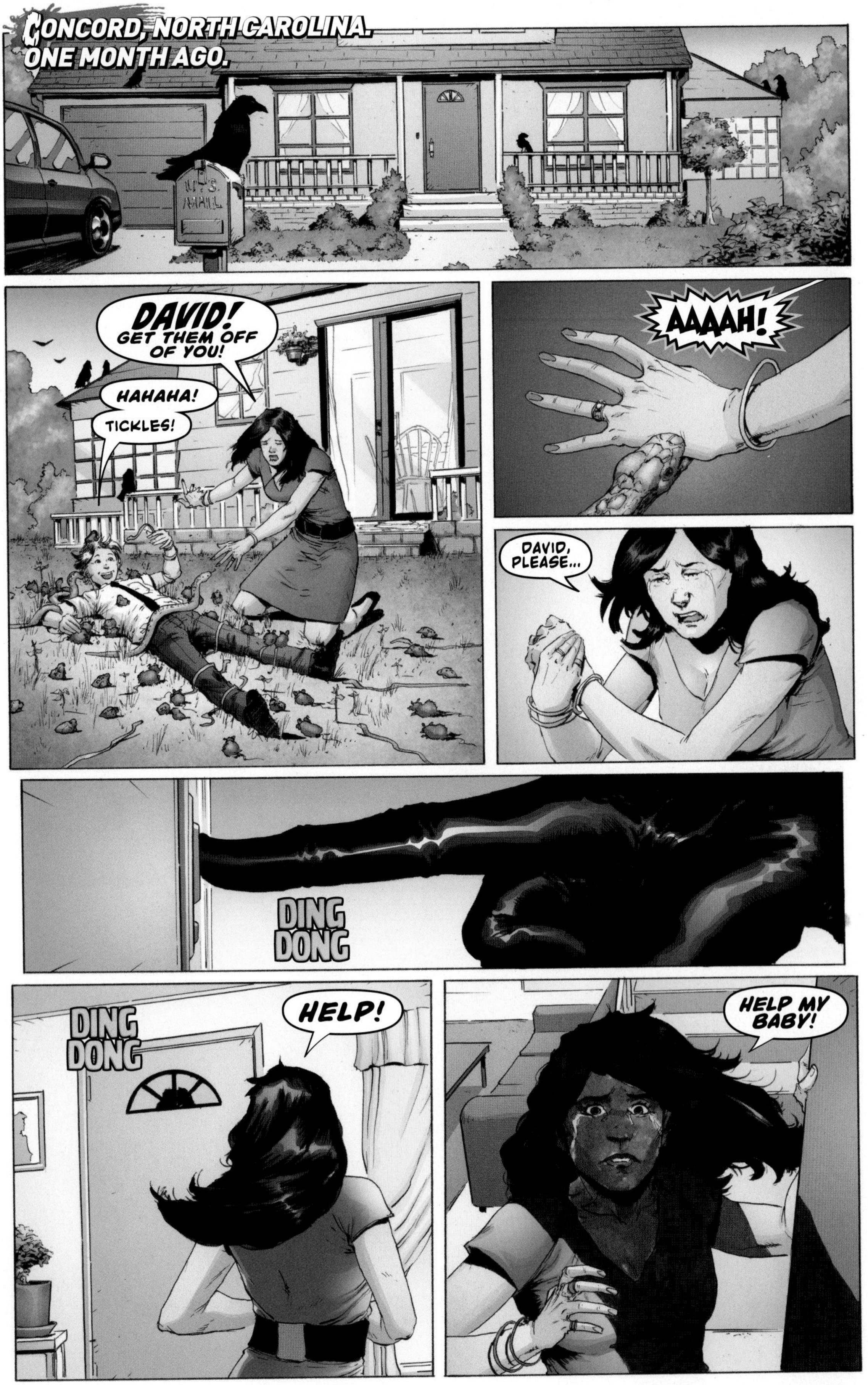
CONCORD, NORTH CAROLINA.
ONE MONTH AGO.
U.S. MAIL
DAVID! GET THEM OFF OF YOU!
HAHAHA!
TICKLES!
AAAAH!
DAVID, PLEASE...
DING DONG
DING DONG
HELP!
HELP MY BABY!

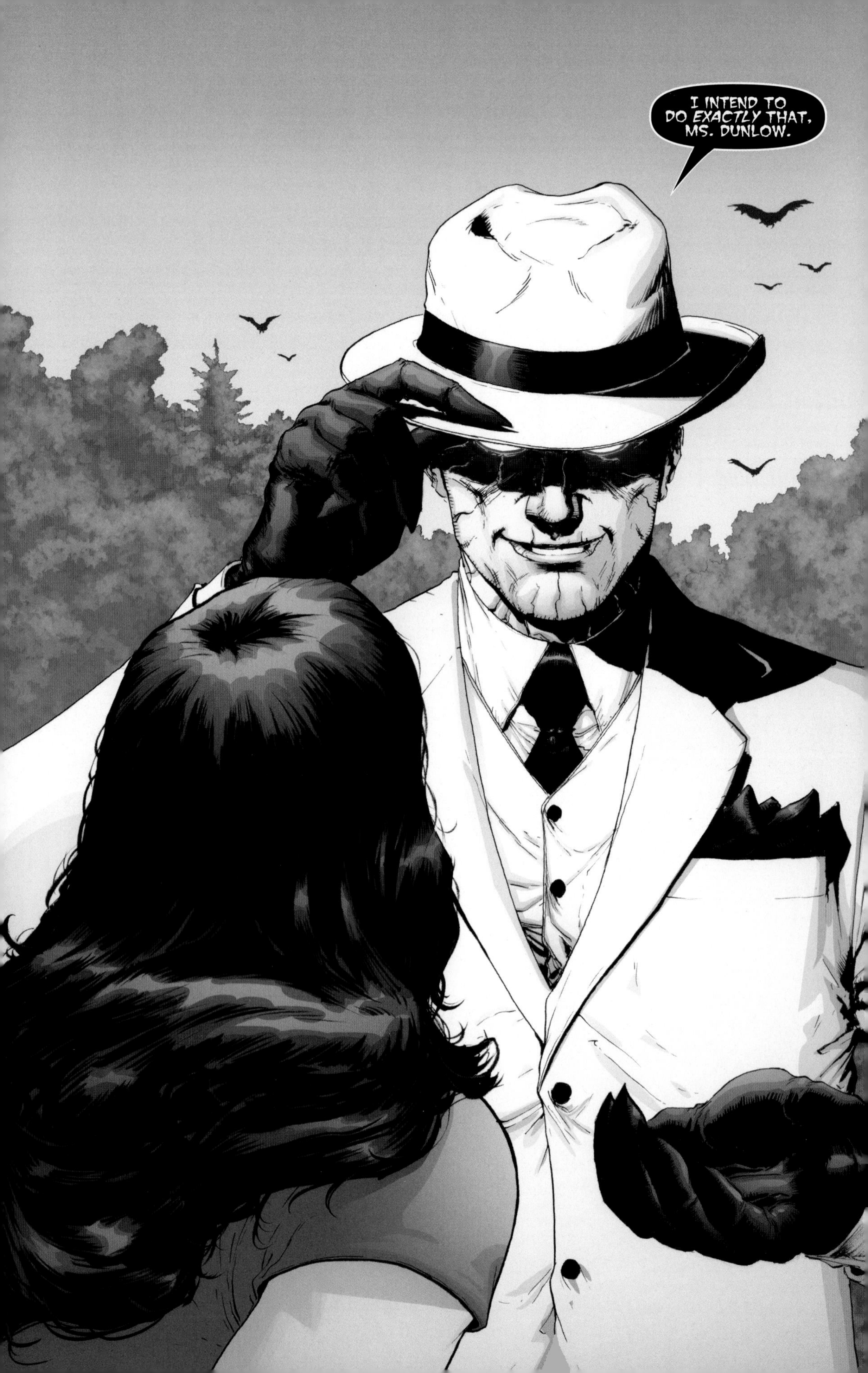
I INTEND TO DO EXACTLY THAT, MS. DUNLOW.

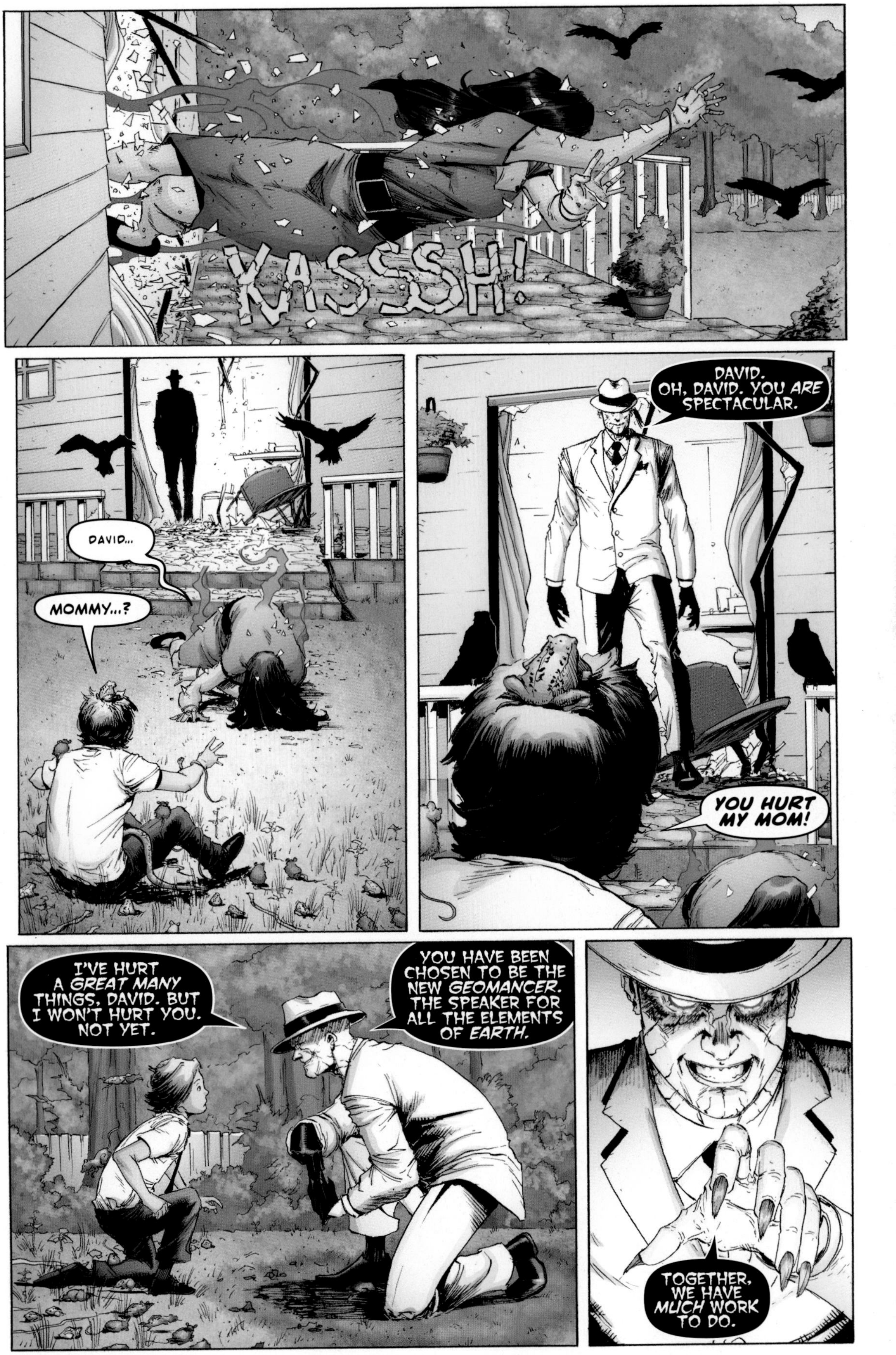
KASSSH!
DAVID...
MOMMY...?
DAVID.
OH, DAVID. YOU ARE SPECTACULAR.
YOU HURT MY MOM!
I'VE HURT A GREAT MANY THINGS, DAVID. BUT I WON'T HURT YOU. NOT YET.
YOU HAVE BEEN CHOSEN TO BE THE NEW GEOMANCER. THE SPEAKER FOR ALL THE ELEMENTS OF EARTH.
TOGETHER, WE HAVE MUCH WORK TO DO.

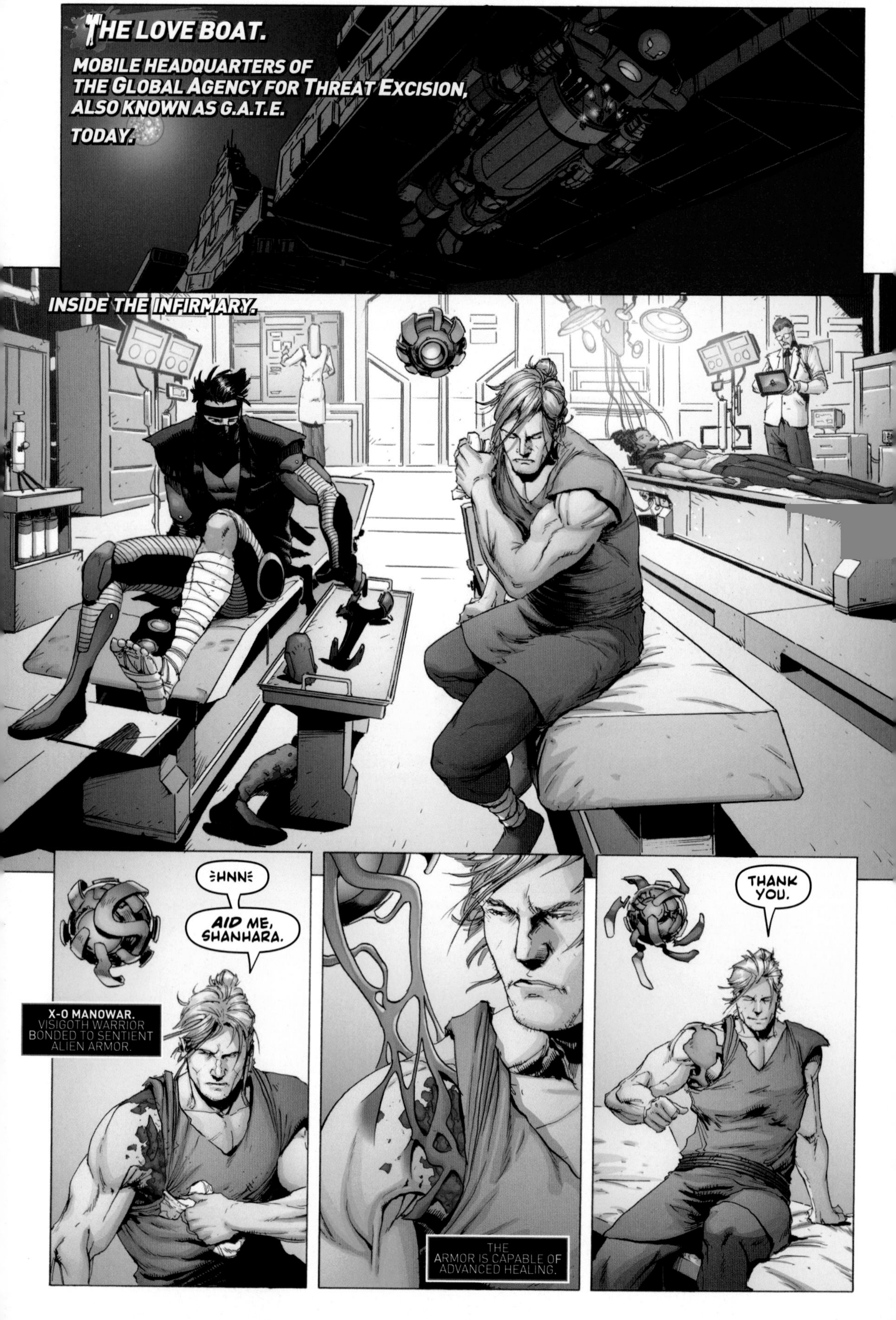
THE LOVE BOAT.
MOBILE HEADQUARTERS OF THE GLOBAL AGENCY FOR THREAT EXCISION, ALSO KNOWN AS G.A.T.E.
TODAY.
INSIDE THE INFIRMARY.
X-O MANOWAR. VISIGOTH WARRIOR BONDED TO SENTIENT ALIEN ARMOR.
HNN
AID ME, SHANHARA.
THE ARMOR IS CAPABLE OF ADVANCED HEALING.
THANK YOU.

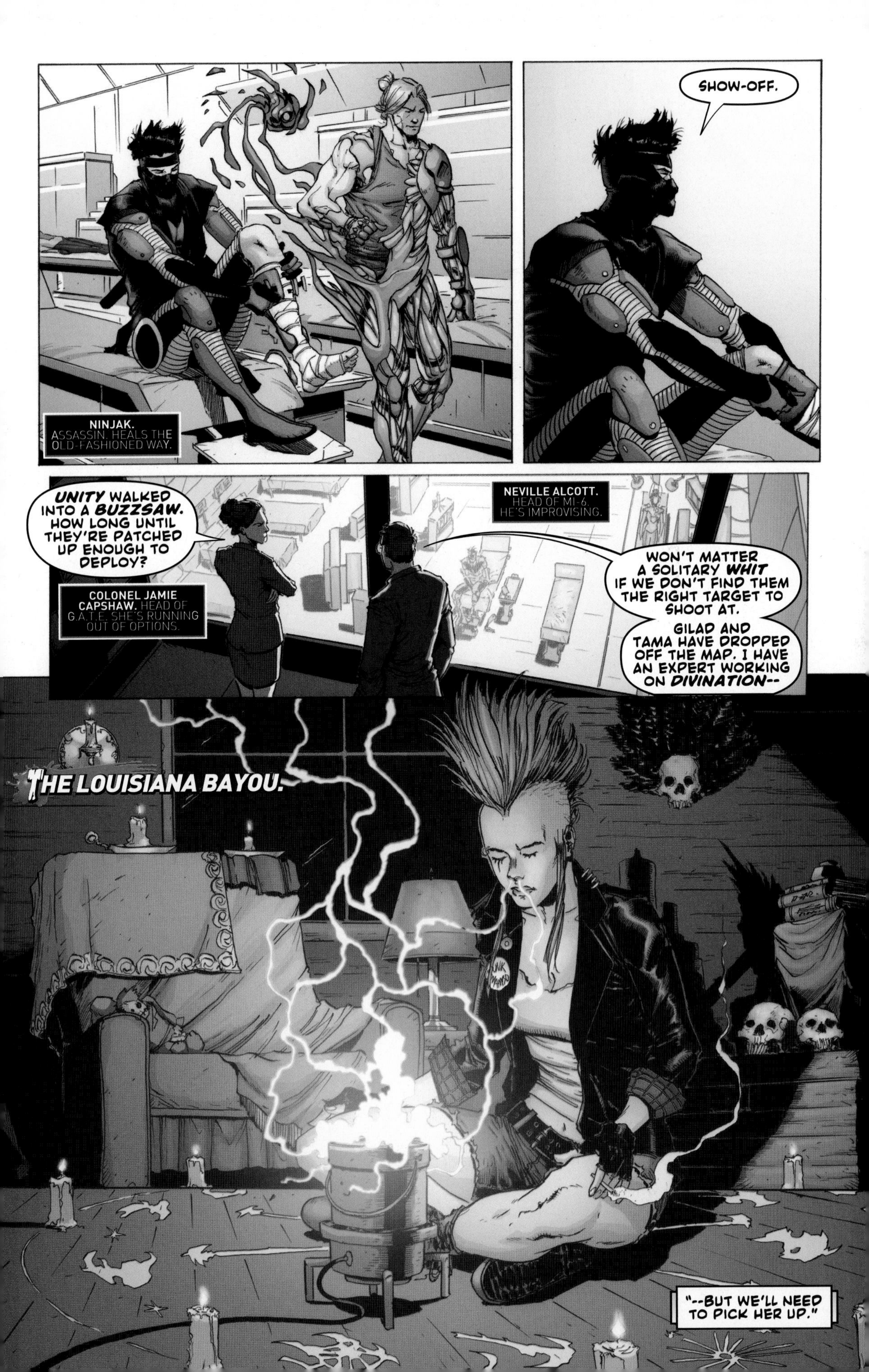

NINJAK. ASSASSIN. HEALS THE OLD-FASHIONED WAY.
SHOW-OFF.
UNITY WALKED INTO A BUZZSAW. HOW LONG UNTIL THEY'RE PATCHED UP ENOUGH TO DEPLOY?
COLONEL JAMIE CAPSHAW. HEAD OF G.A.T.E. SHE'S RUNNING OUT OF OPTIONS.
NEVILLE ALCOTT. HEAD OF MI-6. HE'S IMPROVISING.
WON'T MATTER A SOLITARY WHIT IF WE DON'T FIND THEM THE RIGHT TARGET TO SHOOT AT.
GILAD AND TAMA HAVE DROPPED OFF THE MAP. I HAVE AN EXPERT WORKING ON DIVINATION--
THE LOUISIANA BAYOU.
"--BUT WE'LL NEED TO PICK HER UP."

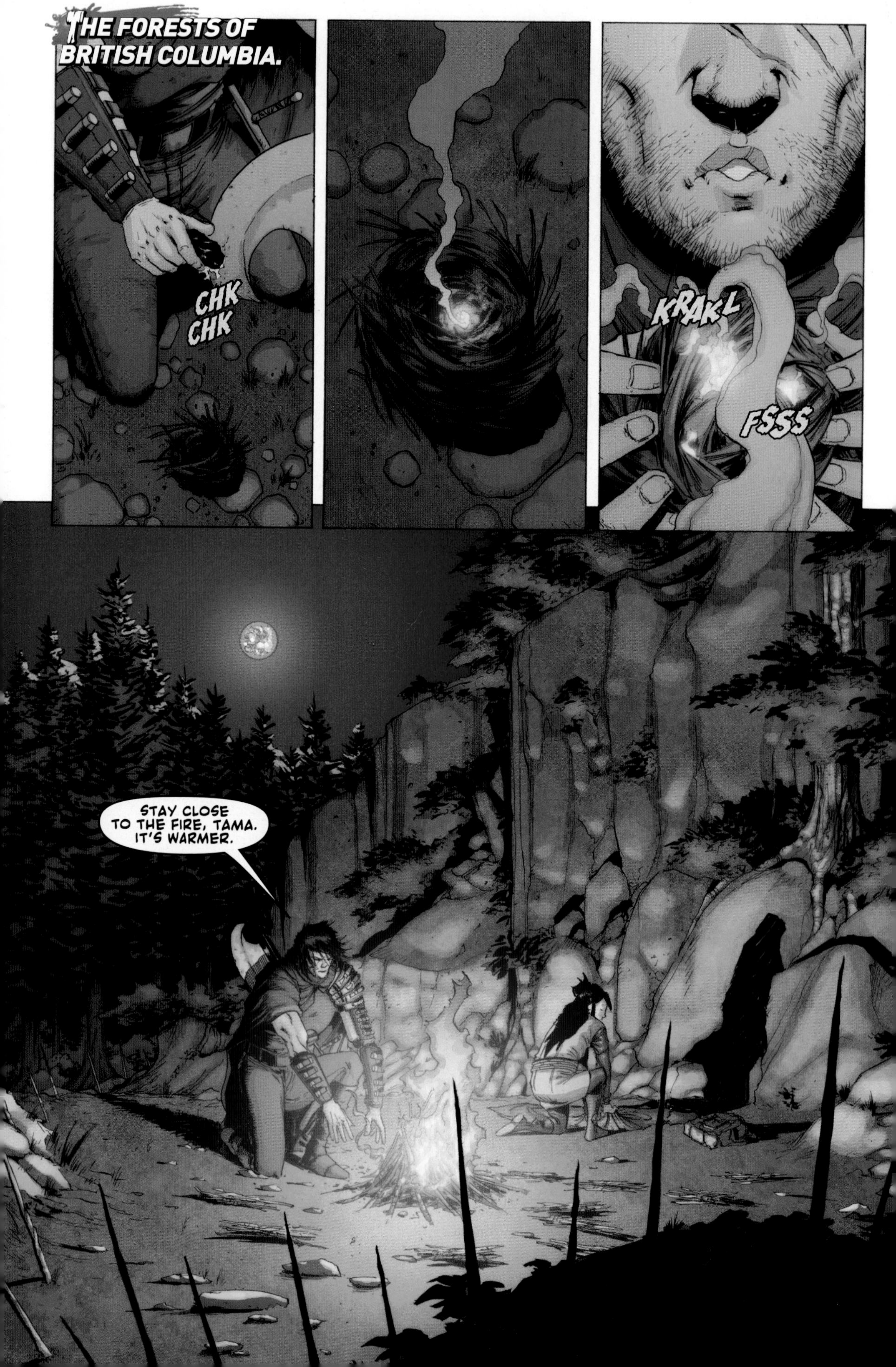
THE FORESTS OF BRITISH COLUMBIA.
CHK CHK
KRAKL
FSSS
STAY CLOSE TO THE FIRE, TAMA. IT'S WARMER.

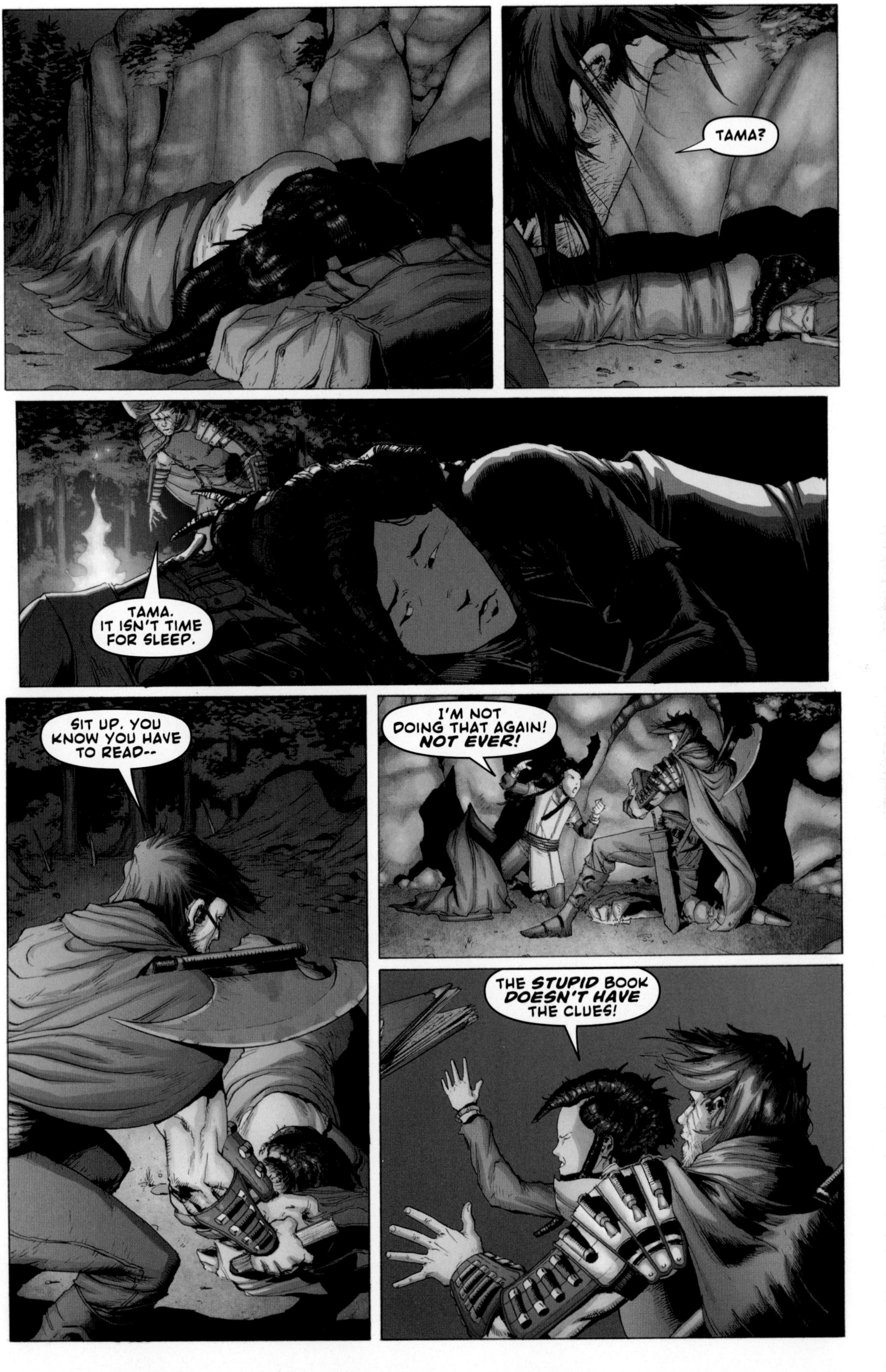
TAMA?
TAMA. IT ISN'T TIME FOR SLEEP.
SIT UP. YOU KNOW YOU HAVE TO READ--
I'M NOT DOING THAT AGAIN! ***NOT EVER!***
THE ***STUPID*** BOOK ***DOESN'T HAVE*** THE CLUES!

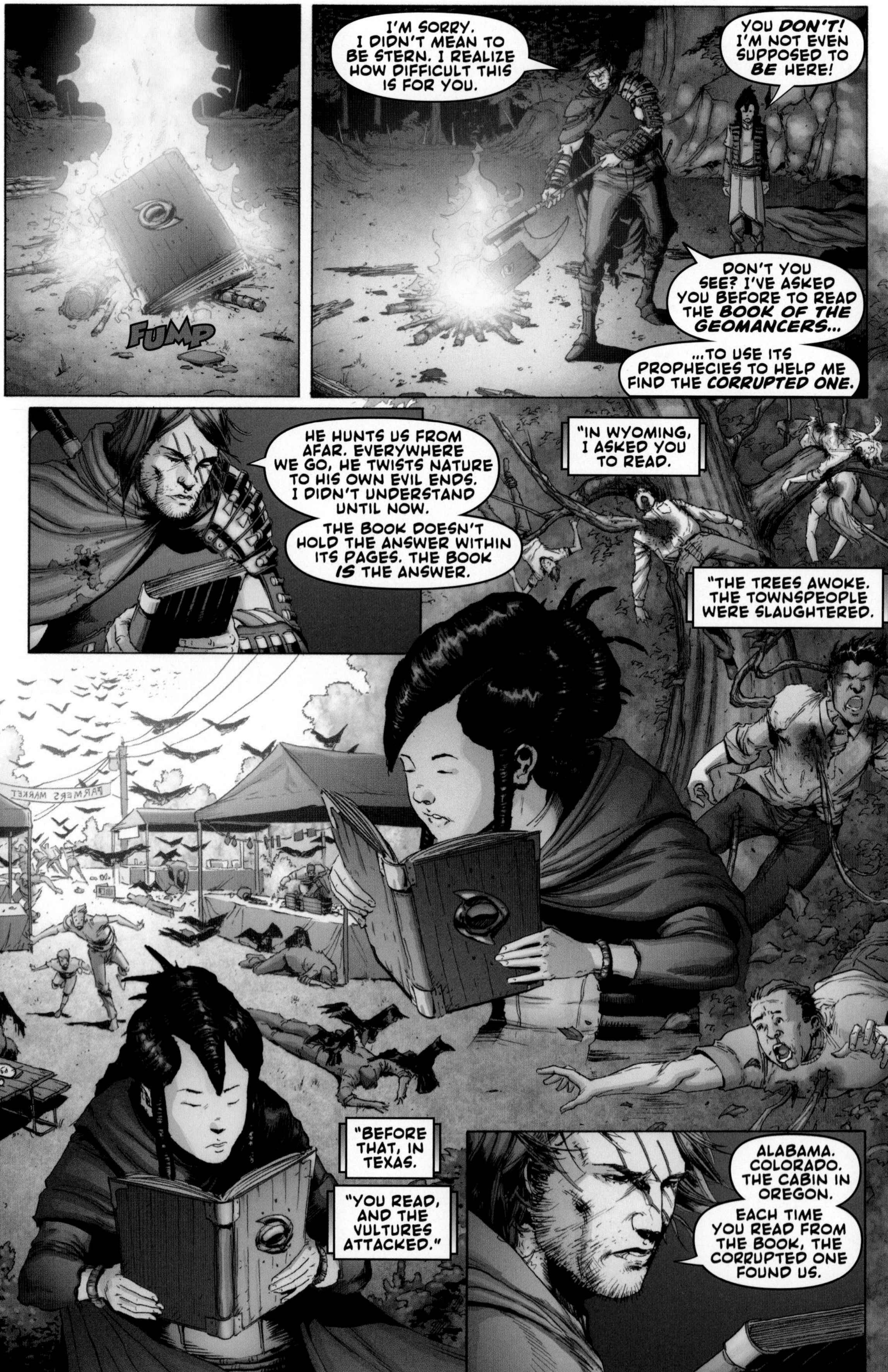
FUMP
I'M SORRY. I DIDN'T MEAN TO BE STERN. I REALIZE HOW DIFFICULT THIS IS FOR YOU.
YOU DON'T! I'M NOT EVEN SUPPOSED TO BE HERE!
DON'T YOU SEE? I'VE ASKED YOU BEFORE TO READ THE BOOK OF THE GEOMANCERS...
...TO USE ITS PROPHECIES TO HELP ME FIND THE CORRUPTED ONE.
HE HUNTS US FROM AFAR. EVERYWHERE WE GO, HE TWISTS NATURE TO HIS OWN EVIL ENDS. I DIDN'T UNDERSTAND UNTIL NOW.
THE BOOK DOESN'T HOLD THE ANSWER WITHIN ITS PAGES. THE BOOK IS THE ANSWER.
"IN WYOMING, I ASKED YOU TO READ.
"THE TREES AWOKE. THE TOWNSPEOPLE WERE SLAUGHTERED.
"BEFORE THAT, IN TEXAS.
"YOU READ, AND THE VULTURES ATTACKED."
ALABAMA. COLORADO. THE CABIN IN OREGON.
EACH TIME YOU READ FROM THE BOOK, THE CORRUPTED ONE FOUND US.

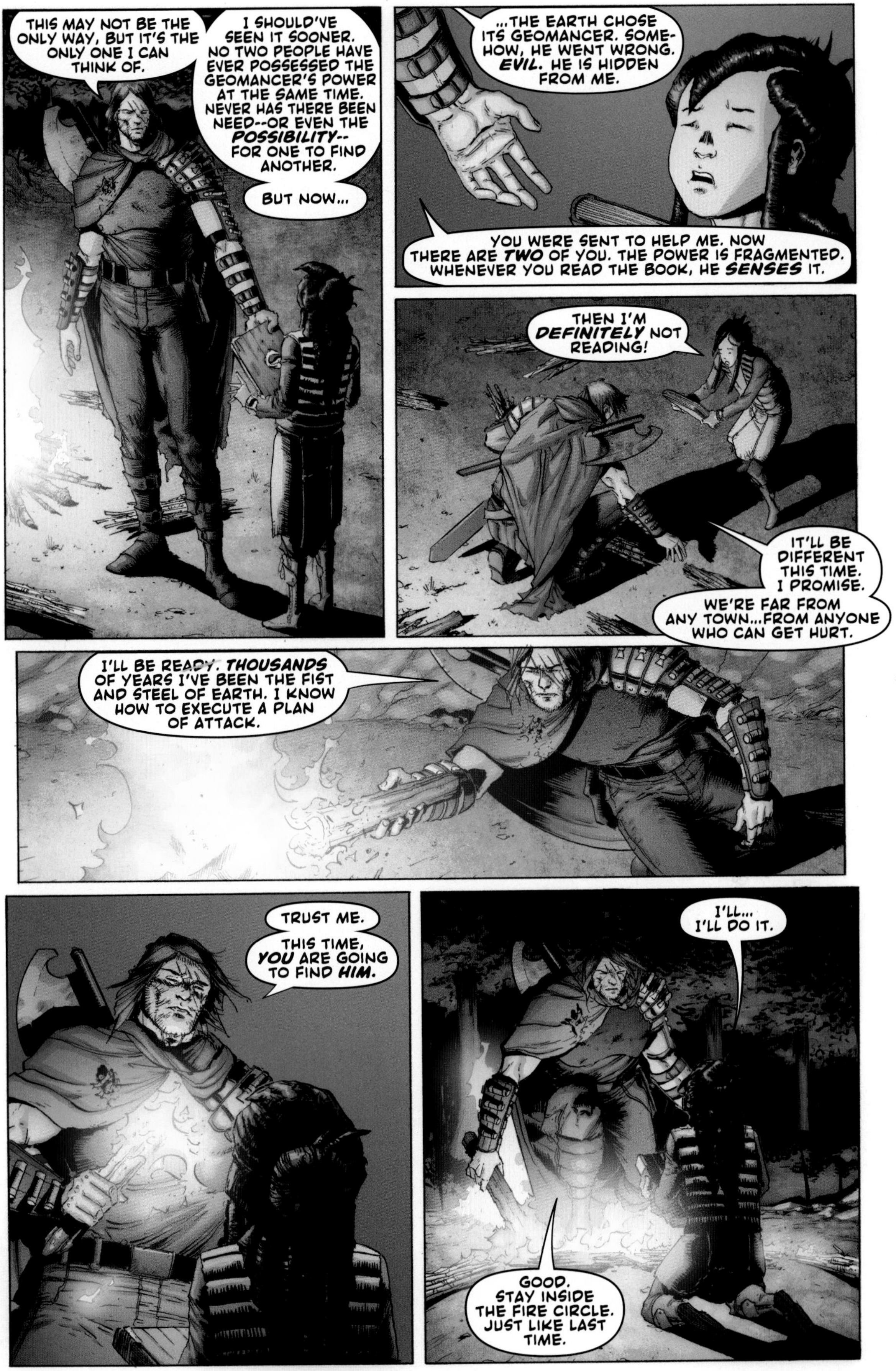
THIS MAY NOT BE THE ONLY WAY, BUT IT'S THE ONLY ONE I CAN THINK OF.
I SHOULD'VE SEEN IT SOONER. NO TWO PEOPLE HAVE EVER POSSESSED THE GEOMANCER'S POWER AT THE SAME TIME. NEVER HAS THERE BEEN NEED--OR EVEN THE *POSSIBILITY*--FOR ONE TO FIND ANOTHER.
BUT NOW...
...THE EARTH CHOSE ITS GEOMANCER. SOMEHOW, HE WENT WRONG. *EVIL.* HE IS HIDDEN FROM ME.
YOU WERE SENT TO HELP ME. NOW THERE ARE *TWO* OF YOU. THE POWER IS FRAGMENTED. WHENEVER YOU READ THE BOOK, HE *SENSES* IT.
THEN I'M *DEFINITELY* NOT READING!
IT'LL BE DIFFERENT THIS TIME. I PROMISE.
WE'RE FAR FROM ANY TOWN...FROM ANYONE WHO CAN GET HURT.
I'LL BE READY. *THOUSANDS* OF YEARS I'VE BEEN THE FIST AND STEEL OF EARTH. I KNOW HOW TO EXECUTE A PLAN OF ATTACK.
TRUST ME.
THIS TIME, *YOU* ARE GOING TO FIND *HIM*.
I'LL... I'LL DO IT.
GOOD. STAY INSIDE THE FIRE CIRCLE. JUST LIKE LAST TIME.

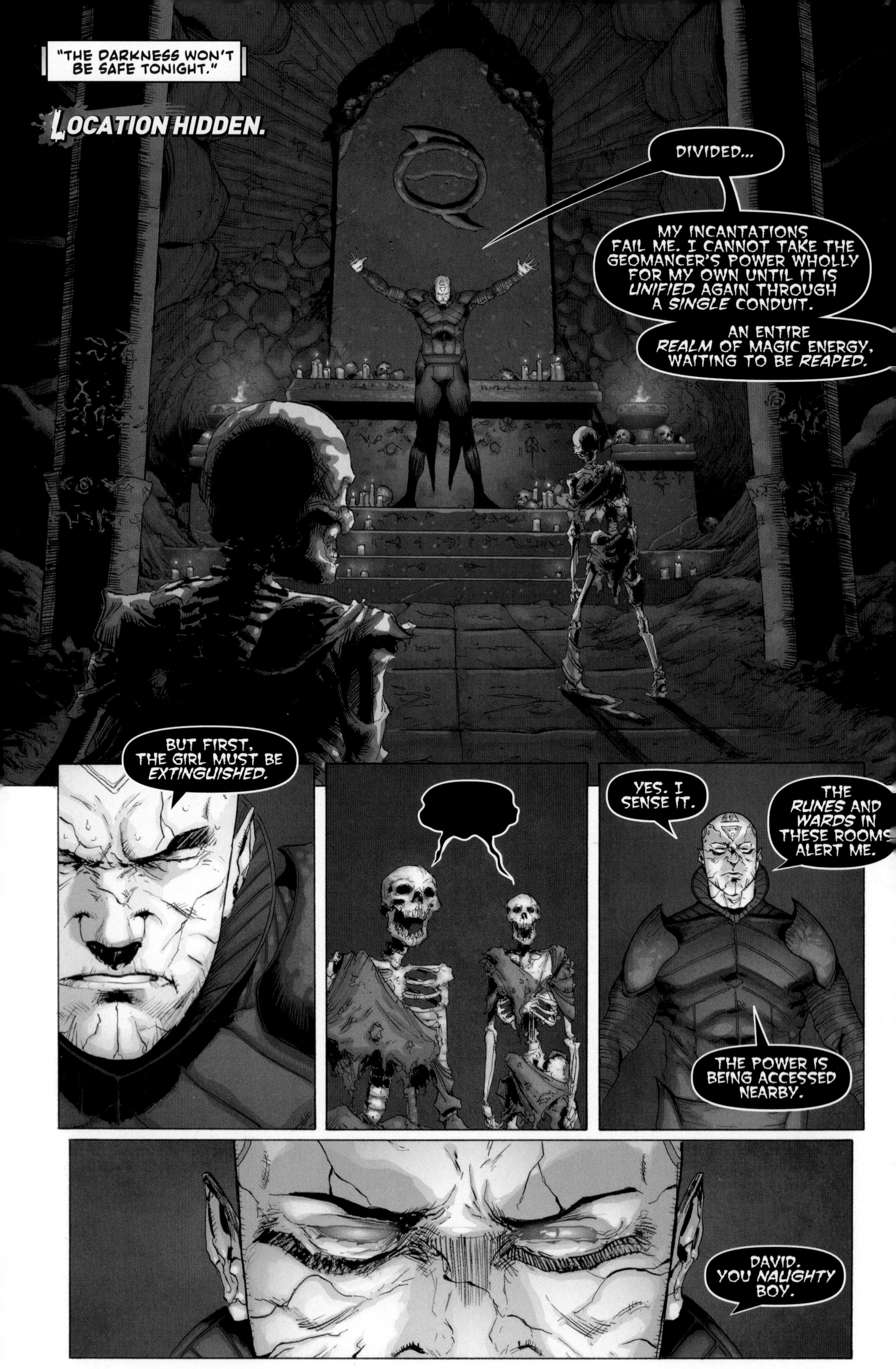
"THE DARKNESS WON'T BE SAFE TONIGHT."
LOCATION HIDDEN.
DIVIDED...
MY INCANTATIONS FAIL ME. I CANNOT TAKE THE GEOMANCER'S POWER WHOLLY FOR MY OWN UNTIL IT IS UNIFIED AGAIN THROUGH A SINGLE CONDUIT.
AN ENTIRE REALM OF MAGIC ENERGY, WAITING TO BE REAPED.
BUT FIRST, THE GIRL MUST BE EXTINGUISHED.
YES. I SENSE IT.
THE RUNES AND WARDS IN THESE ROOMS ALERT ME.
THE POWER IS BEING ACCESSED NEARBY.
DAVID. YOU NAUGHTY BOY.

"SHE'S VIOLATING *OUR BOOK*."

"WITH THE VALIANT FALLEN, SO BEGAN THE REIGN OF THE *CORRUPTED ONE*."

GOOD, TAMA. DON'T STOP READING UNTIL I TELL YOU.

R-READING...

THE GIRL *DIES NOW!*

"NEVER CHOSEN TO BE A GEOMANCER, THE CORRUPTED ONE INSTEAD TOOK THE MANTLE THROUGH *DECEIT* AND *CRUEL MAGIC*."

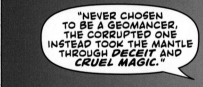

THE USURPER DOESN'T B-BELONG HERE. *I'M* THE R-RIGHTFUL GEOMANCER.

"IN ALL OF EARTH'S EXISTENCE, THIS HAD NEVER HAPPENED BEFORE."

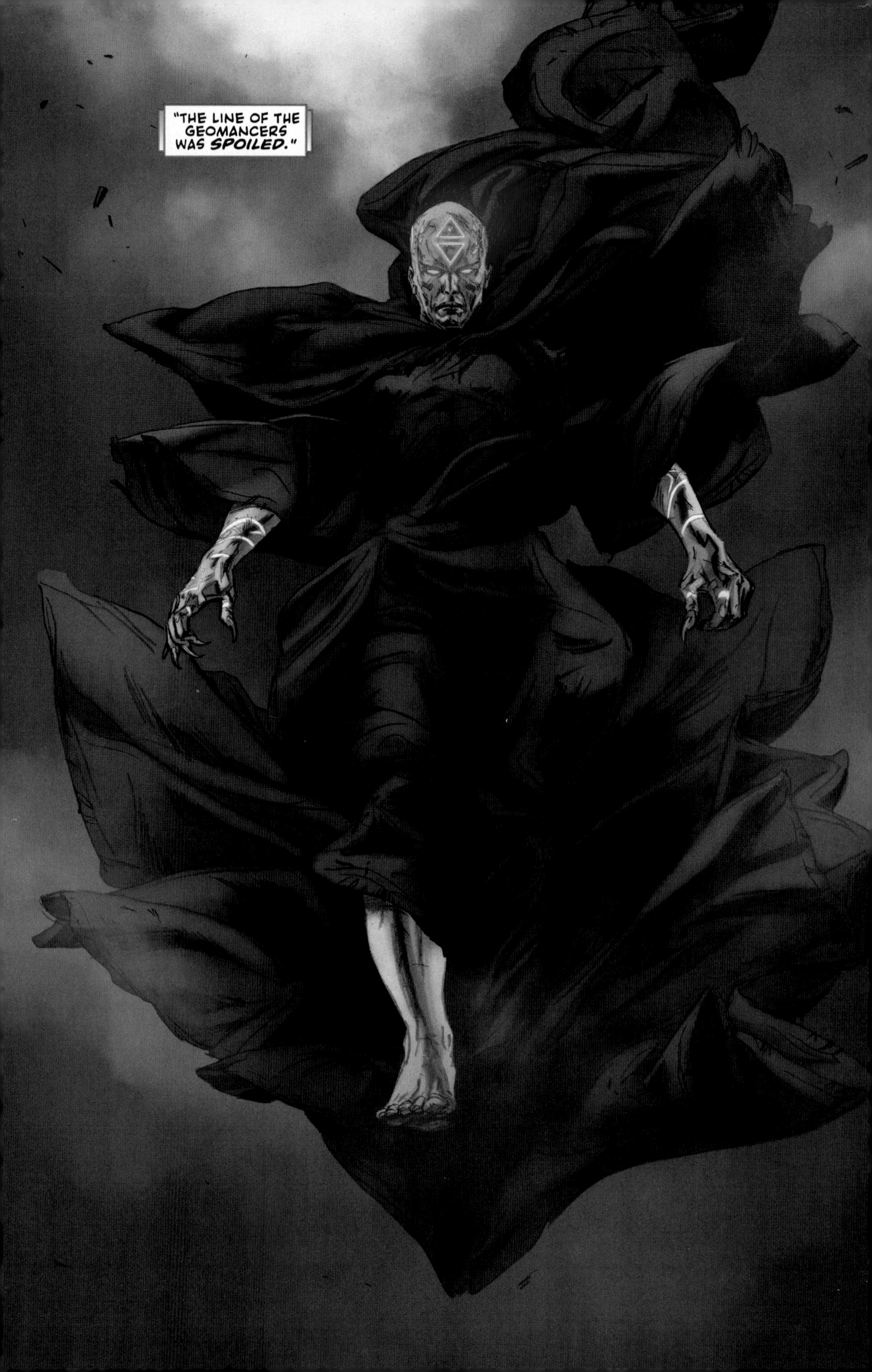
"THE LINE OF THE GEOMANCERS WAS SPOILED."

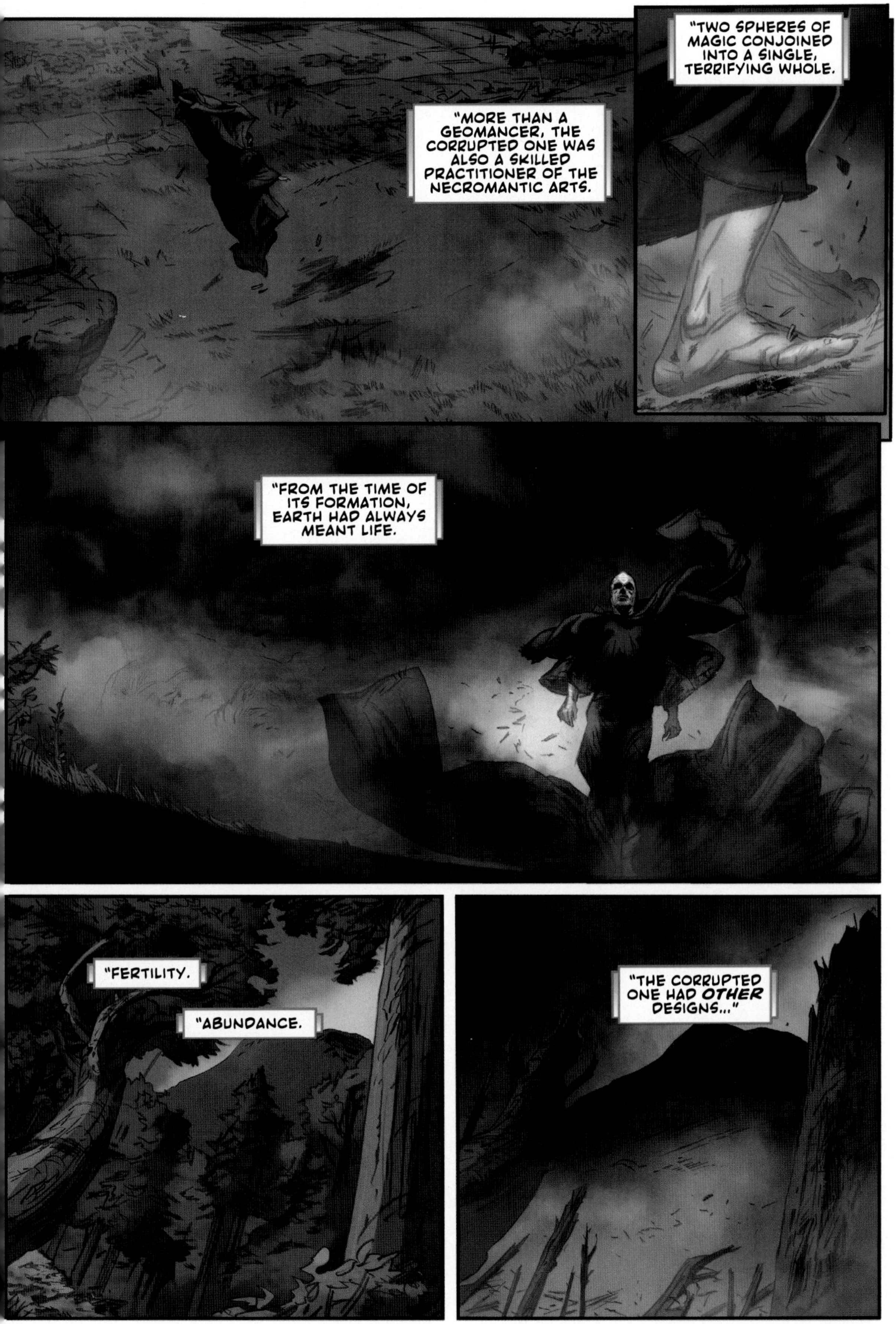
"MORE THAN A GEOMANCER, THE CORRUPTED ONE WAS ALSO A SKILLED PRACTITIONER OF THE NECROMANTIC ARTS.
"TWO SPHERES OF MAGIC CONJOINED INTO A SINGLE, TERRIFYING WHOLE.
"FROM THE TIME OF ITS FORMATION, EARTH HAD ALWAYS MEANT LIFE.
"FERTILITY.
"ABUNDANCE.
"THE CORRUPTED ONE HAD *OTHER* DESIGNS..."

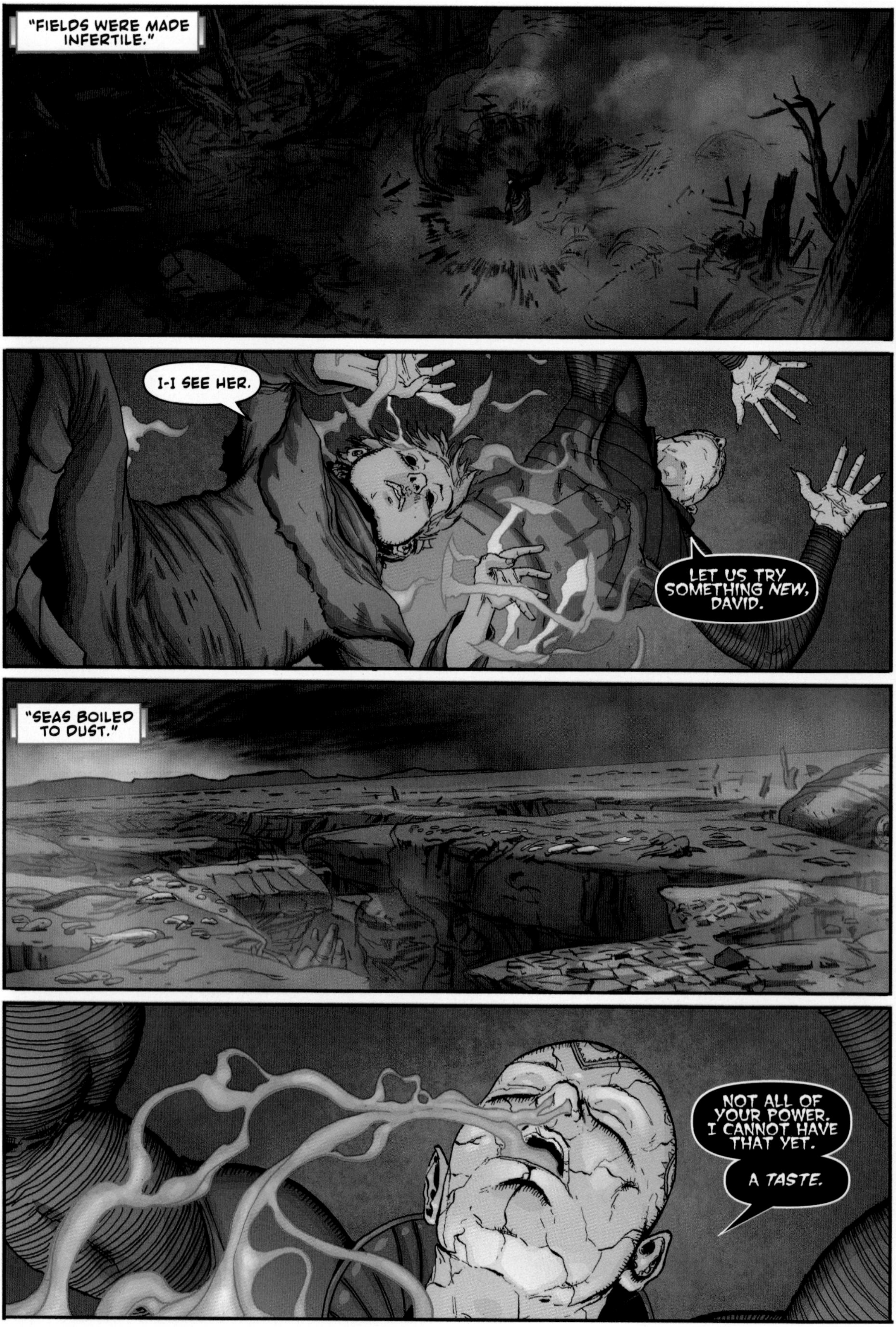
"FIELDS WERE MADE INFERTILE."
I-I SEE HER.
LET US TRY SOMETHING NEW, DAVID.
"SEAS BOILED TO DUST."
NOT ALL OF YOUR POWER. I CANNOT HAVE THAT YET.
A TASTE.

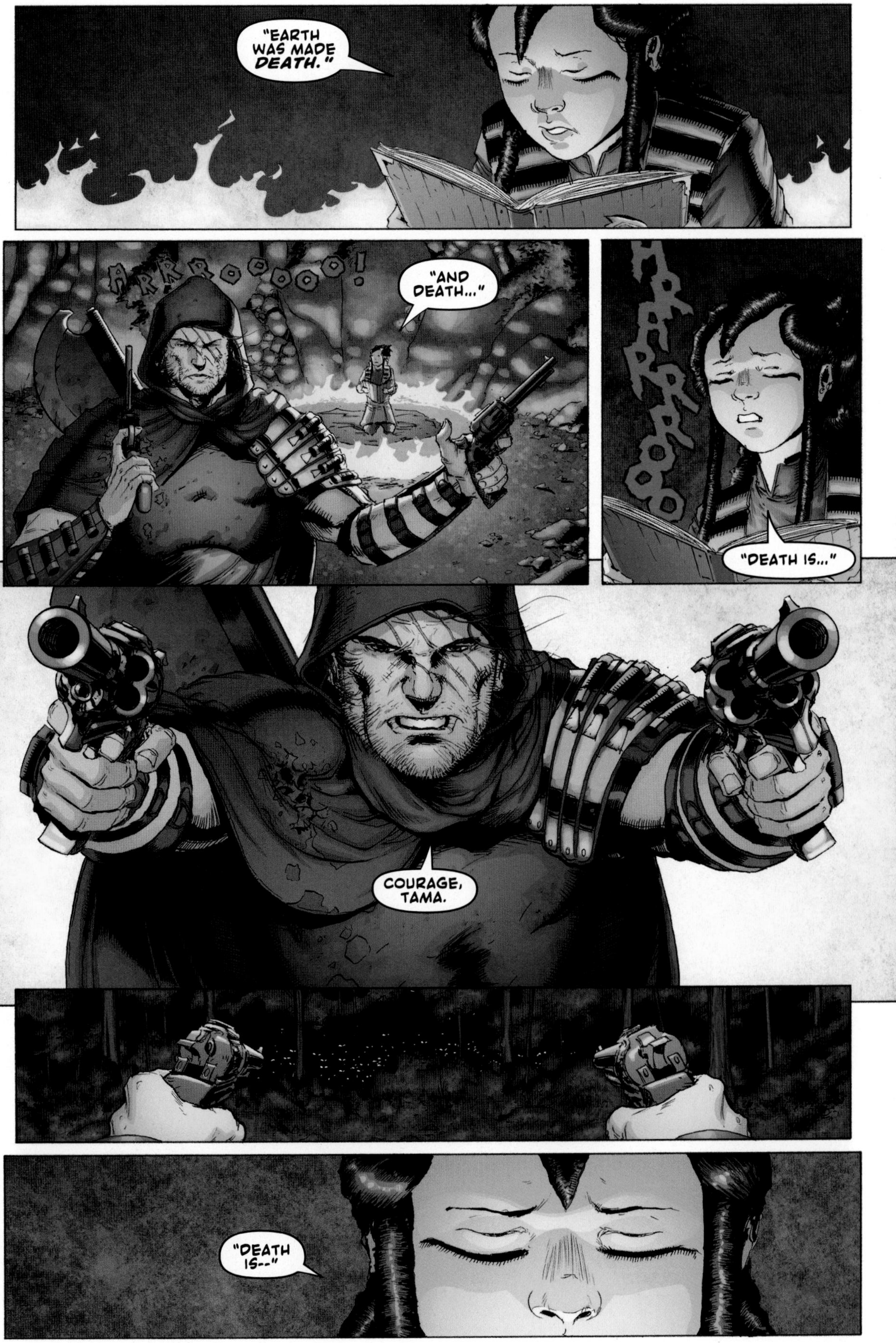
"EARTH WAS MADE DEATH."
ARRROOOOOO!
"AND DEATH..."
HARROOO
"DEATH IS..."
COURAGE, TAMA.
"DEATH IS--"

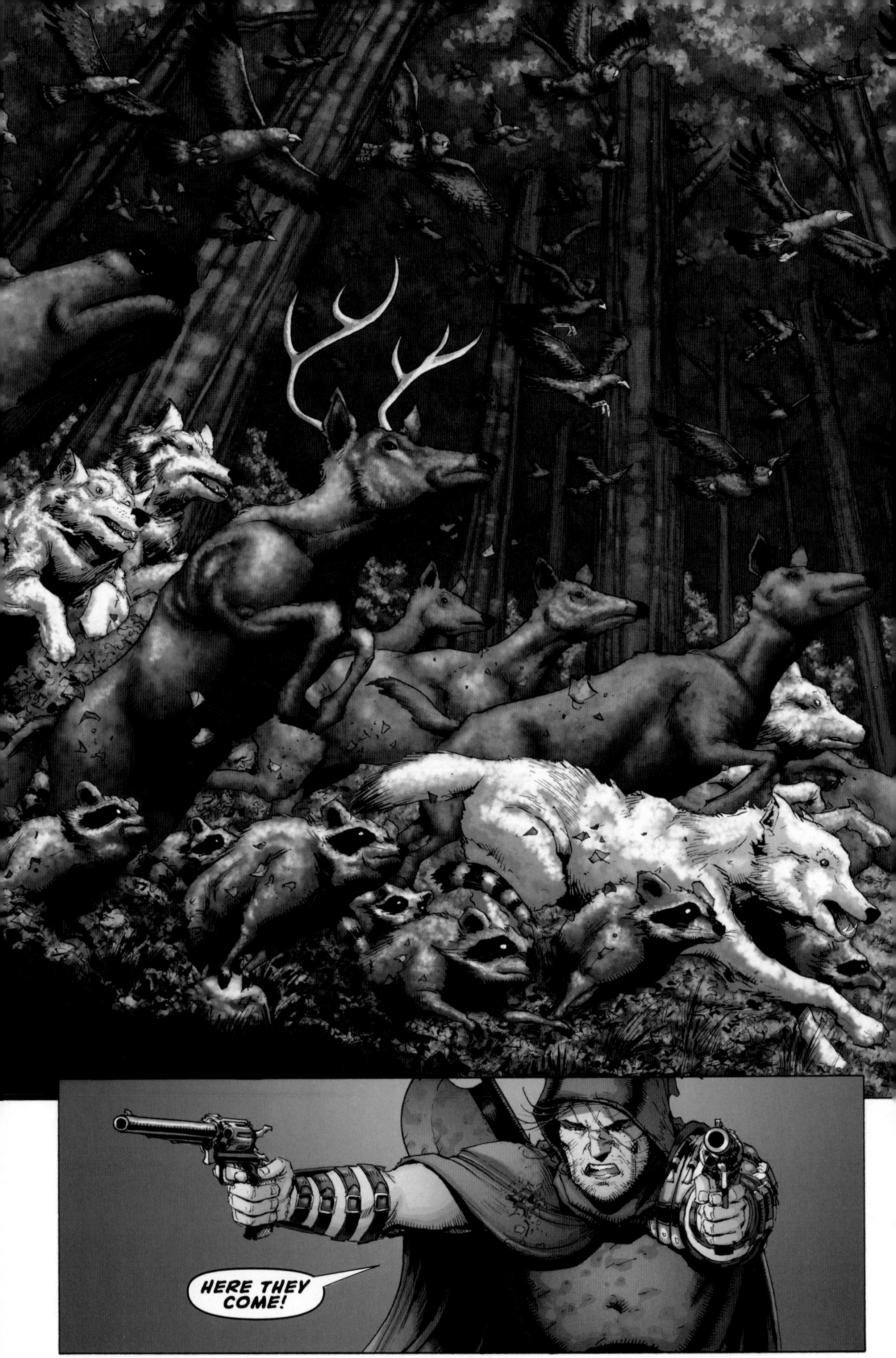
HERE THEY COME!

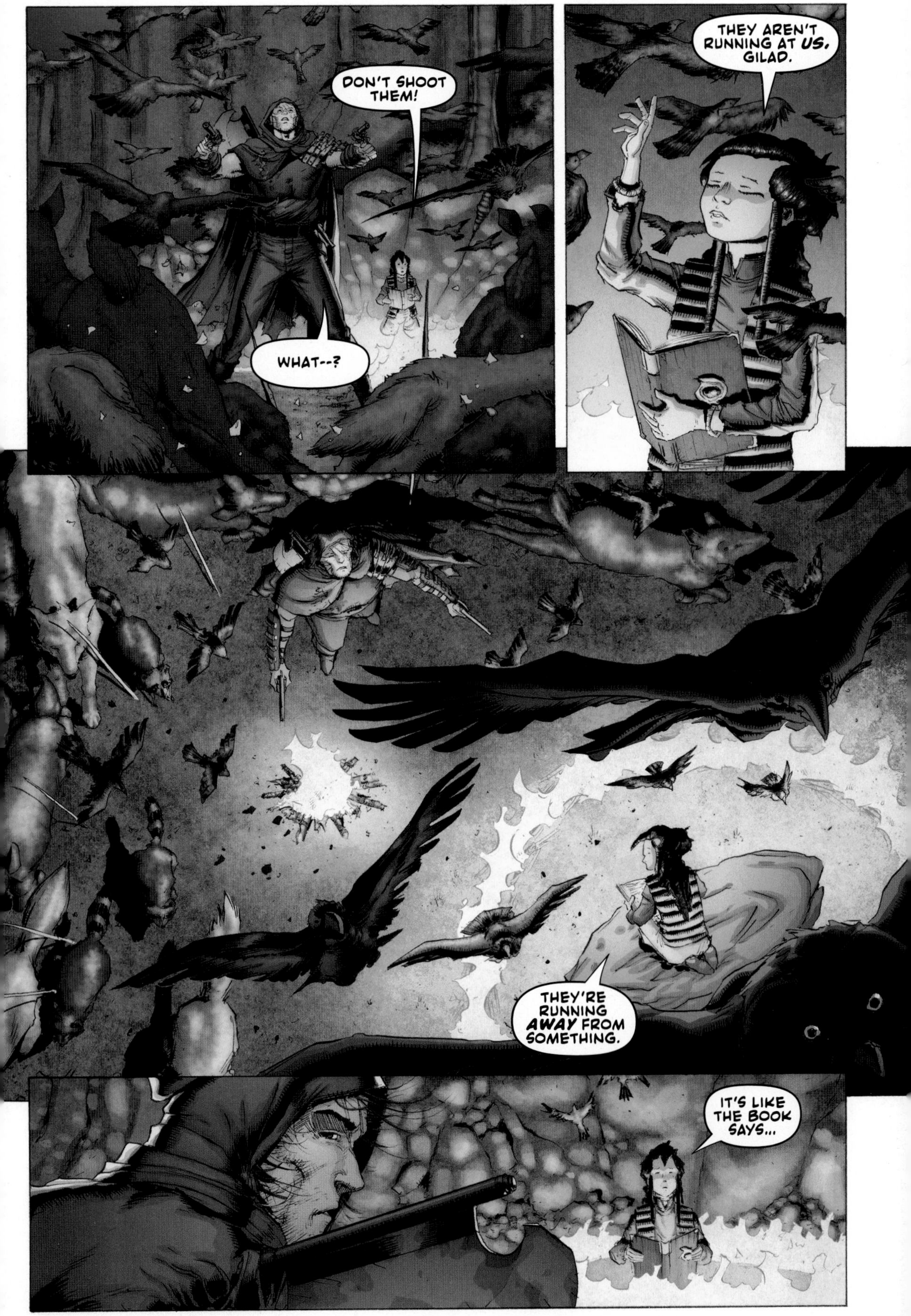
DON'T SHOOT THEM!
WHAT--?
THEY AREN'T RUNNING AT US, GILAD.
THEY'RE RUNNING AWAY FROM SOMETHING.
IT'S LIKE THE BOOK SAYS...

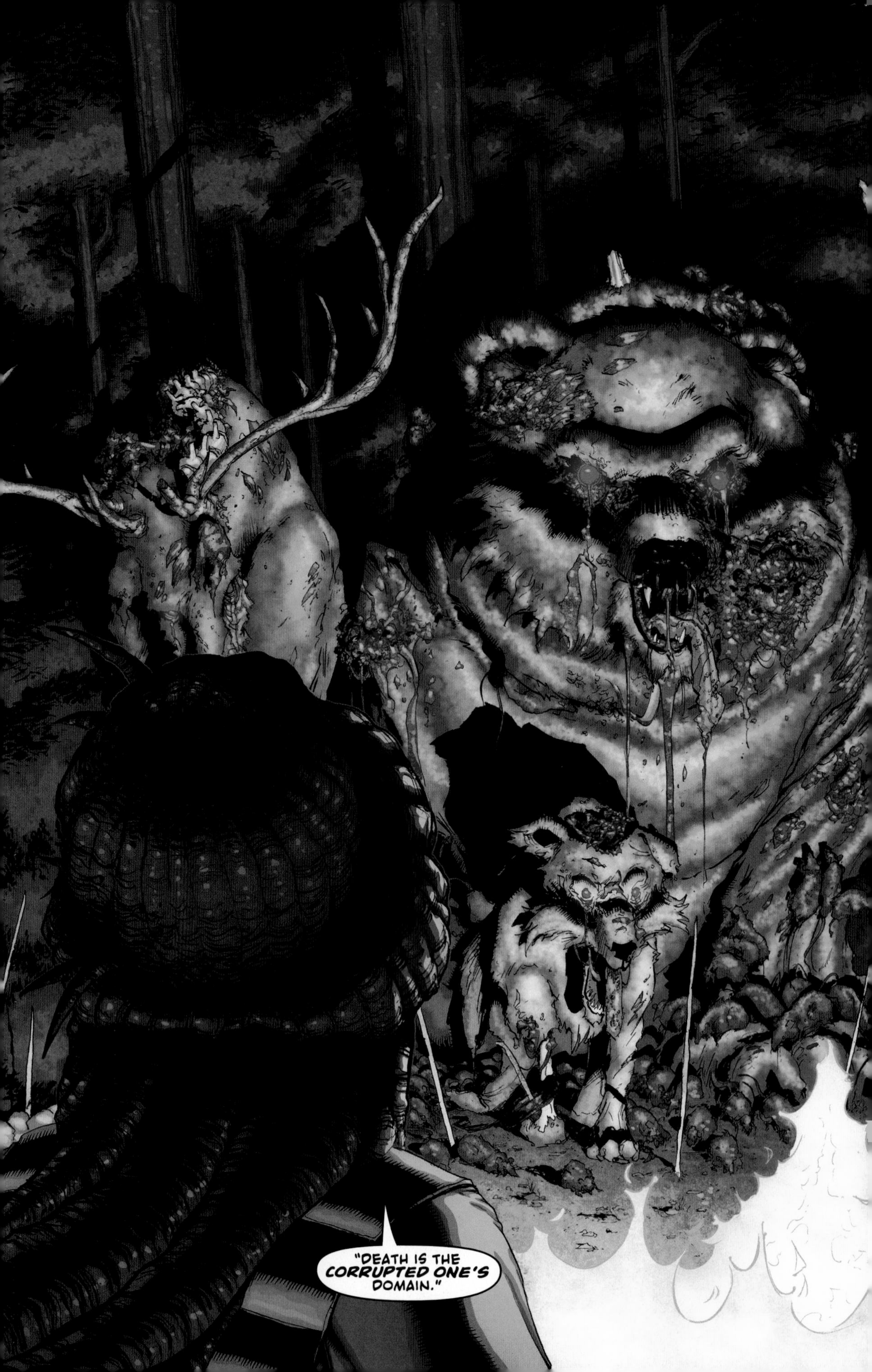
"DEATH IS THE CORRUPTED ONE'S DOMAIN."

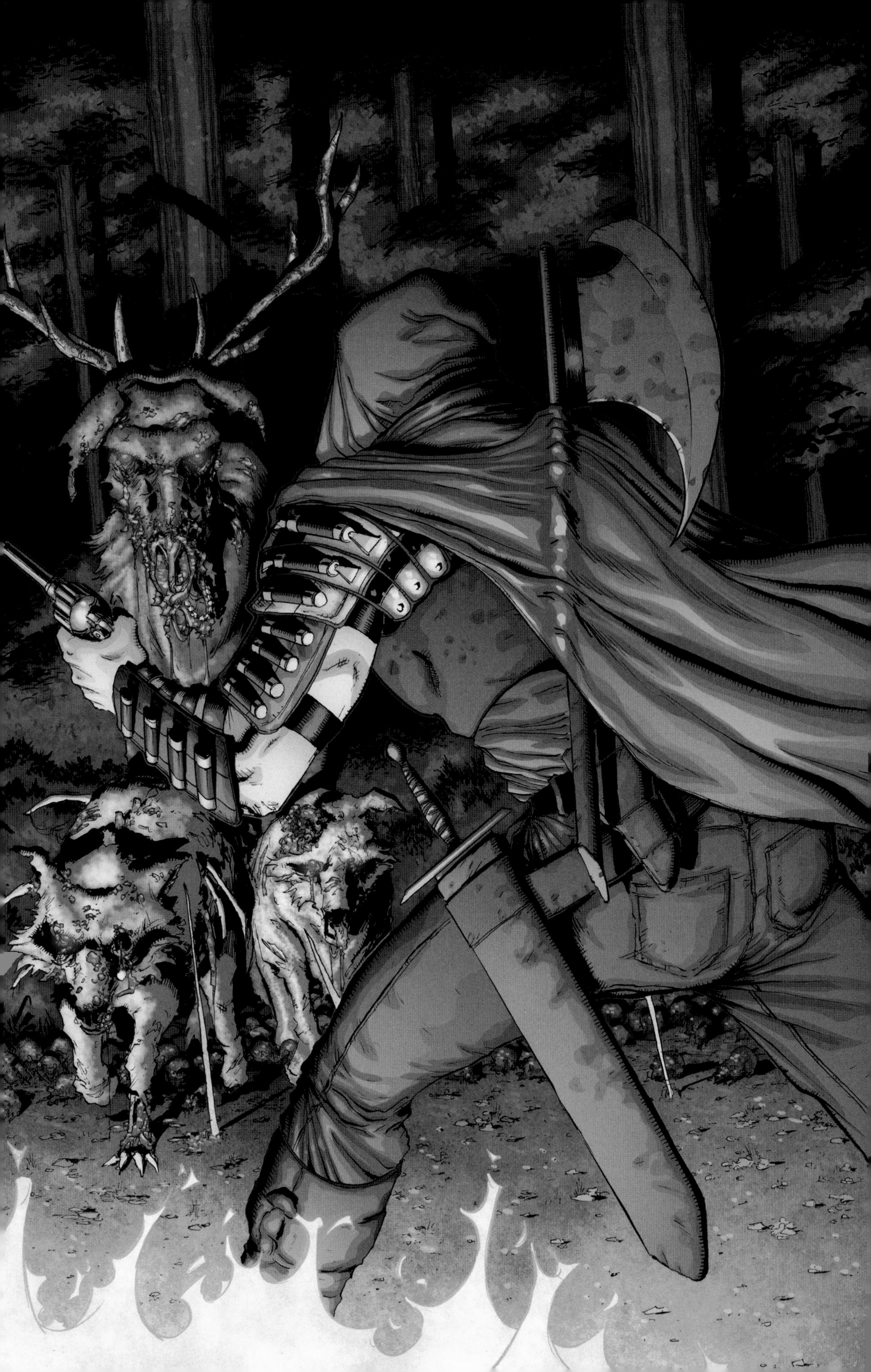

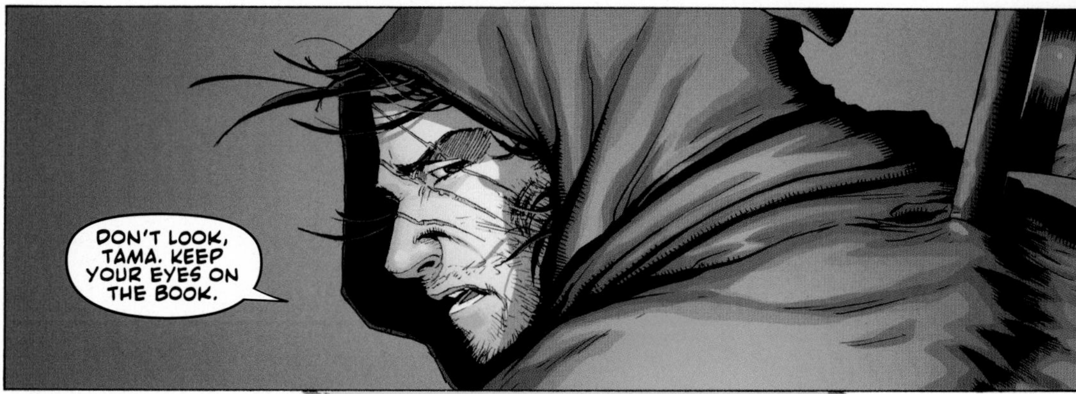
DON'T LOOK, TAMA. KEEP YOUR EYES ON THE BOOK.

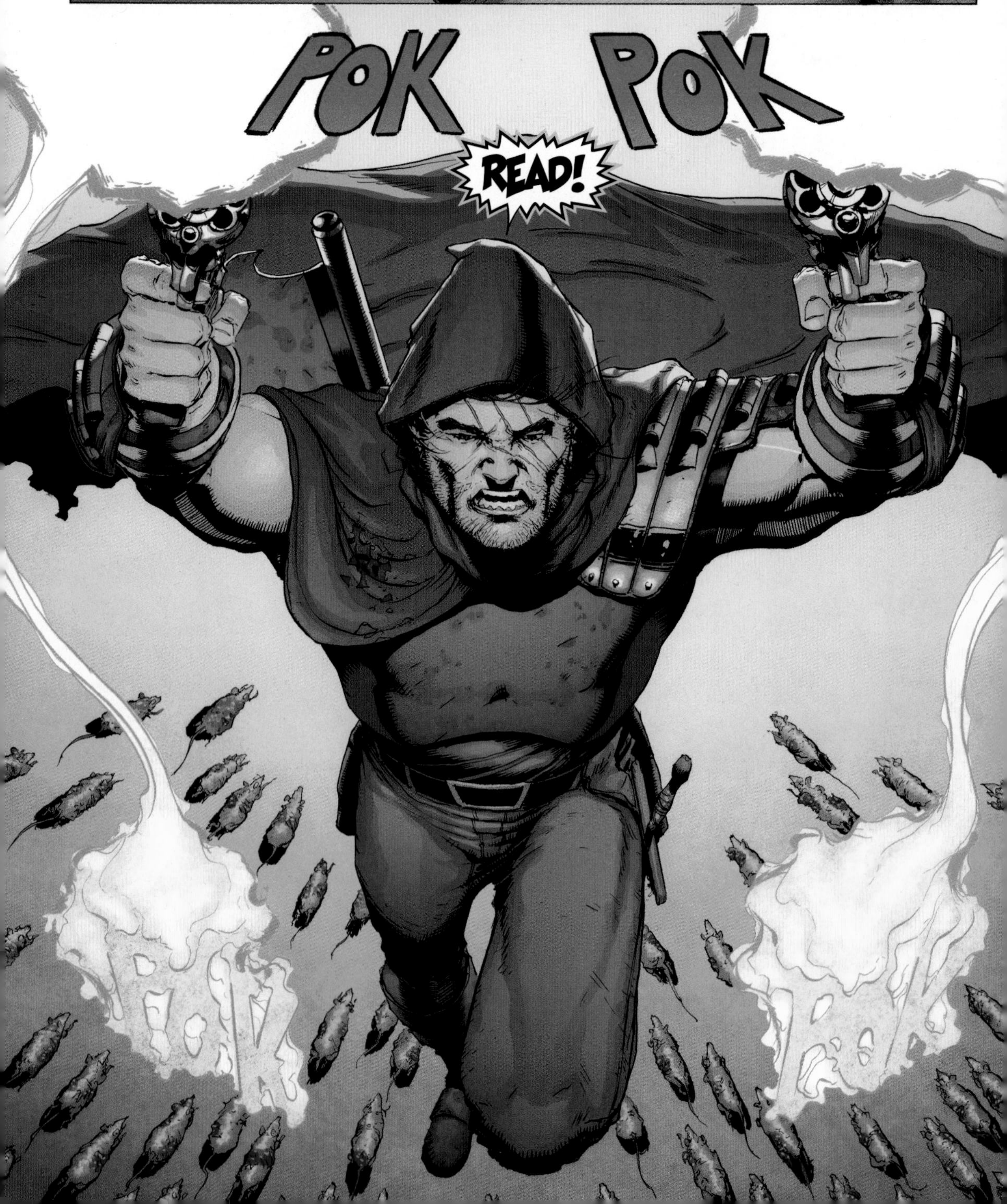
POK POK
READ!

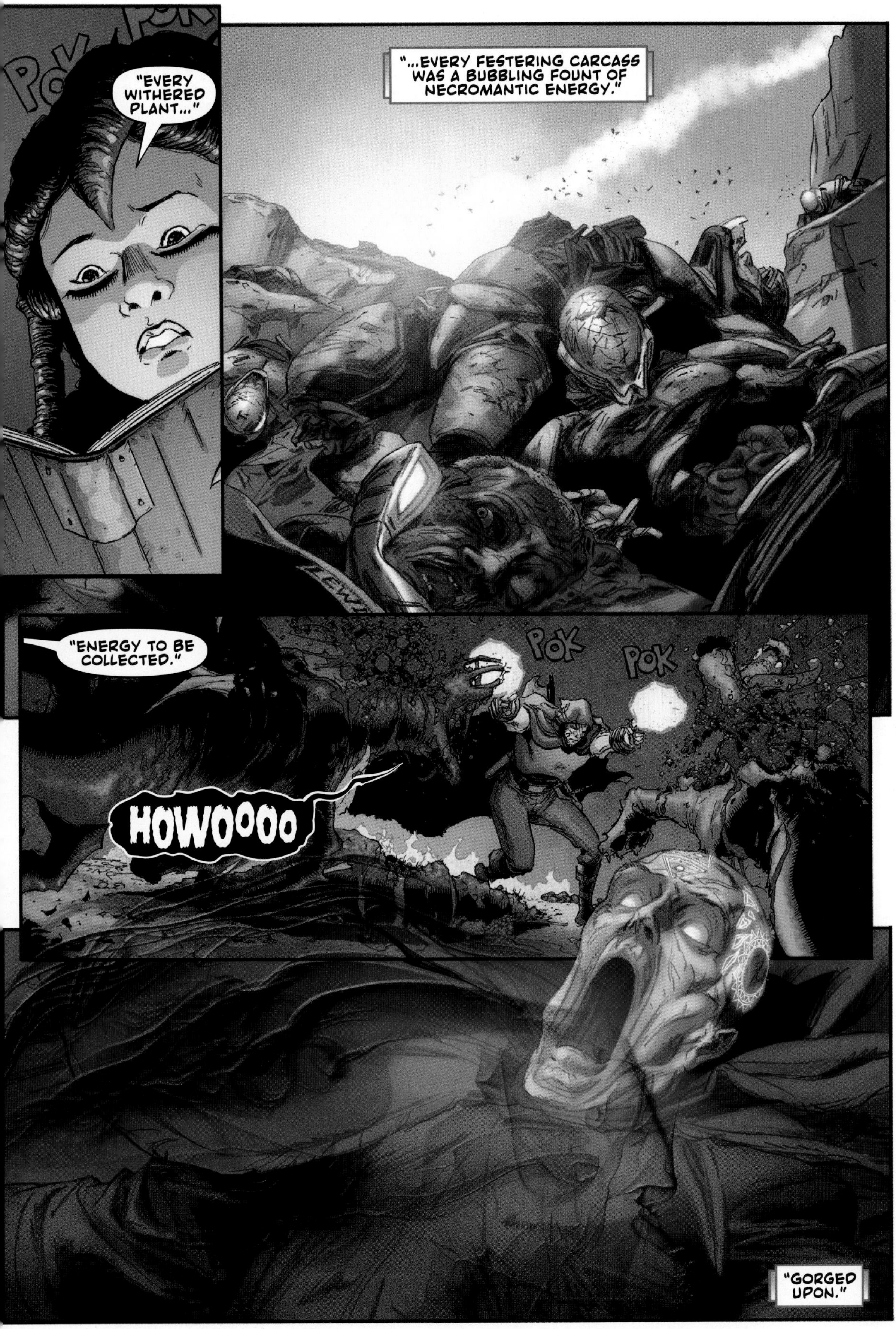
POK
POK
"EVERY WITHERED PLANT..."
"...EVERY FESTERING CARCASS WAS A BUBBLING FOUNT OF NECROMANTIC ENERGY."
"ENERGY TO BE COLLECTED."
POK
POK
HOWOOOO
"GORGED UPON."

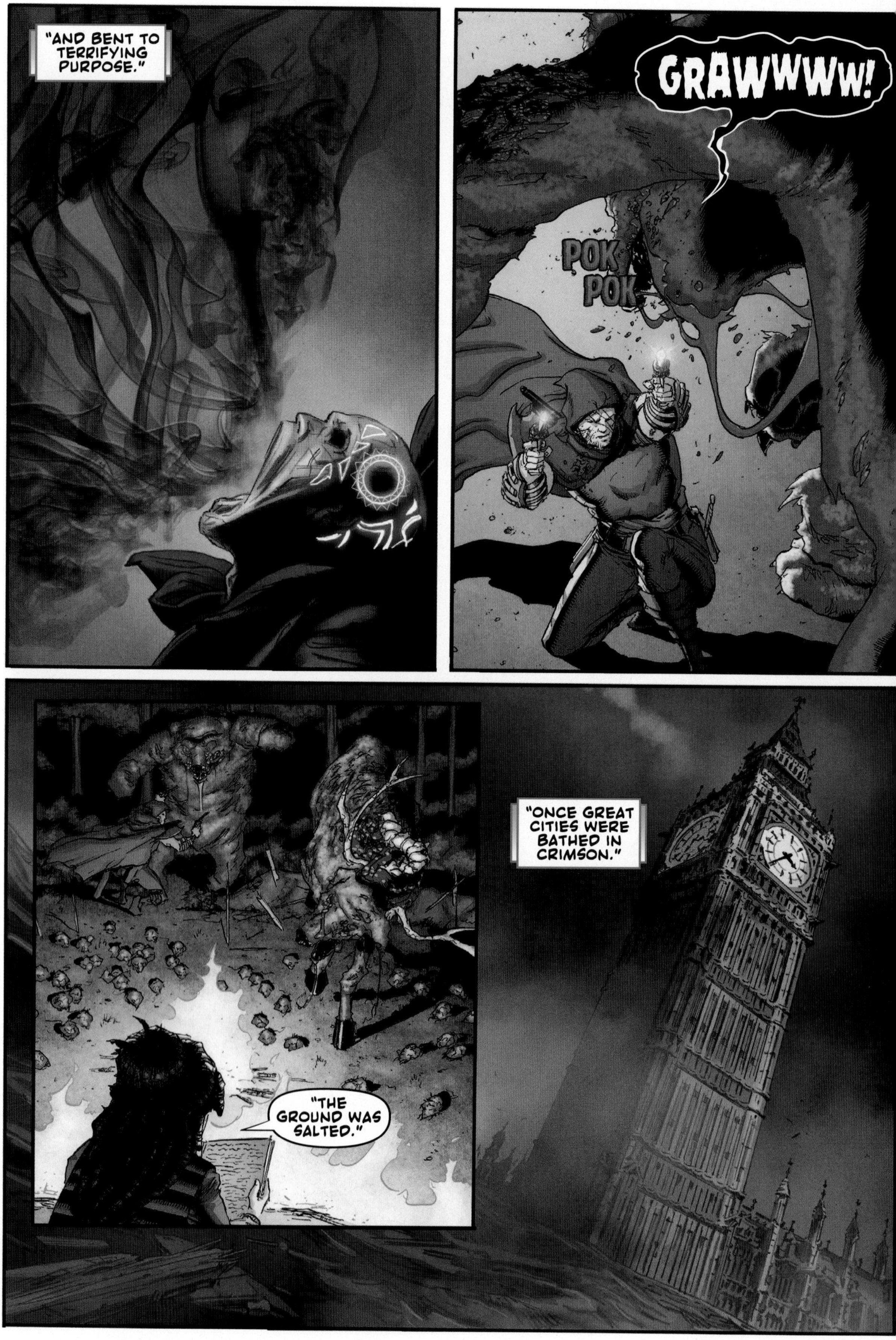
"AND BENT TO TERRIFYING PURPOSE."
GRAWWWW!
POK POK
"THE GROUND WAS SALTED."
"ONCE GREAT CITIES WERE BATHED IN CRIMSON."

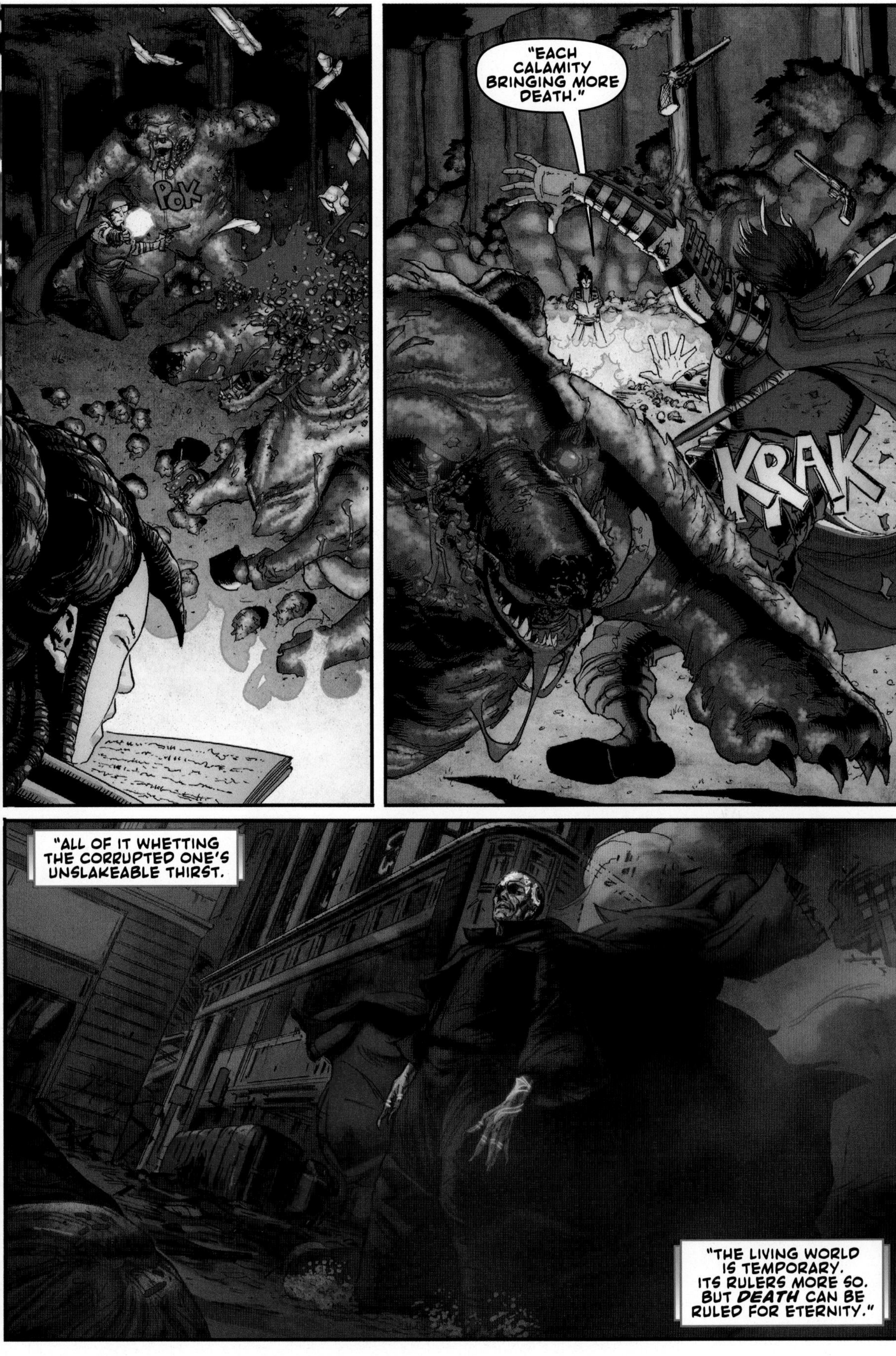
POK
"EACH CALAMITY BRINGING MORE DEATH."
KRAK
"ALL OF IT WHETTING THE CORRUPTED ONE'S UNSLAKEABLE THIRST.
"THE LIVING WORLD IS TEMPORARY. ITS RULERS MORE SO. BUT *DEATH* CAN BE RULED FOR ETERNITY."

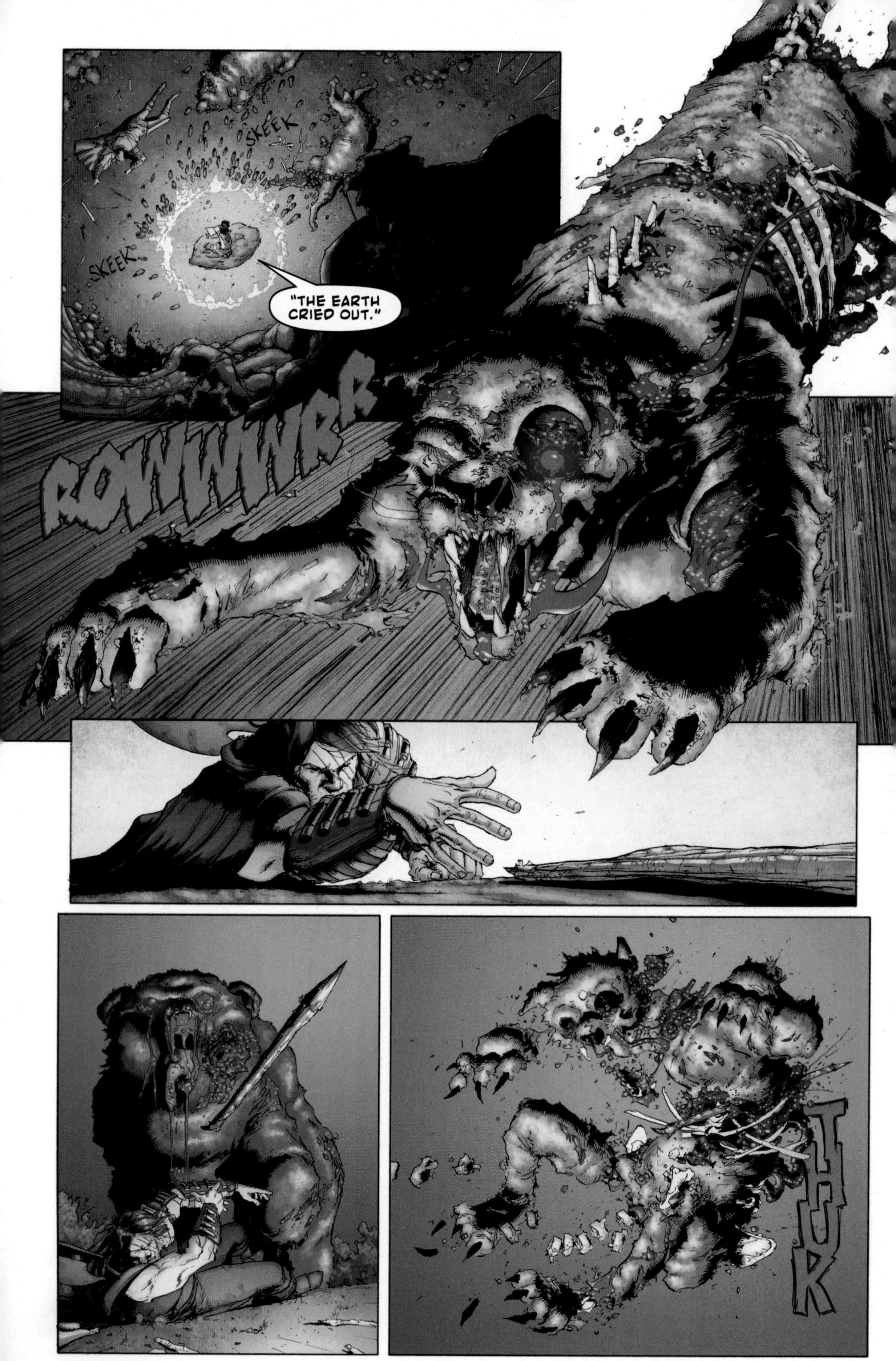
SKEEK
SKEEK
"THE EARTH CRIED OUT."
ROWWWRR
THUK

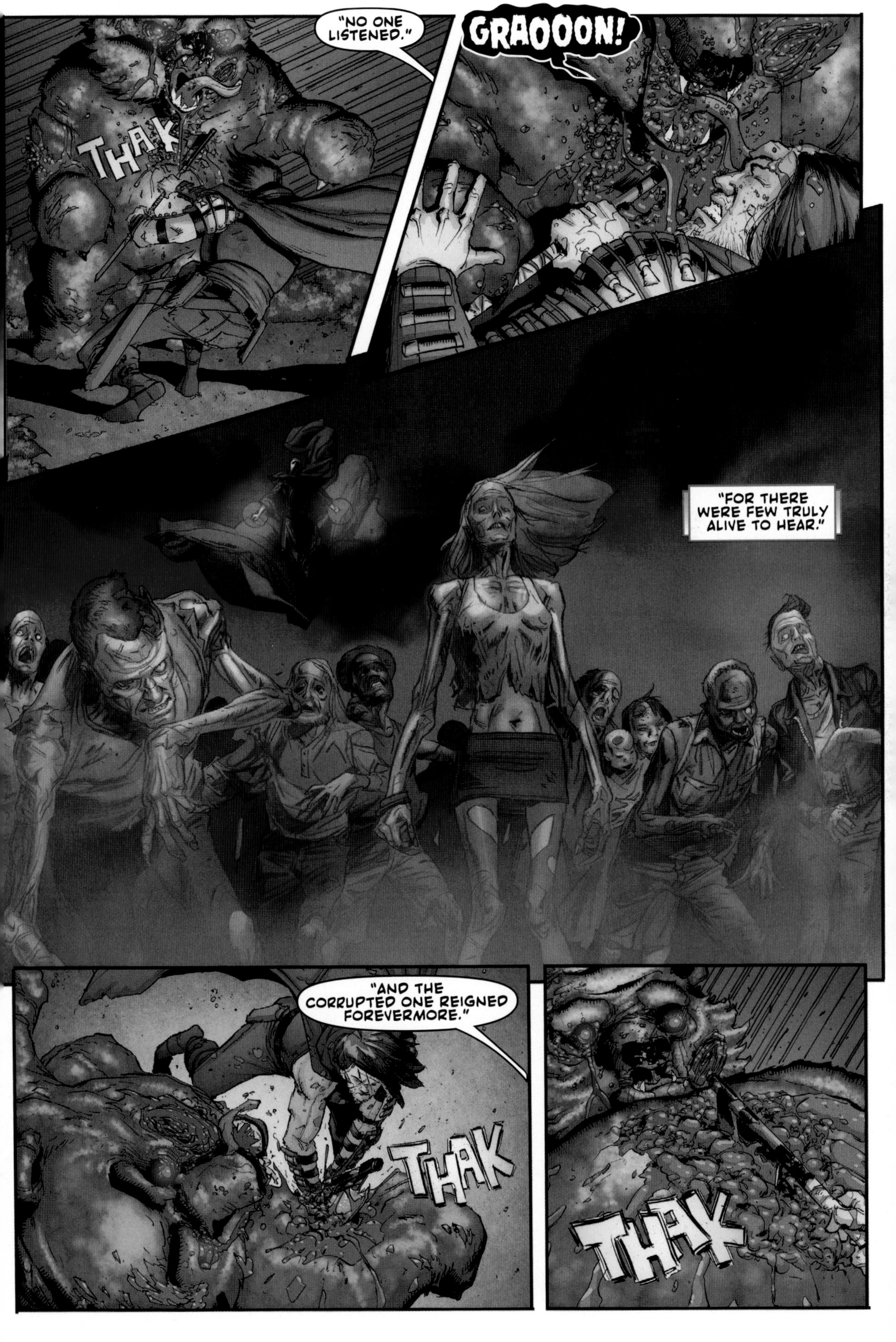
THAK
"NO ONE LISTENED."
GRAOOON!
"FOR THERE WERE FEW TRULY ALIVE TO HEAR."
"AND THE CORRUPTED ONE REIGNED FOREVERMORE."
THAK
THAK

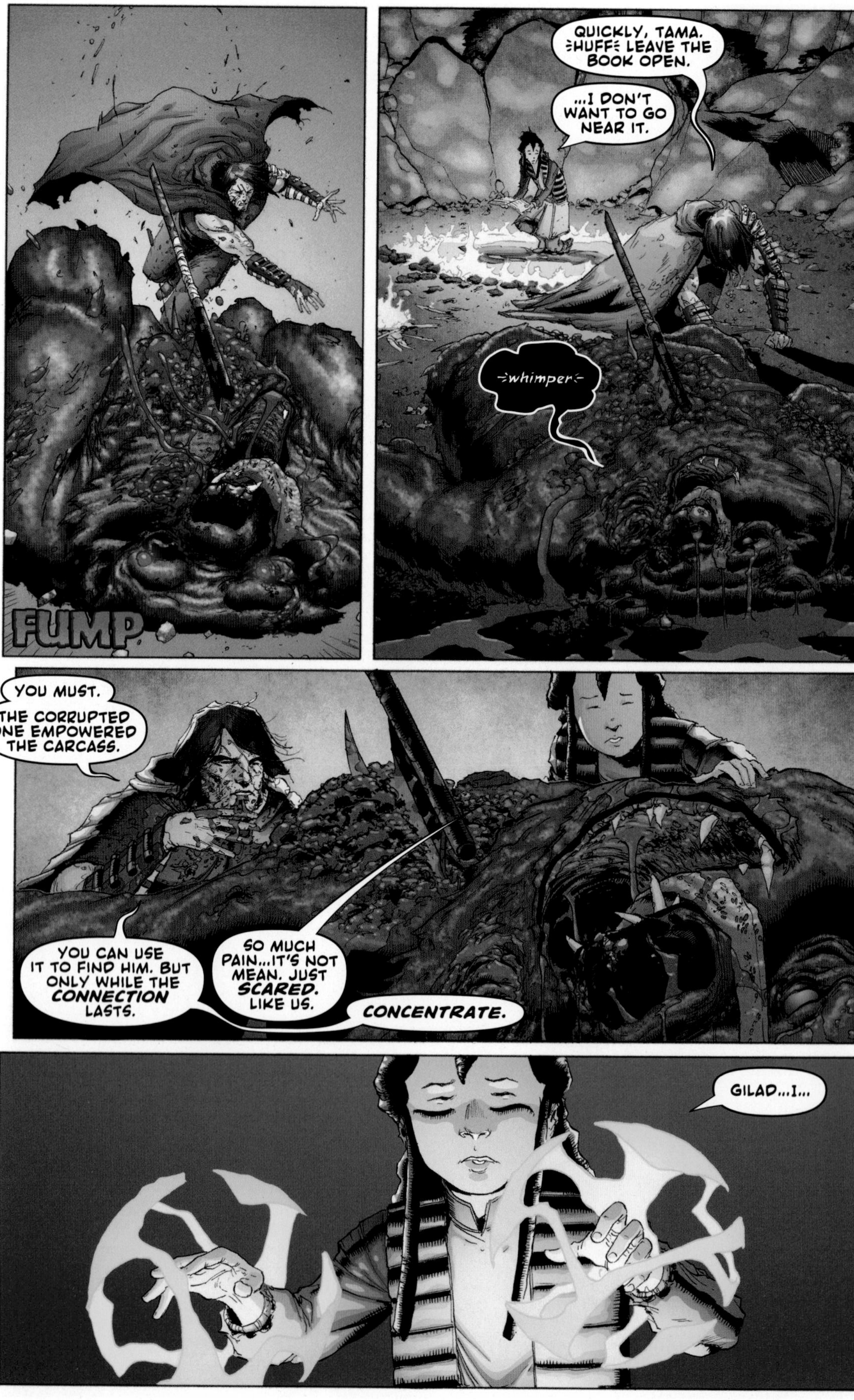
FUMP
QUICKLY, TAMA. ≷HUFF≶ LEAVE THE BOOK OPEN.
...I DON'T WANT TO GO NEAR IT.
≷whimper≶
YOU MUST.
THE CORRUPTED ONE EMPOWERED THE CARCASS.
YOU CAN USE IT TO FIND HIM. BUT ONLY WHILE THE CONNECTION LASTS.
SO MUCH PAIN...IT'S NOT MEAN. JUST SCARED. LIKE US.
CONCENTRATE.
GILAD...I...

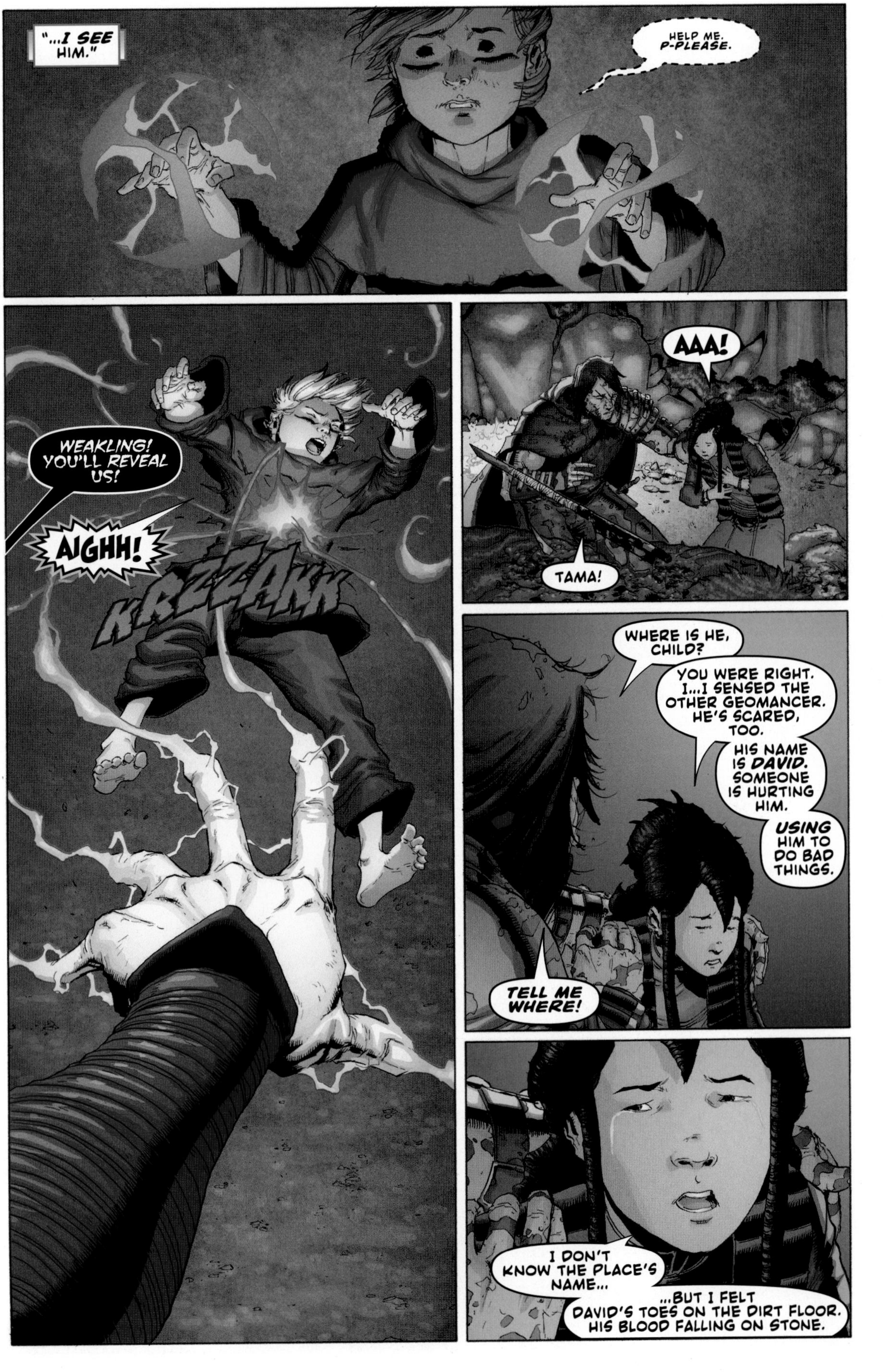
"...I SEE HIM."
HELP ME. P-PLEASE.
WEAKLING! YOU'LL REVEAL US!
AIGHH!
KRZZAKK
AAA!
TAMA!
WHERE IS HE, CHILD?
YOU WERE RIGHT. I...I SENSED THE OTHER GEOMANCER. HE'S SCARED, TOO.
HIS NAME IS DAVID. SOMEONE IS HURTING HIM.
USING HIM TO DO BAD THINGS.
TELL ME WHERE!
I DON'T KNOW THE PLACE'S NAME...
...BUT I FELT DAVID'S TOES ON THE DIRT FLOOR. HIS BLOOD FALLING ON STONE.

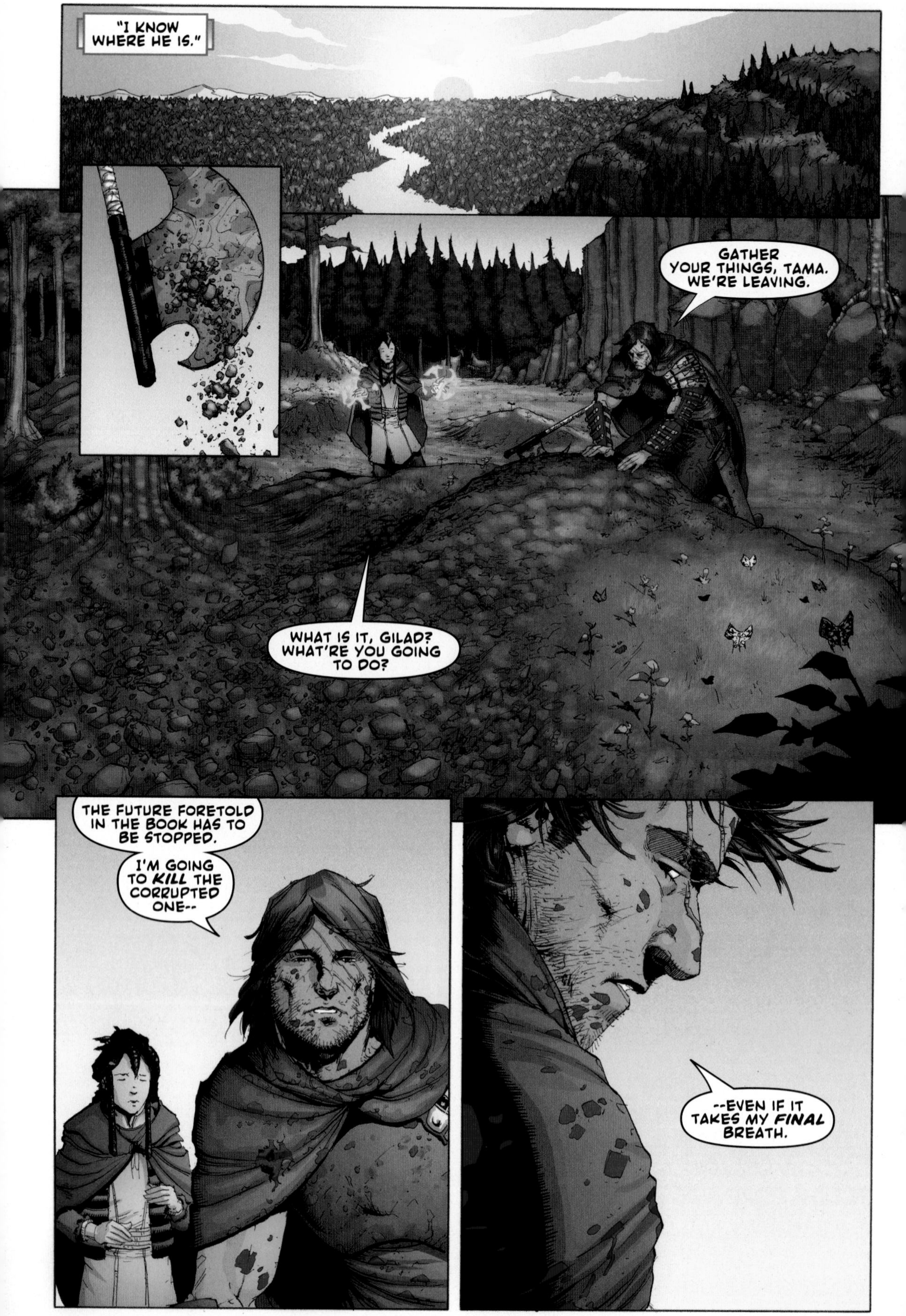
"I KNOW WHERE HE IS."
GATHER YOUR THINGS, TAMA. WE'RE LEAVING.
WHAT IS IT, GILAD? WHAT'RE YOU GOING TO DO?
THE FUTURE FORETOLD IN THE BOOK HAS TO BE STOPPED.
I'M GOING TO KILL THE CORRUPTED ONE--
--EVEN IF IT TAKES MY FINAL BREATH.

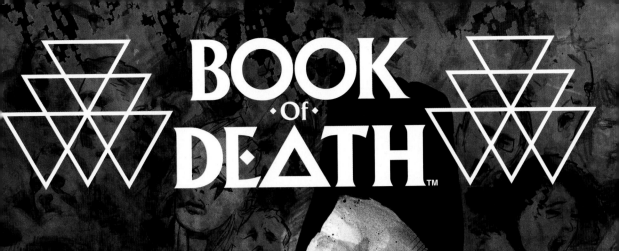

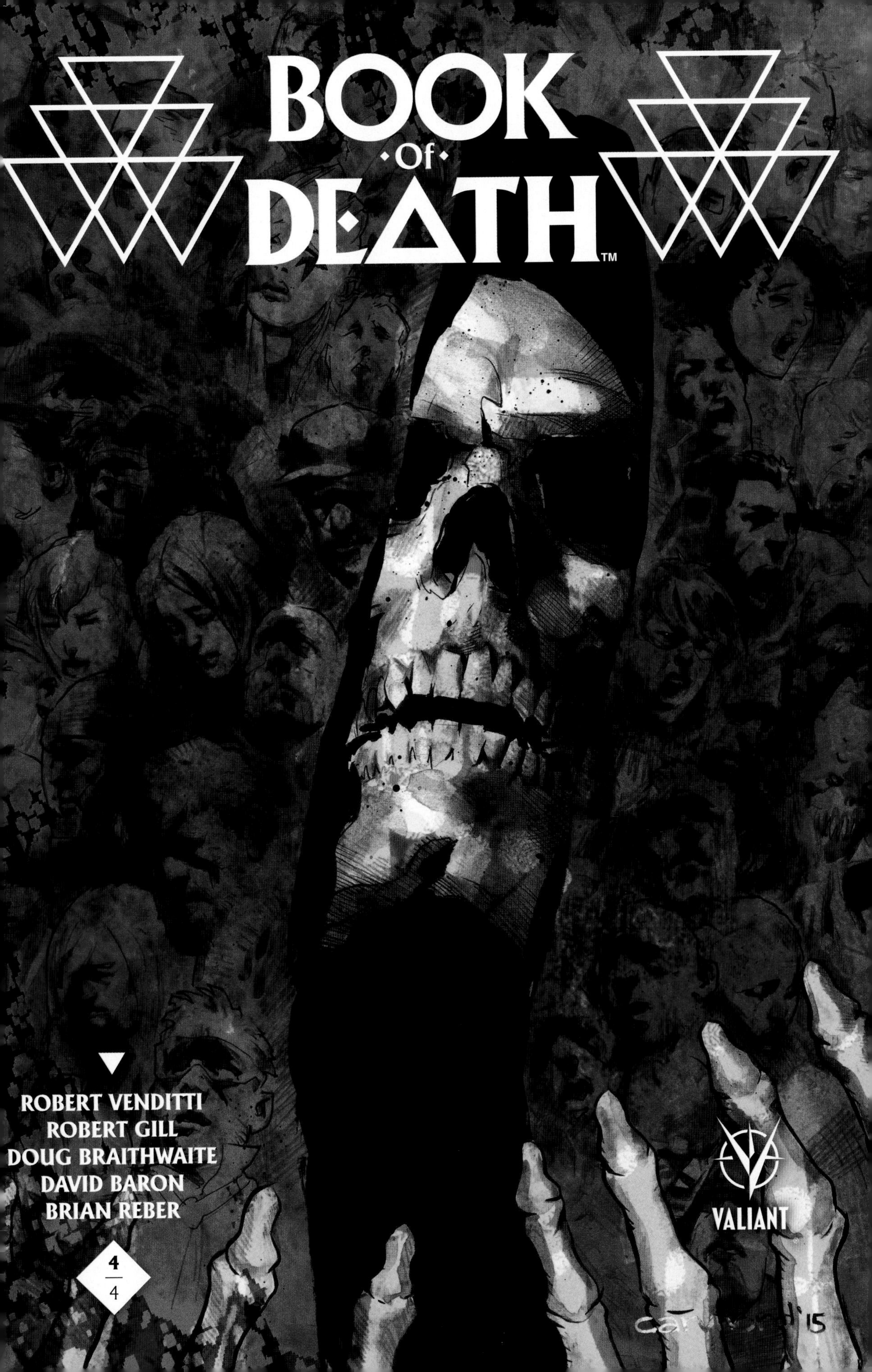

BOOK OF DEATH

·OF·

ROBERT VENDITTI
ROBERT GILL
DOUG BRAITHWAITE
DAVID BARON
BRIAN REBER

4/4

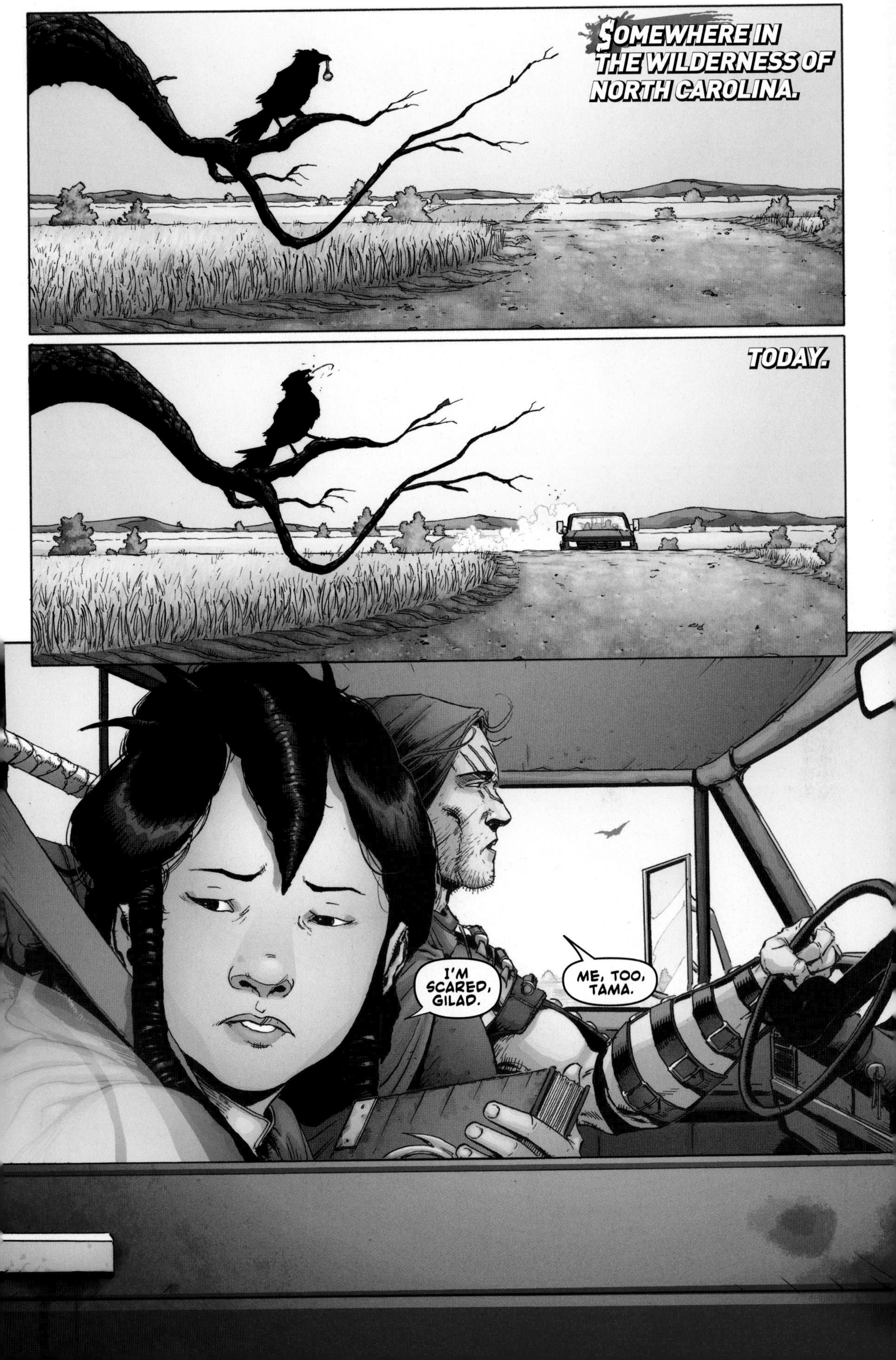
SOMEWHERE IN THE WILDERNESS OF NORTH CAROLINA.
TODAY.
I'M SCARED, GILAD.
ME, TOO, TAMA.

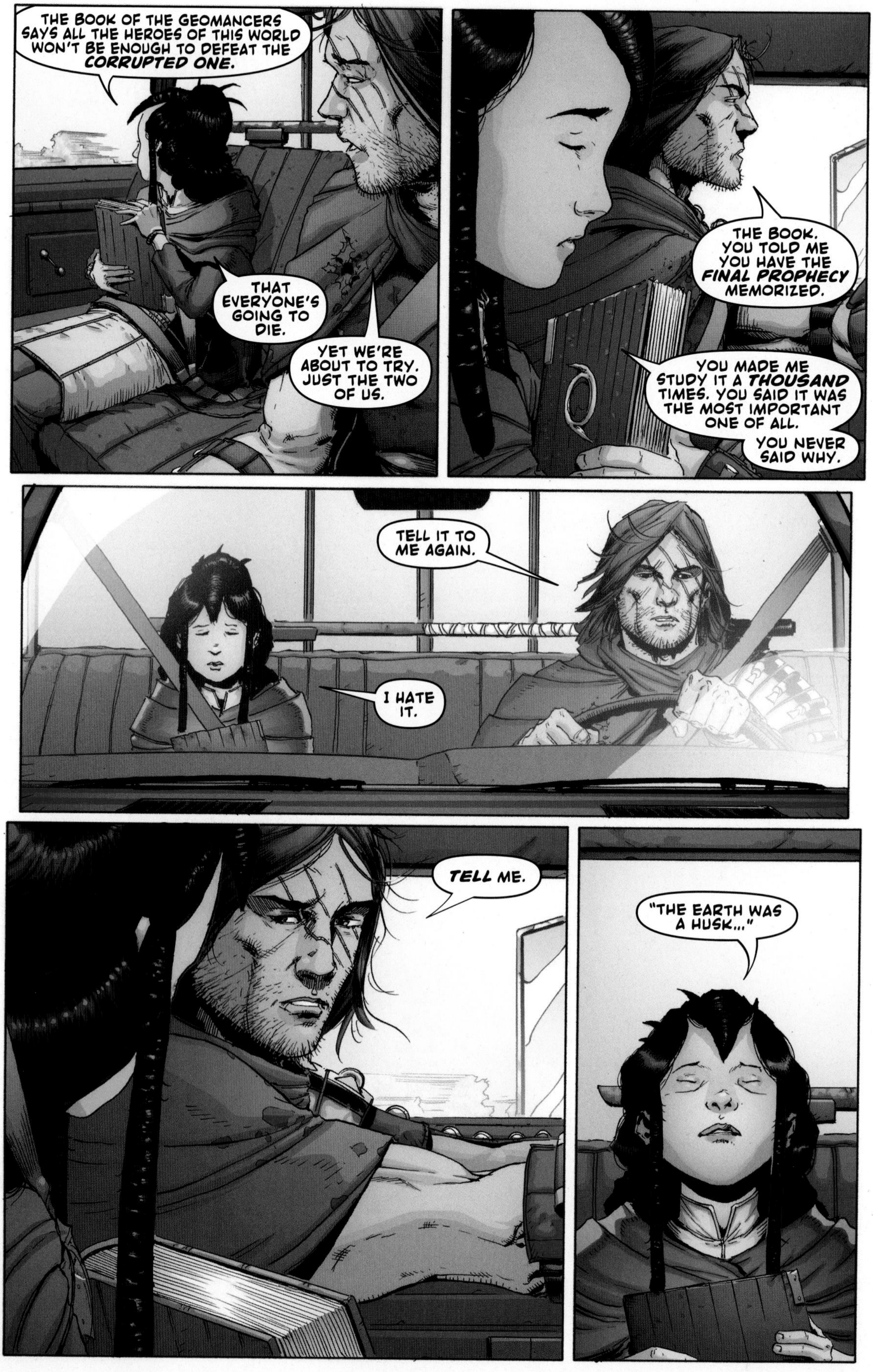
THE BOOK OF THE GEOMANCERS SAYS ALL THE HEROES OF THIS WORLD WON'T BE ENOUGH TO DEFEAT THE CORRUPTED ONE.
THAT EVERYONE'S GOING TO DIE.
YET WE'RE ABOUT TO TRY. JUST THE TWO OF US.
THE BOOK. YOU TOLD ME YOU HAVE THE FINAL PROPHECY MEMORIZED.
YOU MADE ME STUDY IT A THOUSAND TIMES. YOU SAID IT WAS THE MOST IMPORTANT ONE OF ALL.
YOU NEVER SAID WHY.
TELL IT TO ME AGAIN.
I HATE IT.
TELL ME.
"THE EARTH WAS A HUSK..."

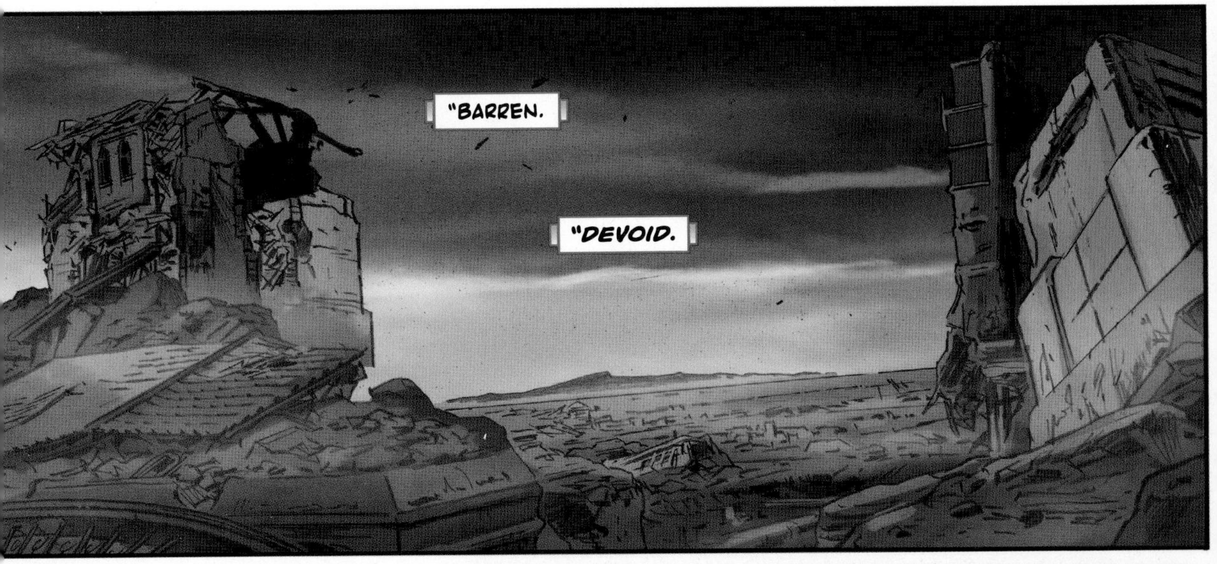
"BARREN.
"DEVOID.

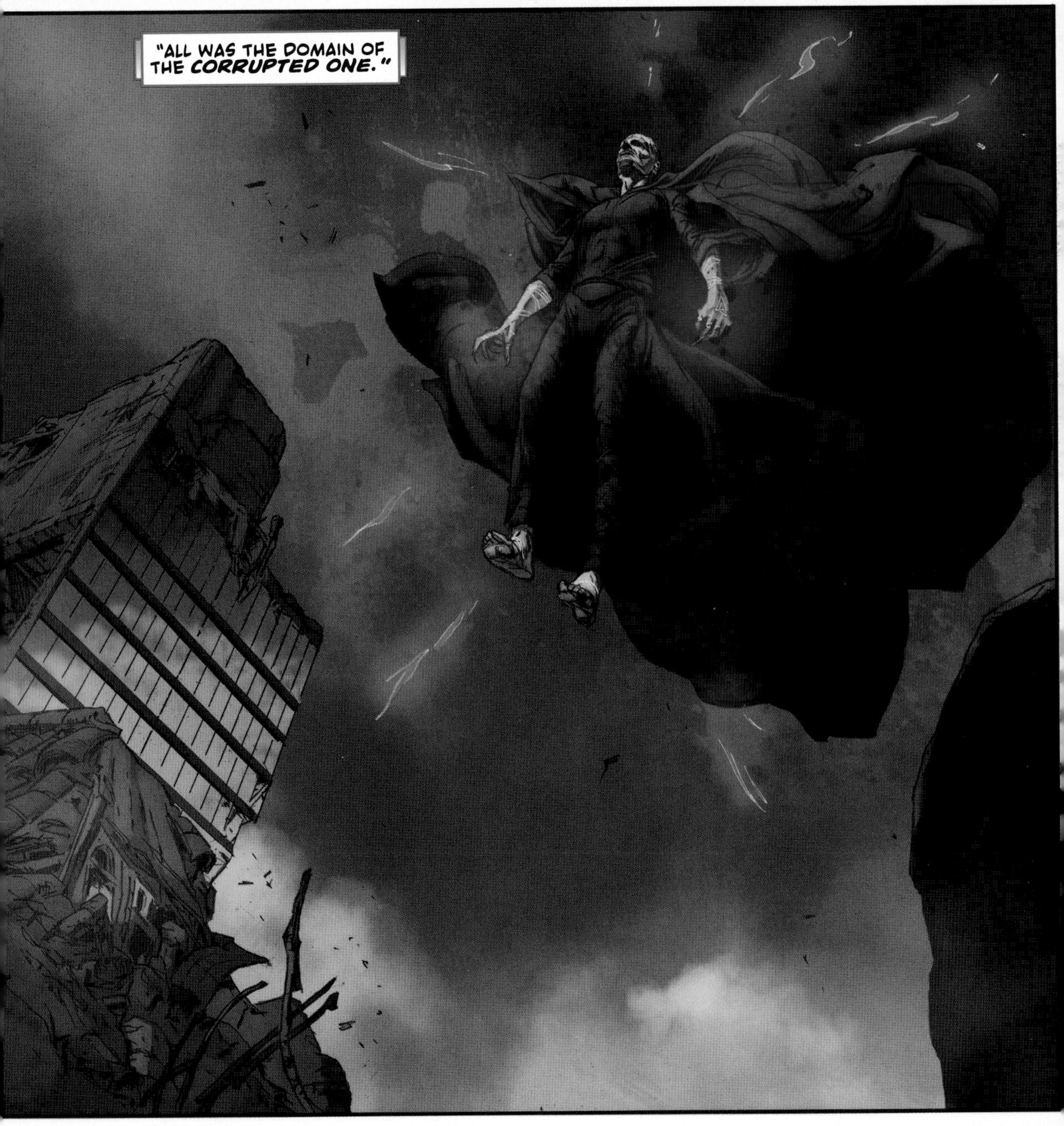
"ALL WAS THE DOMAIN OF THE CORRUPTED ONE."

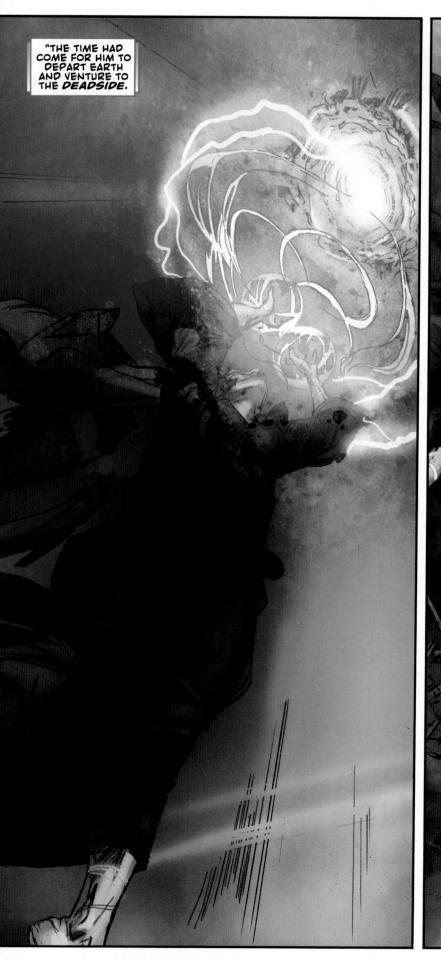

"THE TIME HAD COME FOR HIM TO DEPART EARTH AND VENTURE TO THE *DEADSIDE*.

"YEARS. DECADES. *CENTURIES* HE HAD TORTURED THE WORLD. THERE WERE NONE WHO COULD OPPOSE HIM.

"DOMINION WAS HIS. WHY DEPART?

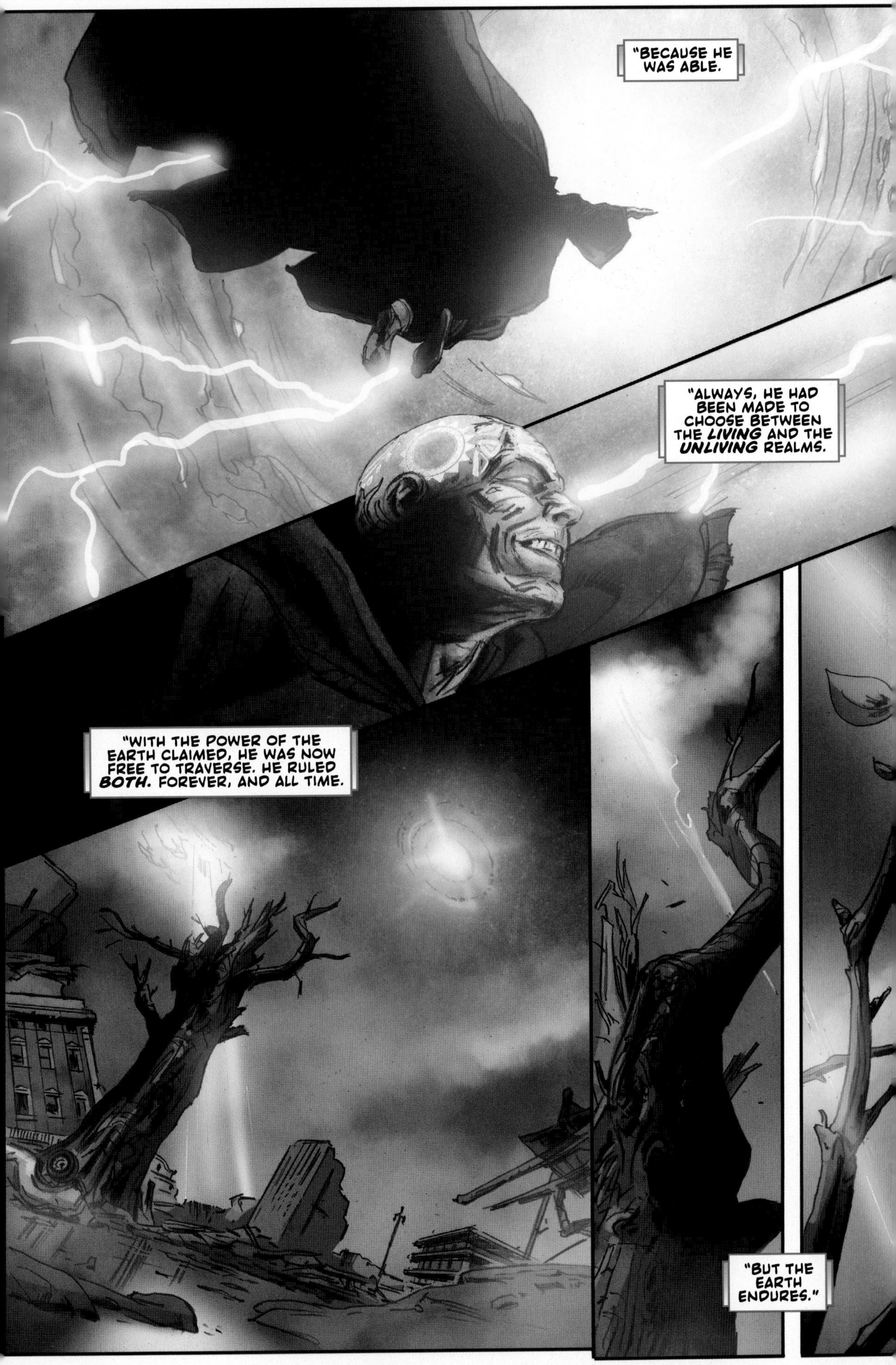
"BECAUSE HE WAS ABLE.
"ALWAYS, HE HAD BEEN MADE TO CHOOSE BETWEEN THE *LIVING* AND THE *UNLIVING* REALMS.
"WITH THE POWER OF THE EARTH CLAIMED, HE WAS NOW FREE TO TRAVERSE. HE RULED **BOTH**. FOREVER, AND ALL TIME.
"BUT THE EARTH ENDURES."

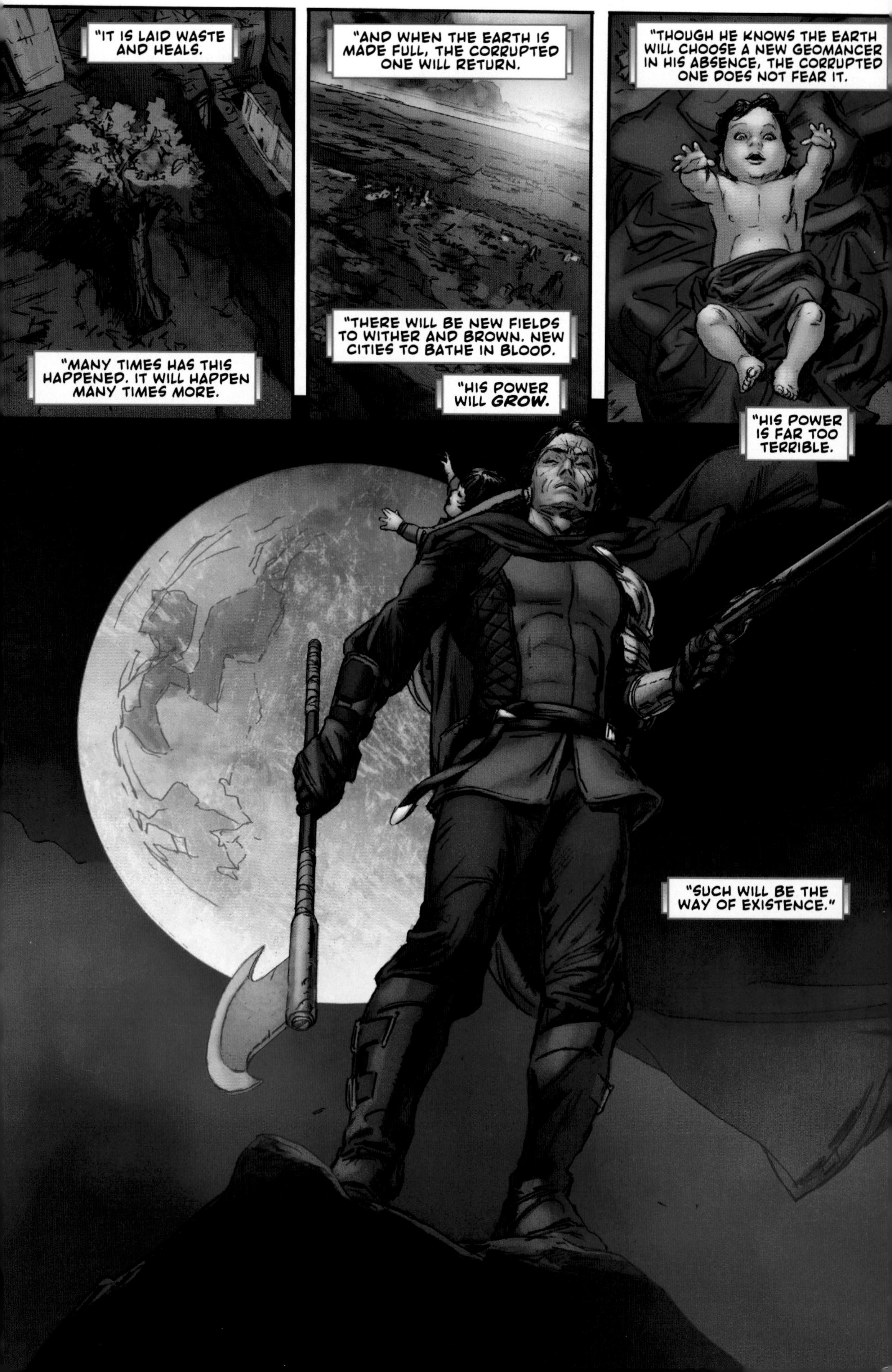
"IT IS LAID WASTE AND HEALS.
"MANY TIMES HAS THIS HAPPENED. IT WILL HAPPEN MANY TIMES MORE.
"AND WHEN THE EARTH IS MADE FULL, THE CORRUPTED ONE WILL RETURN.
"THERE WILL BE NEW FIELDS TO WITHER AND BROWN. NEW CITIES TO BATHE IN BLOOD.
"HIS POWER WILL GROW.
"THOUGH HE KNOWS THE EARTH WILL CHOOSE A NEW GEOMANCER IN HIS ABSENCE, THE CORRUPTED ONE DOES NOT FEAR IT.
"HIS POWER IS FAR TOO TERRIBLE.
"SUCH WILL BE THE WAY OF EXISTENCE."

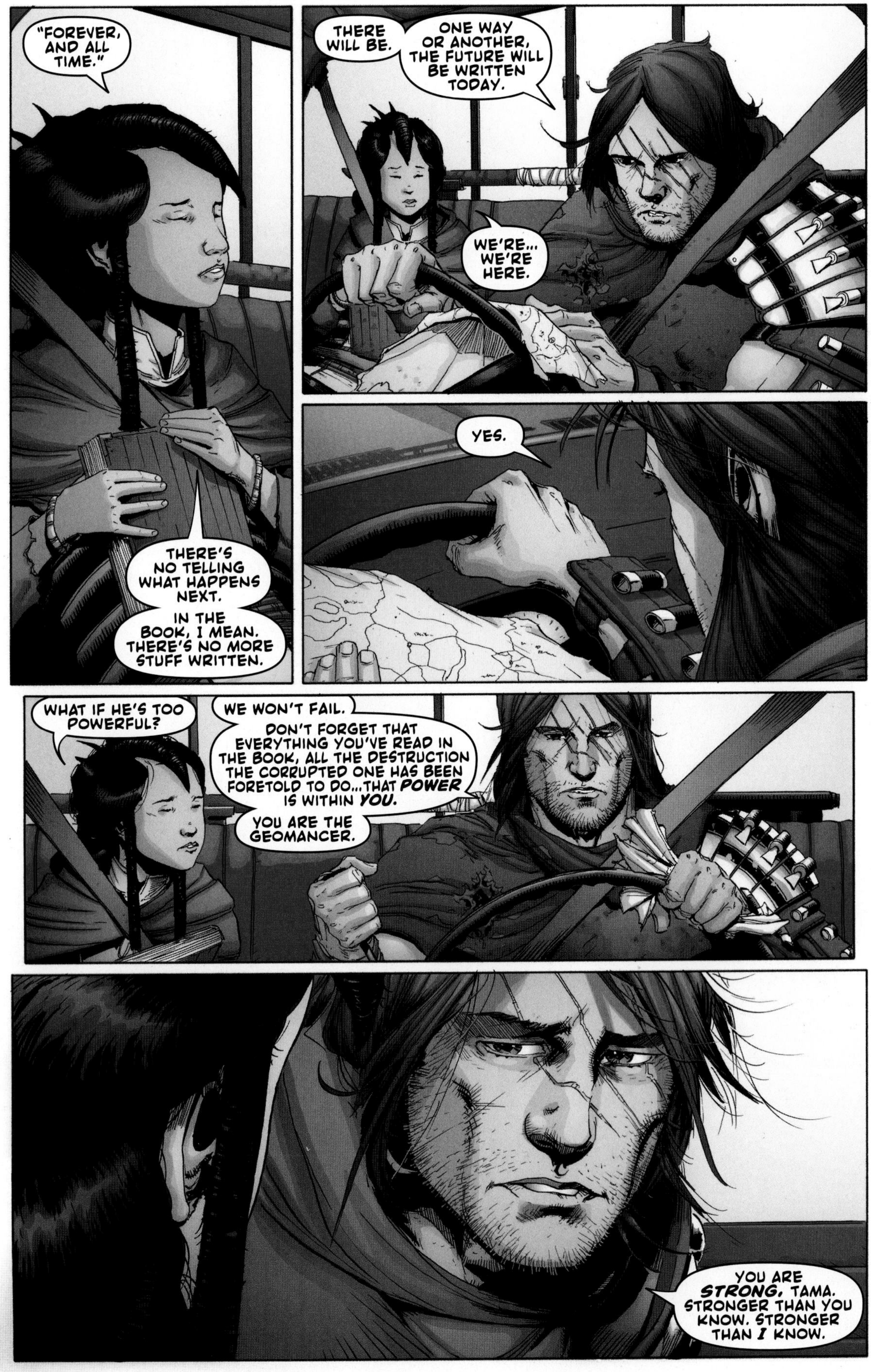
"FOREVER, AND ALL TIME."
THERE WILL BE.
ONE WAY OR ANOTHER, THE FUTURE WILL BE WRITTEN TODAY.
WE'RE... WE'RE HERE.
YES.
THERE'S NO TELLING WHAT HAPPENS NEXT.
IN THE BOOK, I MEAN. THERE'S NO MORE STUFF WRITTEN.
WHAT IF HE'S TOO POWERFUL?
WE WON'T FAIL.
DON'T FORGET THAT EVERYTHING YOU'VE READ IN THE BOOK, ALL THE DESTRUCTION THE CORRUPTED ONE HAS BEEN FORETOLD TO DO...THAT POWER IS WITHIN YOU.
YOU ARE THE GEOMANCER.
YOU ARE STRONG, TAMA. STRONGER THAN YOU KNOW. STRONGER THAN I KNOW.

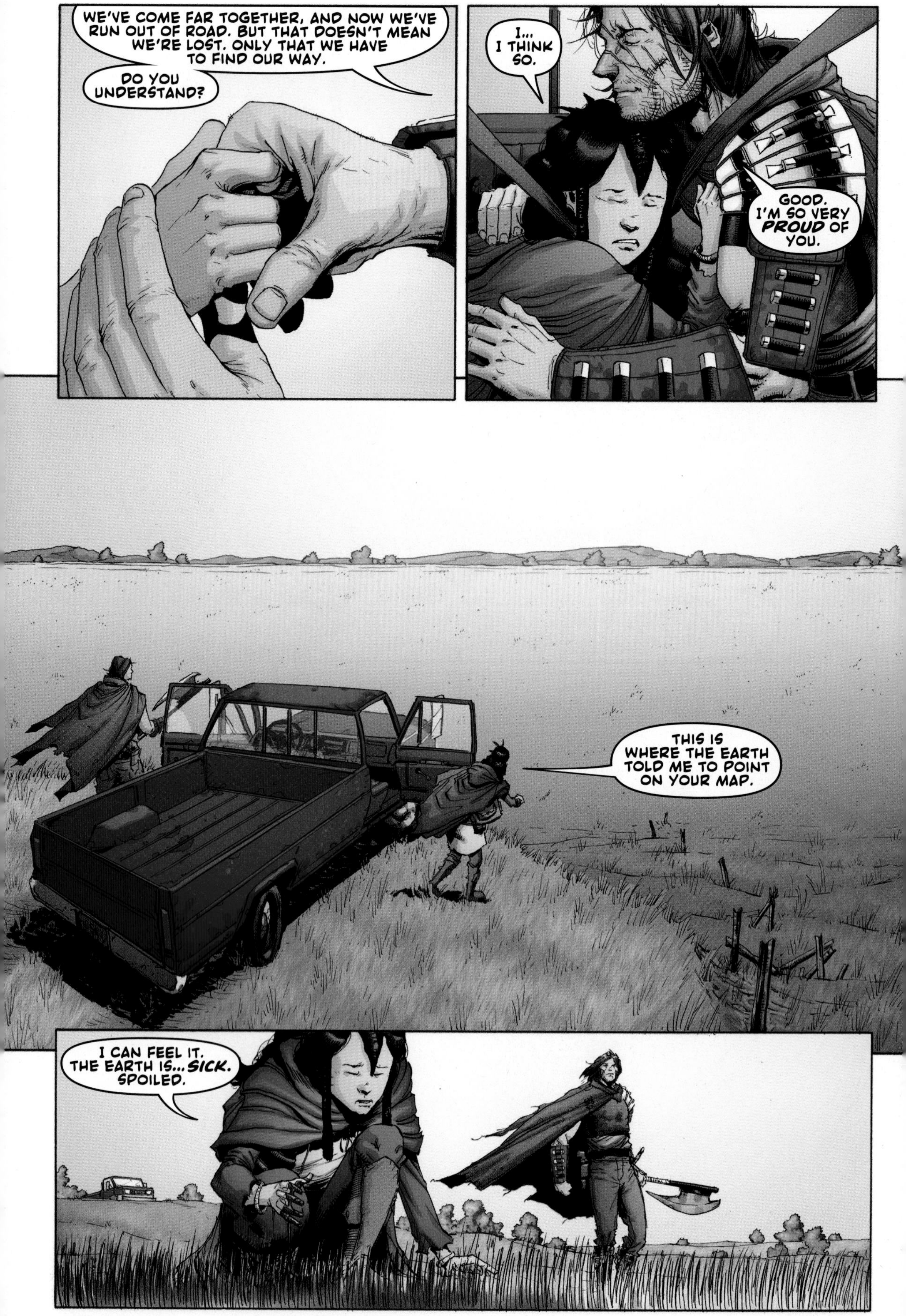
WE'VE COME FAR TOGETHER, AND NOW WE'VE RUN OUT OF ROAD. BUT THAT DOESN'T MEAN WE'RE LOST. ONLY THAT WE HAVE TO FIND OUR WAY.
DO YOU UNDERSTAND?
I... I THINK SO.
GOOD. I'M SO VERY PROUD OF YOU.
THIS IS WHERE THE EARTH TOLD ME TO POINT ON YOUR MAP.
I CAN FEEL IT. THE EARTH IS... SICK. SPOILED.

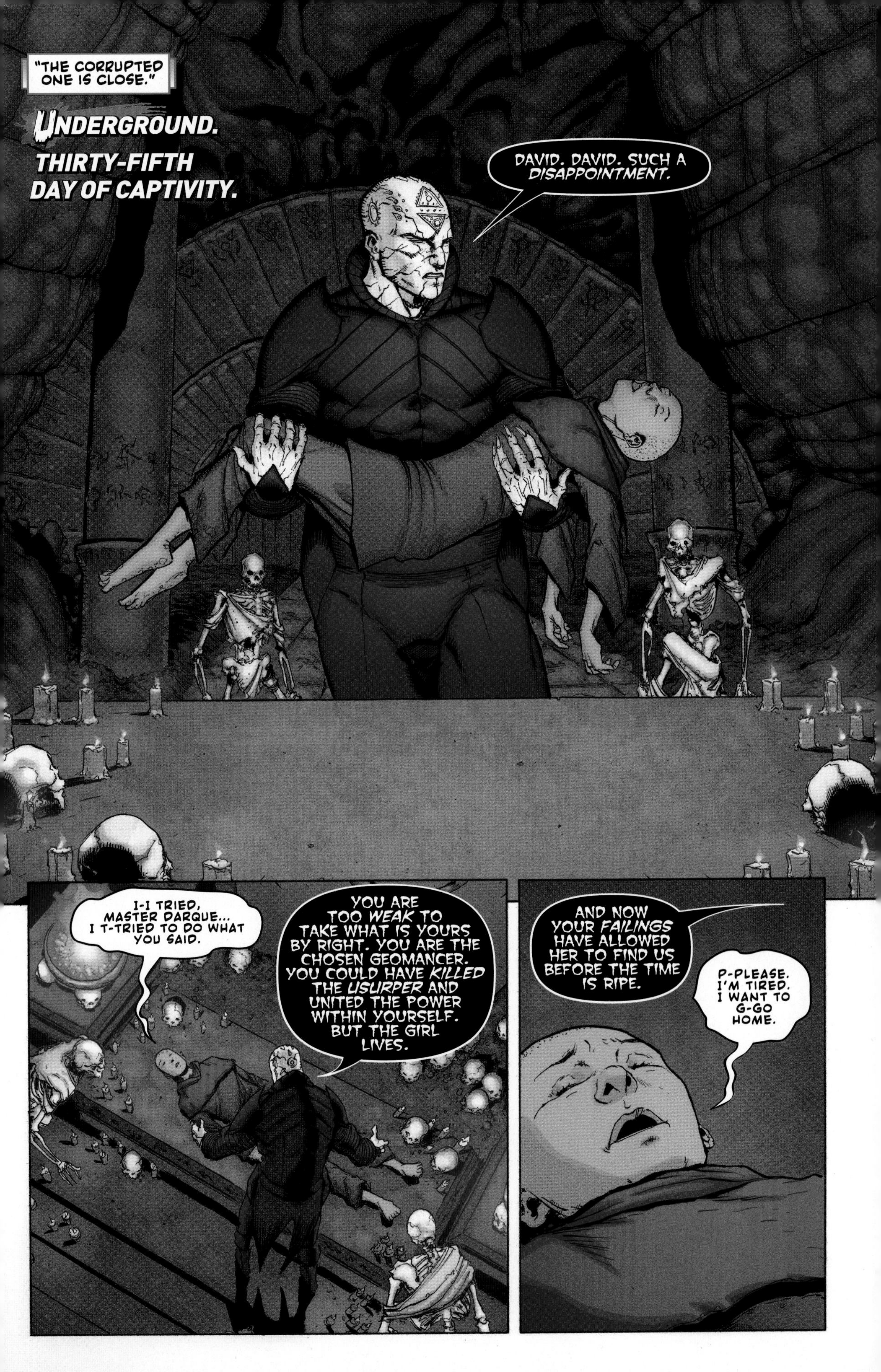
"THE CORRUPTED ONE IS CLOSE."
UNDERGROUND.
THIRTY-FIFTH DAY OF CAPTIVITY.
DAVID. DAVID. SUCH A DISAPPOINTMENT.
I-I TRIED, MASTER DARQUE... I T-TRIED TO DO WHAT YOU SAID.
YOU ARE TOO WEAK TO TAKE WHAT IS YOURS BY RIGHT. YOU ARE THE CHOSEN GEOMANCER. YOU COULD HAVE KILLED THE USURPER AND UNITED THE POWER WITHIN YOURSELF. BUT THE GIRL LIVES.
AND NOW YOUR FAILINGS HAVE ALLOWED HER TO FIND US BEFORE THE TIME IS RIPE.
P-PLEASE. I'M TIRED. I WANT TO G-GO HOME.

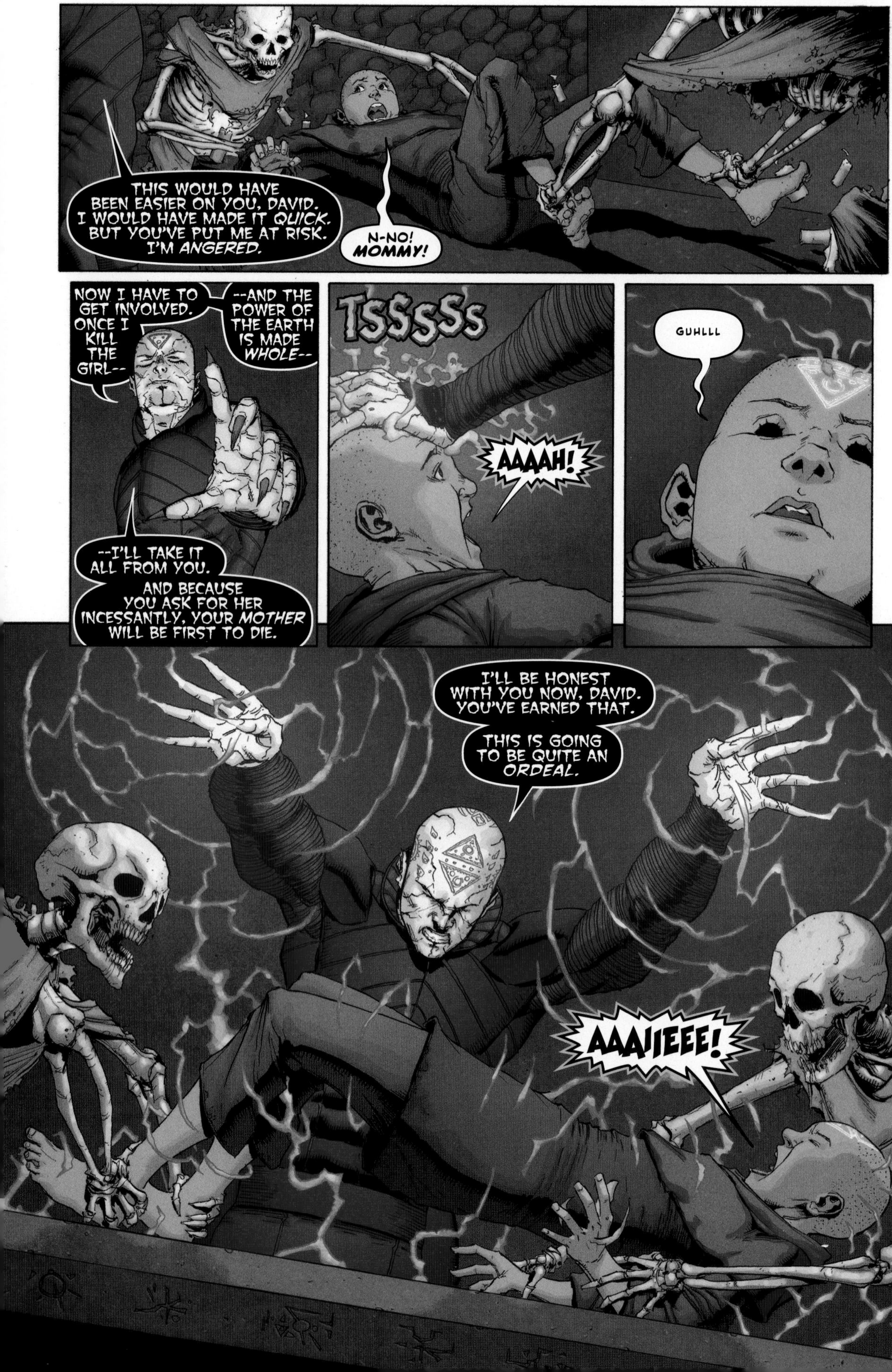
THIS WOULD HAVE BEEN EASIER ON YOU, DAVID. I WOULD HAVE MADE IT QUICK. BUT YOU'VE PUT ME AT RISK. I'M ANGERED.
N-NO! MOMMY!
NOW I HAVE TO GET INVOLVED. ONCE I KILL THE GIRL--
--AND THE POWER OF THE EARTH IS MADE WHOLE--
--I'LL TAKE IT ALL FROM YOU.
AND BECAUSE YOU ASK FOR HER INCESSANTLY, YOUR MOTHER WILL BE FIRST TO DIE.
TSSSSS
AAAAH!
GUHLLL
I'LL BE HONEST WITH YOU NOW, DAVID. YOU'VE EARNED THAT.
THIS IS GOING TO BE QUITE AN ORDEAL.
AAAIIEEE!

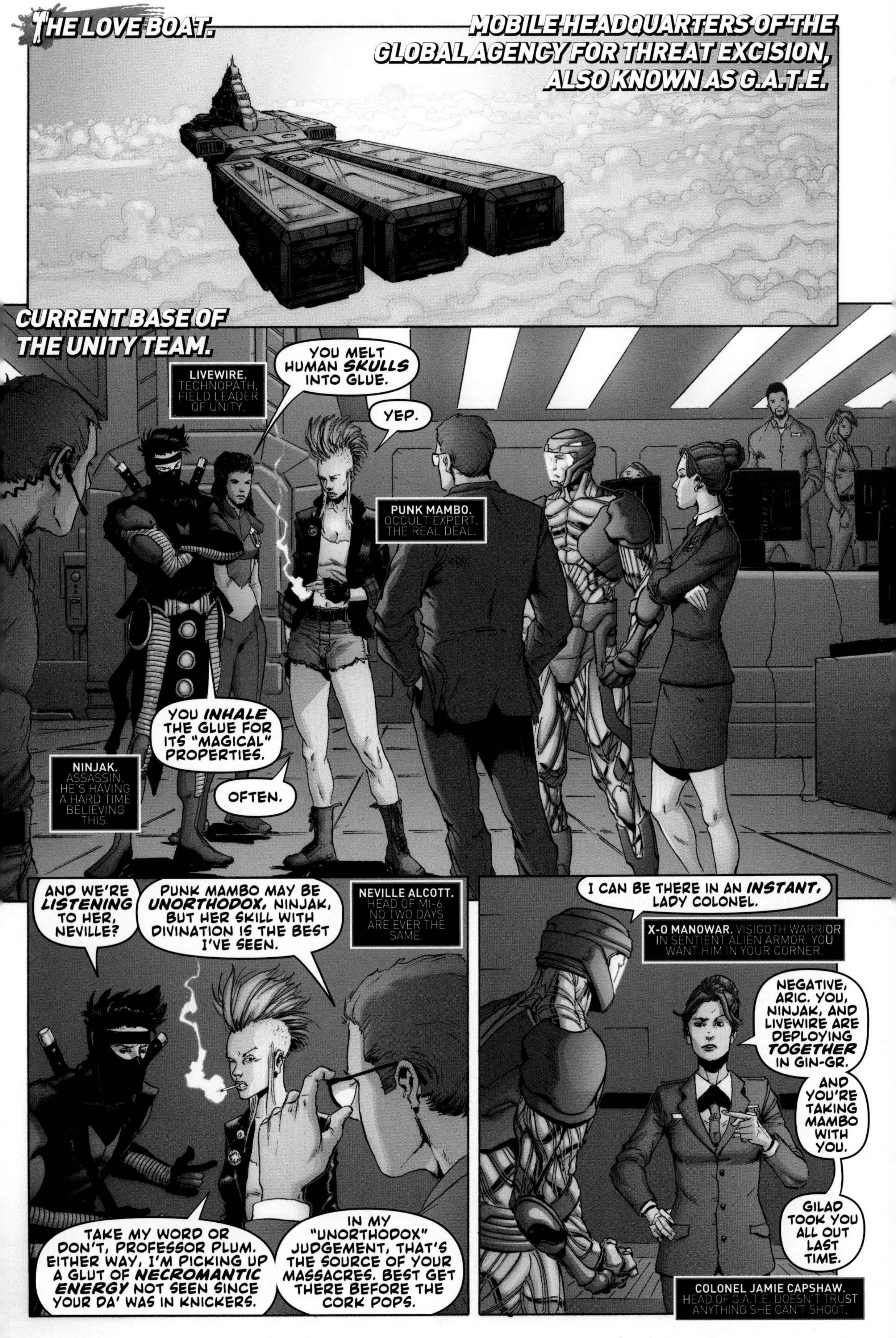
THE LOVE BOAT.
MOBILE HEADQUARTERS OF THE GLOBAL AGENCY FOR THREAT EXCISION, ALSO KNOWN AS G.A.T.E.
CURRENT BASE OF THE UNITY TEAM.
LIVEWIRE. TECHNOPATH. FIELD LEADER OF UNITY.
YOU MELT HUMAN SKULLS INTO GLUE.
YEP.
PUNK MAMBO. OCCULT EXPERT. THE REAL DEAL.
YOU INHALE THE GLUE FOR ITS "MAGICAL" PROPERTIES.
OFTEN.
NINJAK. ASSASSIN. HE'S HAVING A HARD TIME BELIEVING THIS.
AND WE'RE LISTENING TO HER, NEVILLE?
PUNK MAMBO MAY BE UNORTHODOX, NINJAK, BUT HER SKILL WITH DIVINATION IS THE BEST I'VE SEEN.
NEVILLE ALCOTT. HEAD OF MI-6. NO TWO DAYS ARE EVER THE SAME.
TAKE MY WORD OR DON'T, PROFESSOR PLUM. EITHER WAY, I'M PICKING UP A GLUT OF NECROMANTIC ENERGY NOT SEEN SINCE YOUR DA' WAS IN KNICKERS.
IN MY "UNORTHODOX" JUDGEMENT, THAT'S THE SOURCE OF YOUR MASSACRES. BEST GET THERE BEFORE THE CORK POPS.
I CAN BE THERE IN AN INSTANT, LADY COLONEL.
X-O MANOWAR. VISIGOTH WARRIOR IN SENTIENT ALIEN ARMOR. YOU WANT HIM IN YOUR CORNER.
NEGATIVE, ARIC. YOU, NINJAK, AND LIVEWIRE ARE DEPLOYING TOGETHER IN GIN-GR.
AND YOU'RE TAKING MAMBO WITH YOU.
GILAD TOOK YOU ALL OUT LAST TIME.
COLONEL JAMIE CAPSHAW. HEAD OF G.A.T.E. DOESN'T TRUST ANYTHING SHE CAN'T SHOOT.

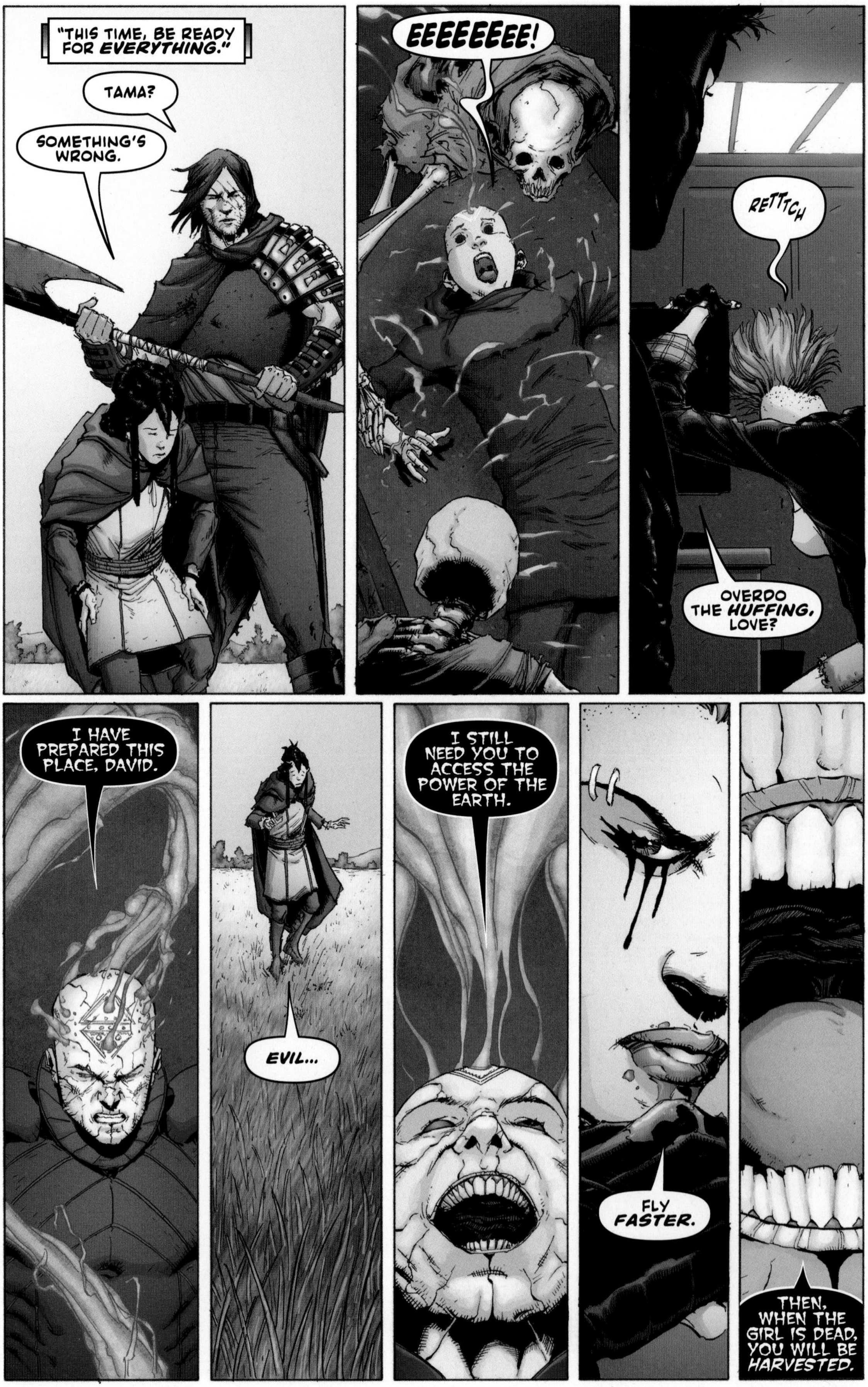
"THIS TIME, BE READY FOR EVERYTHING."
TAMA?
SOMETHING'S WRONG.
EEEEEEEE!
RETTTCH
OVERDO THE HUFFING, LOVE?
I HAVE PREPARED THIS PLACE, DAVID.
EVIL...
I STILL NEED YOU TO ACCESS THE POWER OF THE EARTH.
FLY FASTER.
THEN, WHEN THE GIRL IS DEAD, YOU WILL BE HARVESTED.

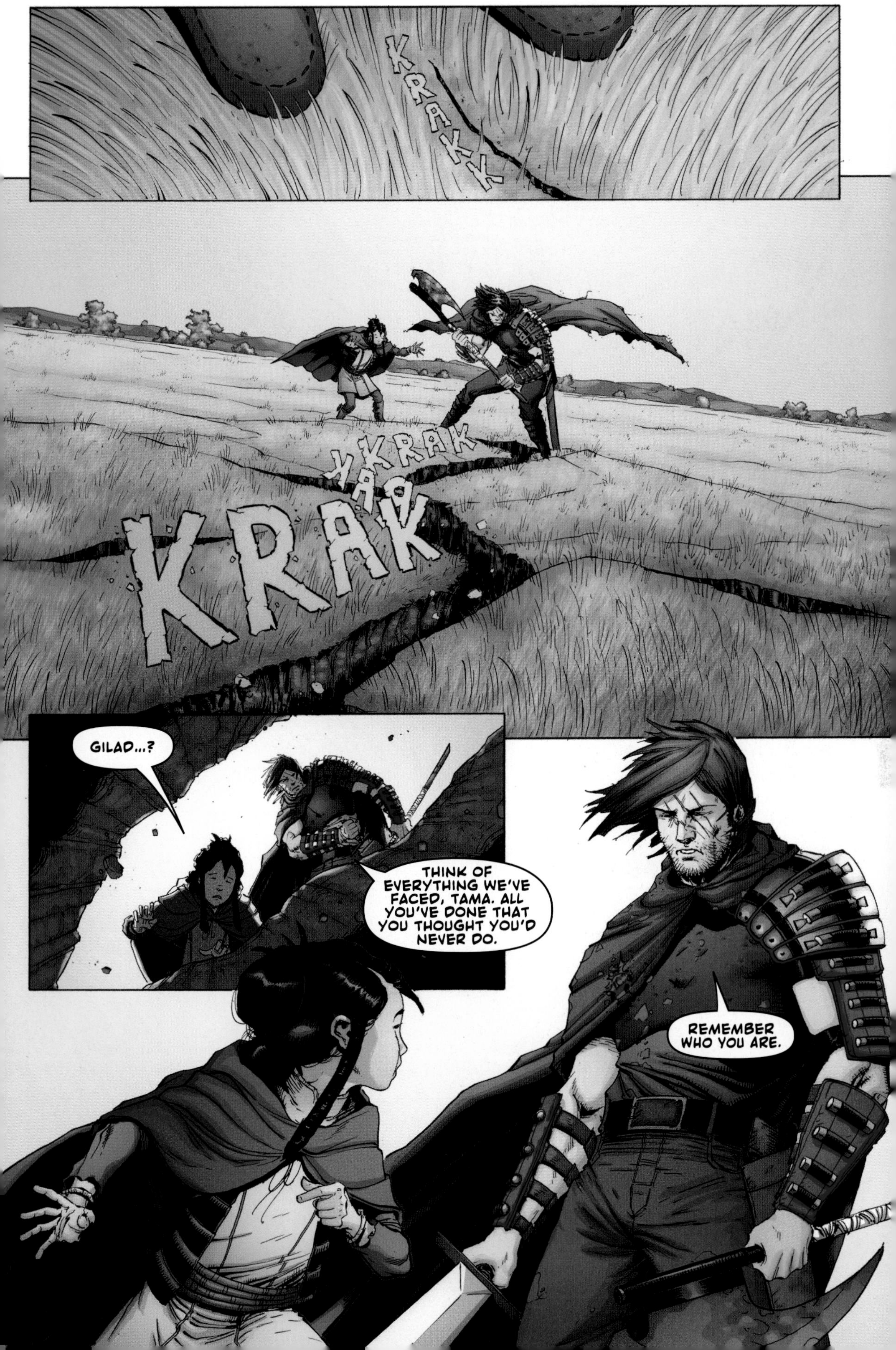
KRAKK
KRAK
KRAK
KRAK
GILAD...?
THINK OF EVERYTHING WE'VE FACED, TAMA. ALL YOU'VE DONE THAT YOU THOUGHT YOU'D NEVER DO.
REMEMBER WHO YOU ARE.

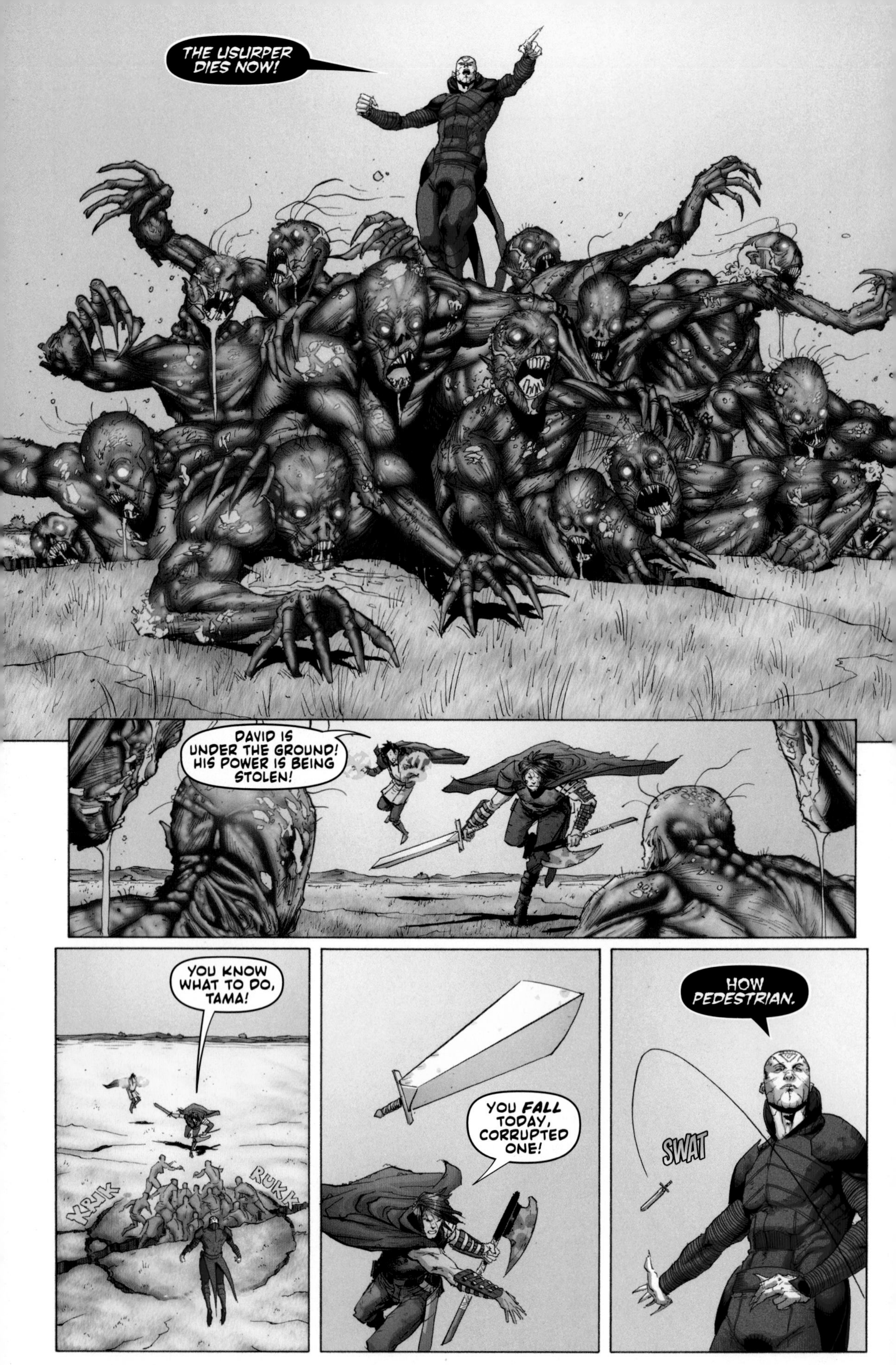
THE USURPER DIES NOW!
DAVID IS UNDER THE GROUND! HIS POWER IS BEING STOLEN!
YOU KNOW WHAT TO DO, TAMA!
KRUK
RUKK
YOU **FALL** TODAY, CORRUPTED ONE!
HOW PEDESTRIAN.
SWAT

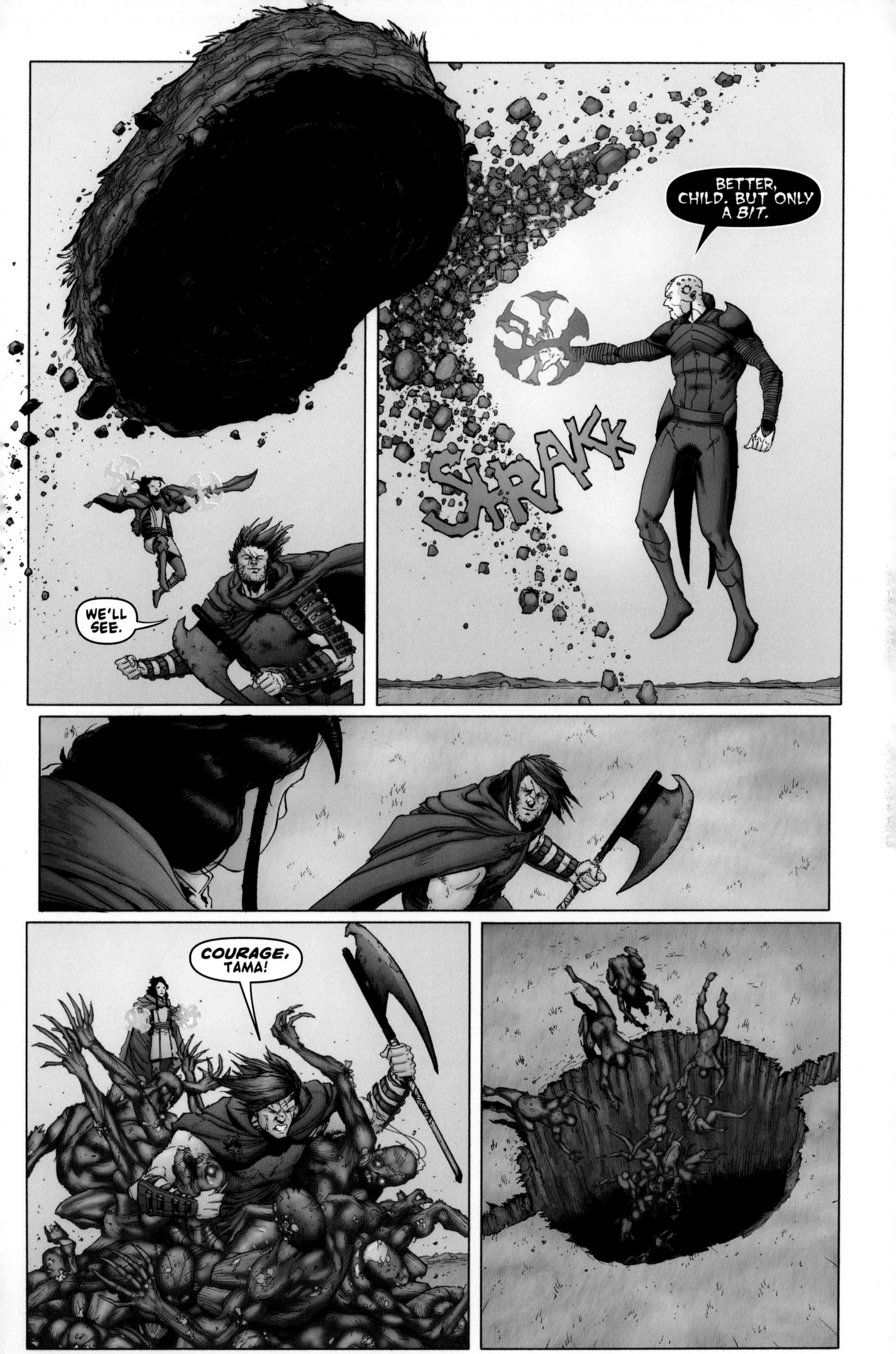

BETTER, CHILD. BUT ONLY A BIT.
SKRAKK
WE'LL SEE.
COURAGE, TAMA!

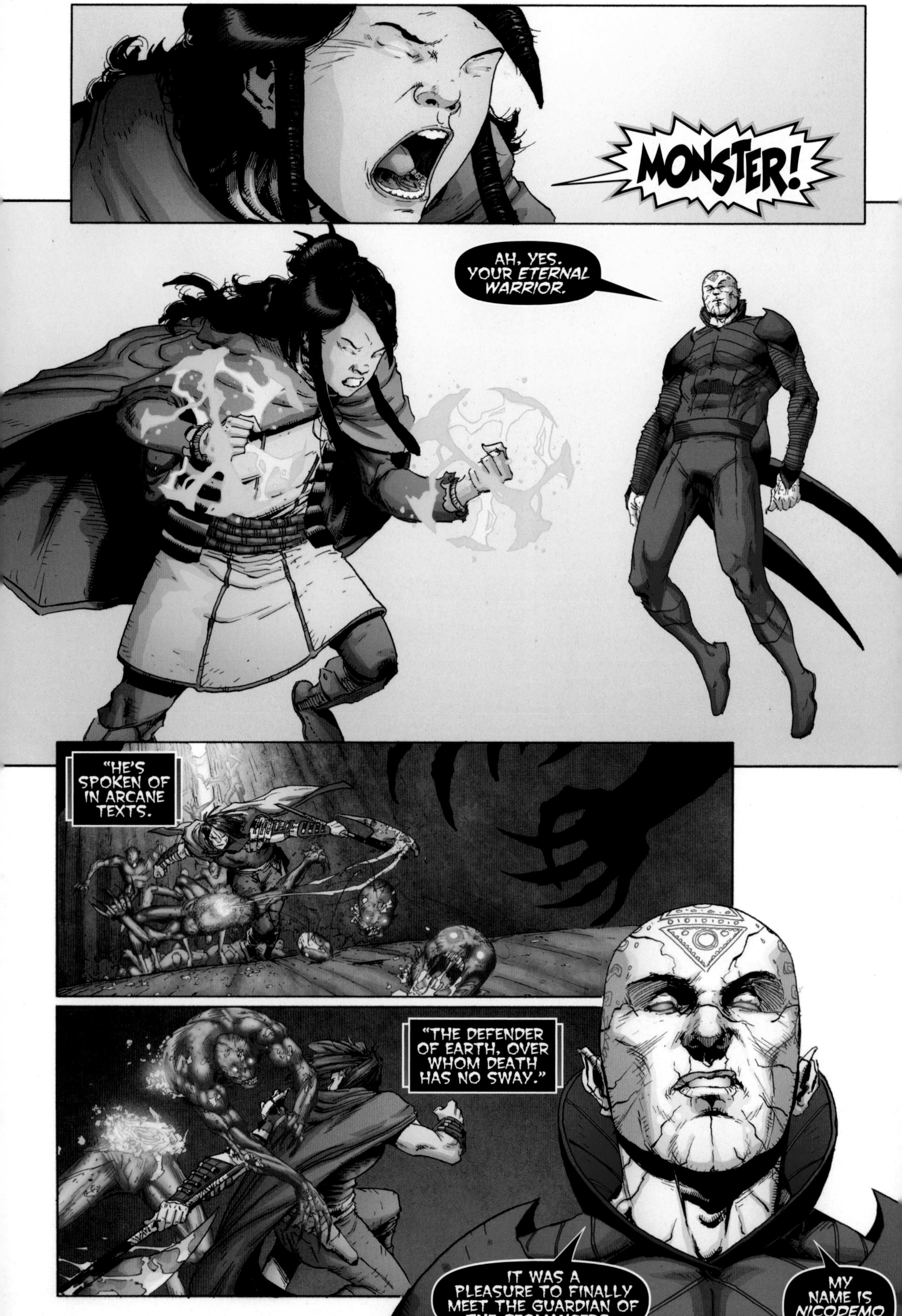
MONSTER!
AH, YES. YOUR ETERNAL WARRIOR.
"HE'S SPOKEN OF IN ARCANE TEXTS.
"THE DEFENDER OF EARTH, OVER WHOM DEATH HAS NO SWAY."
IT WAS A PLEASURE TO FINALLY MEET THE GUARDIAN OF THE GEOMANCERS.
MY NAME IS NICODEMO DARQUE.

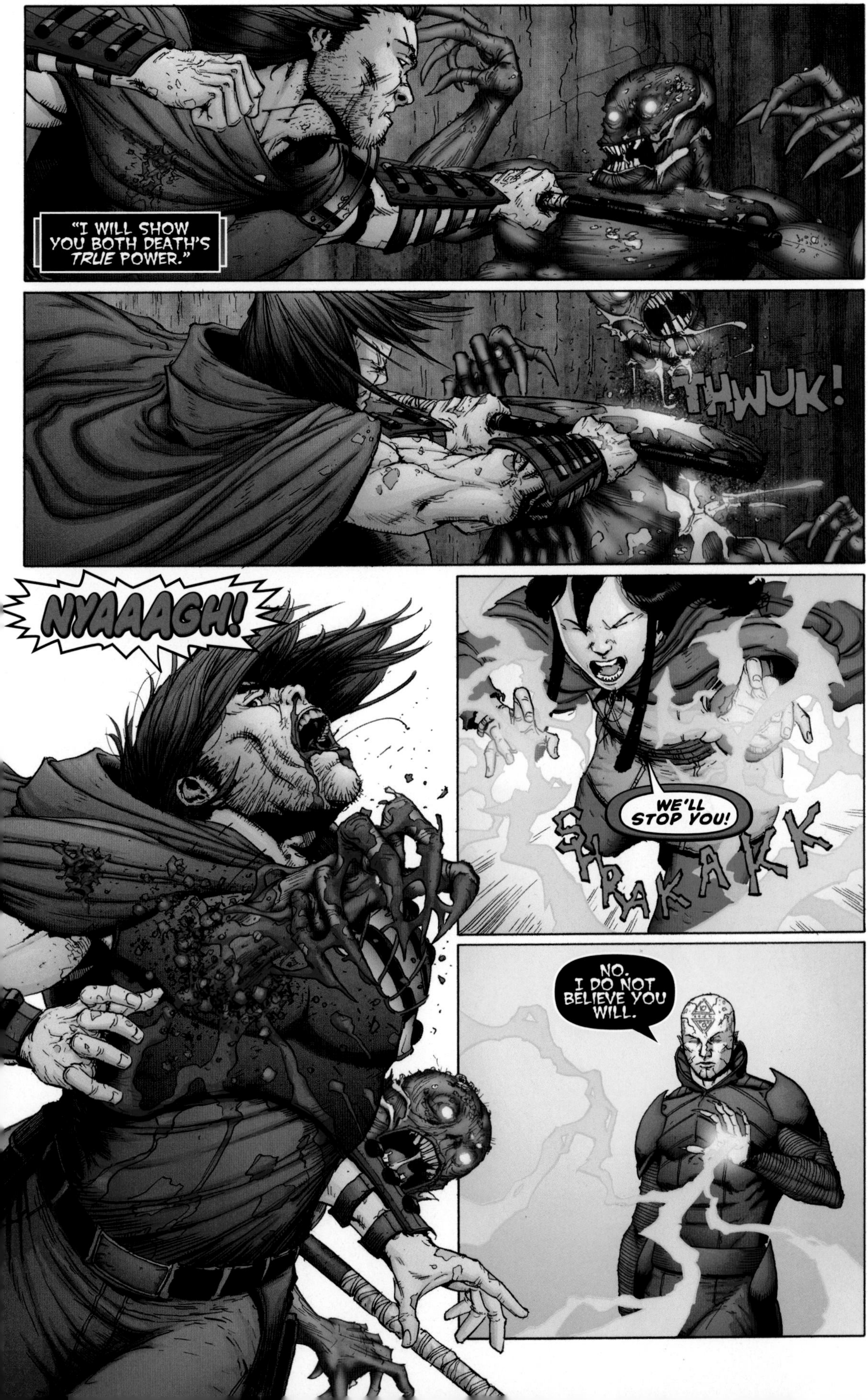
"I WILL SHOW YOU BOTH DEATH'S *TRUE* POWER."
THWUK!
NYAAAGH!
WE'LL STOP YOU!
SHRAKAKK
NO. I DO NOT BELIEVE YOU WILL.

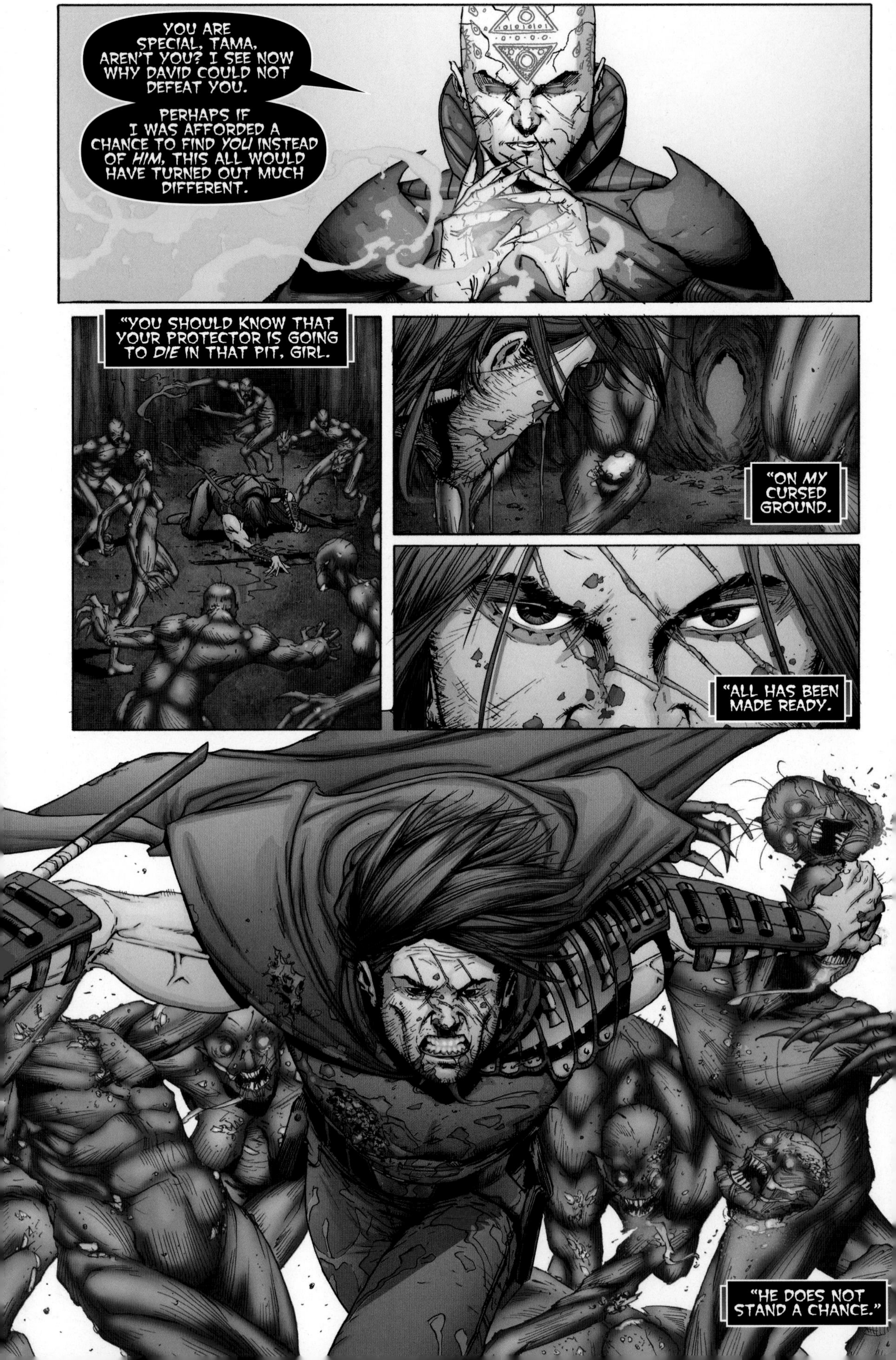

YOU ARE SPECIAL, TAMA, AREN'T YOU? I SEE NOW WHY DAVID COULD NOT DEFEAT YOU.
PERHAPS IF I WAS AFFORDED A CHANCE TO FIND *YOU* INSTEAD OF *HIM*, THIS ALL WOULD HAVE TURNED OUT MUCH DIFFERENT.
"YOU SHOULD KNOW THAT YOUR PROTECTOR IS GOING TO *DIE* IN THAT PIT, GIRL.
"ON *MY* CURSED GROUND.
"ALL HAS BEEN MADE READY.
"HE DOES NOT STAND A CHANCE."

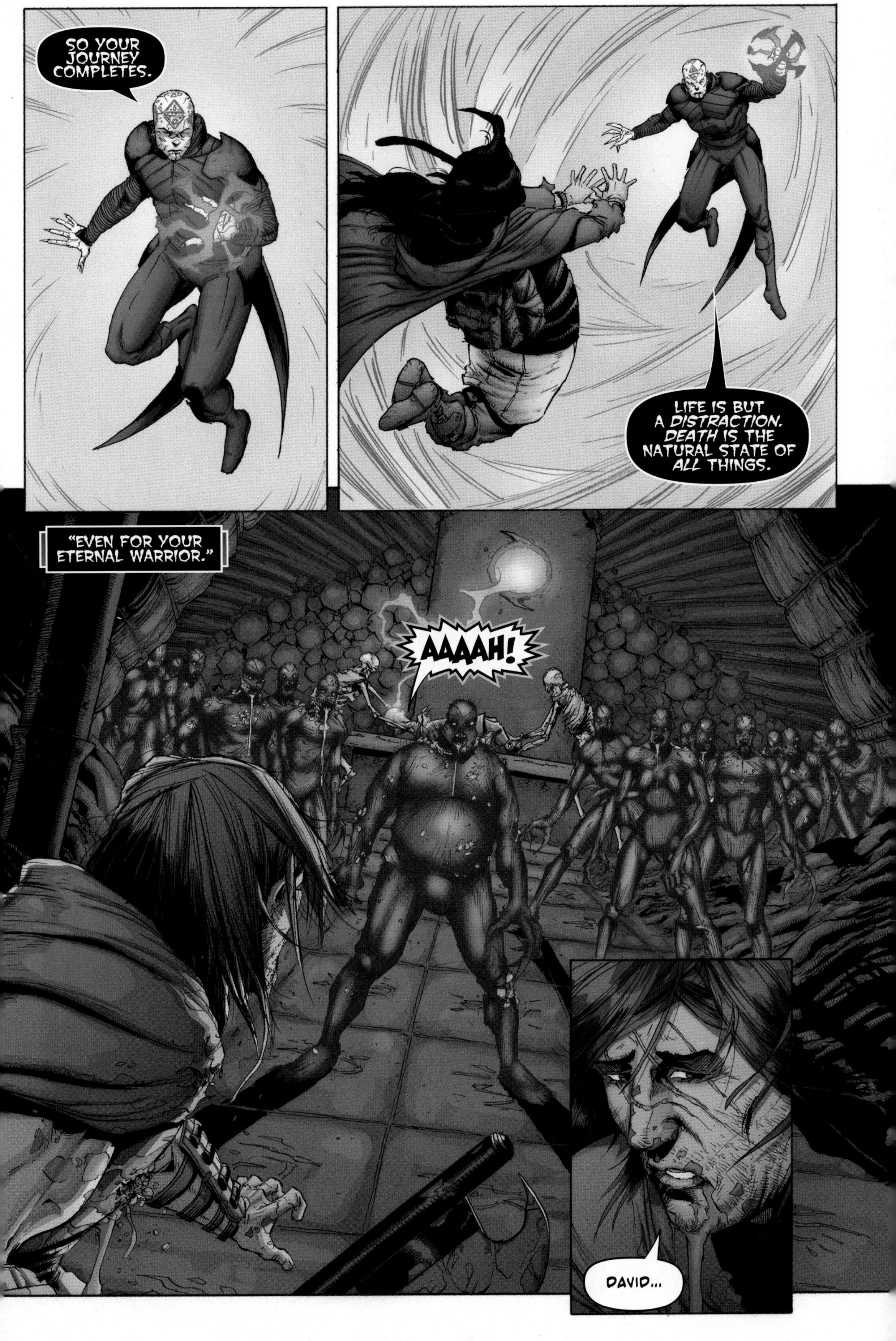
SO YOUR JOURNEY COMPLETES.
LIFE IS BUT A DISTRACTION. DEATH IS THE NATURAL STATE OF ALL THINGS.
"EVEN FOR YOUR ETERNAL WARRIOR."
AAAAH!
DAVID...

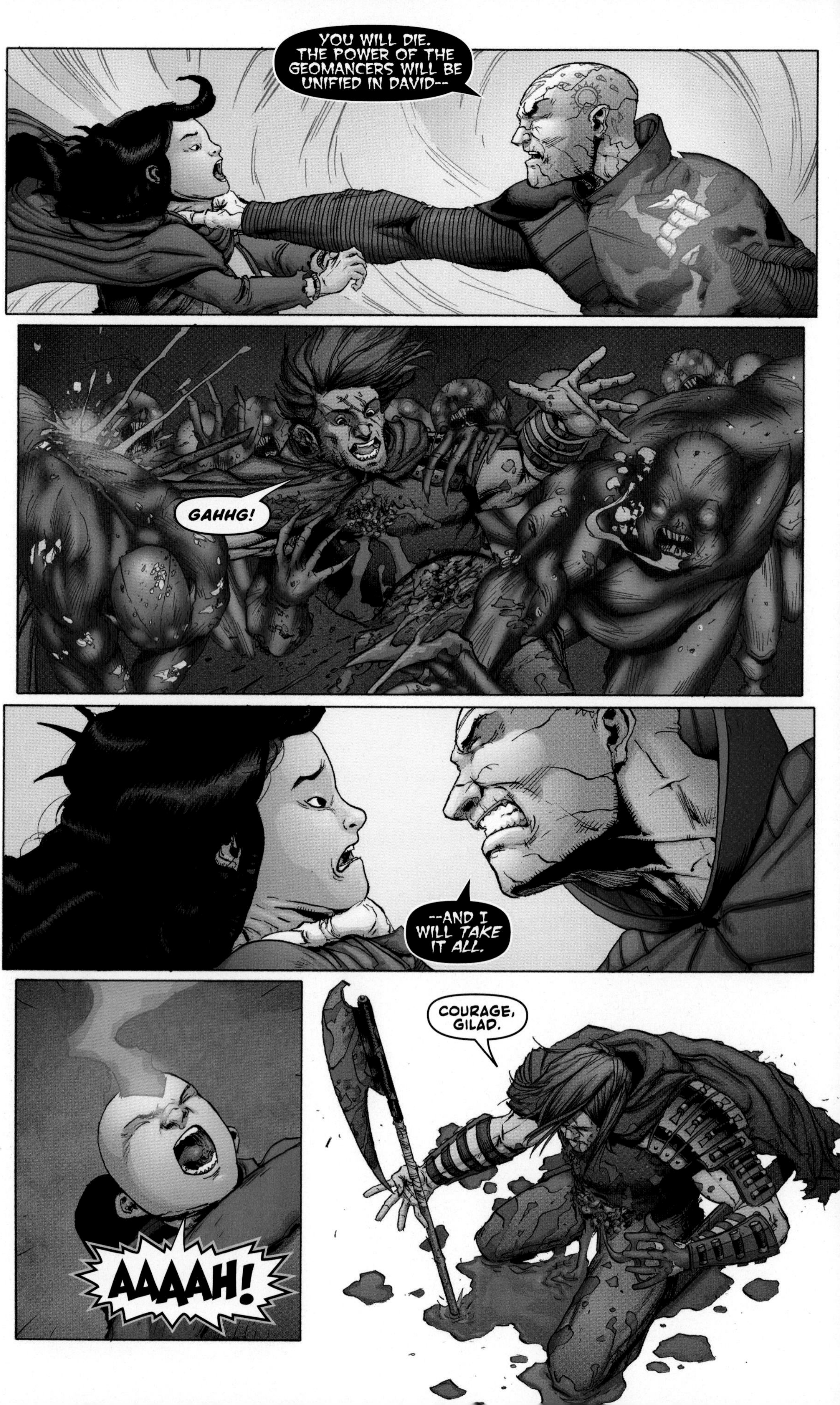
YOU WILL DIE. THE POWER OF THE GEOMANCERS WILL BE UNIFIED IN DAVID--
GAHHG!
--AND I WILL TAKE IT ALL.
AAAAH!
COURAGE, GILAD.

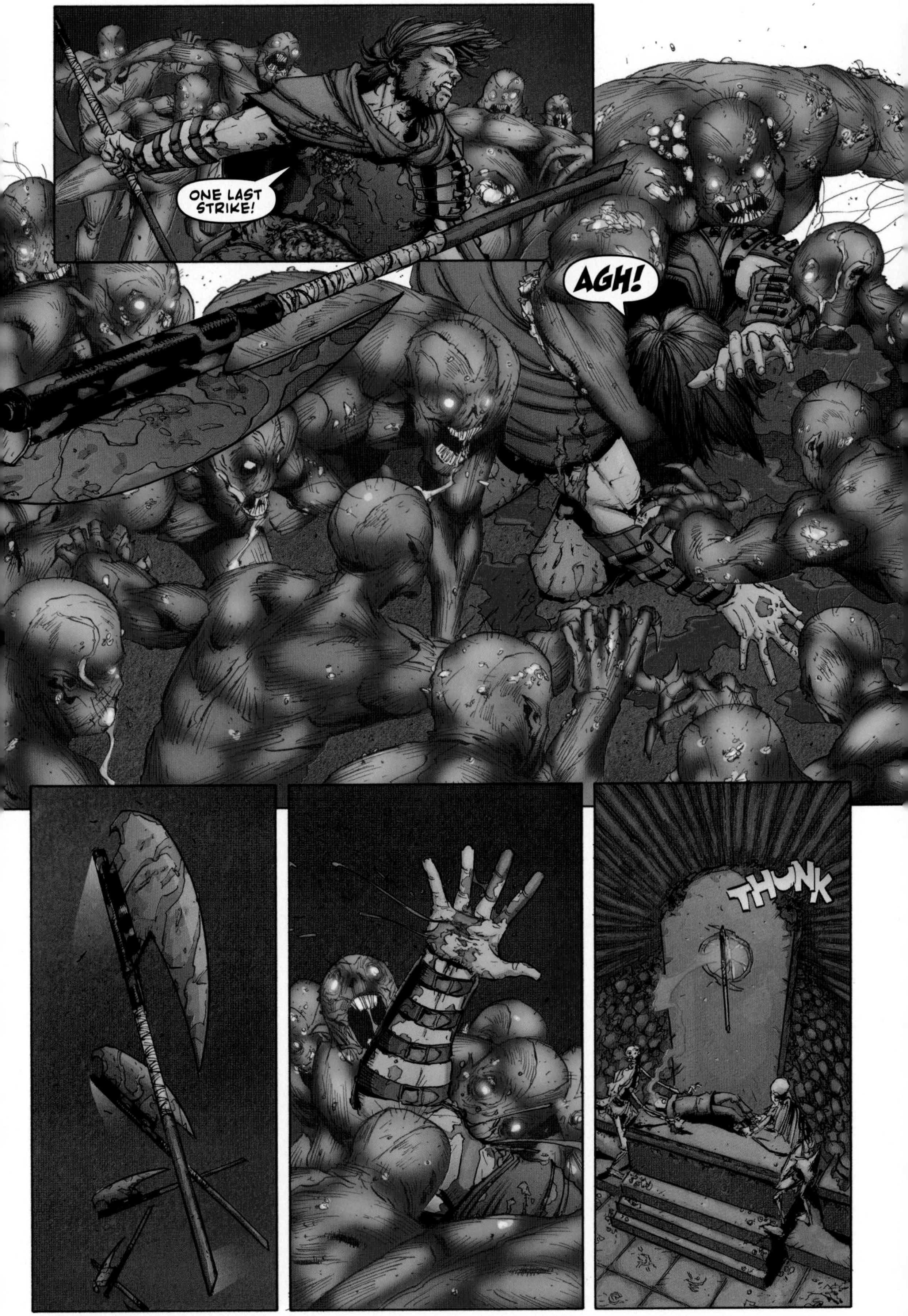
ONE LAST STRIKE!
AGH!
THUNK

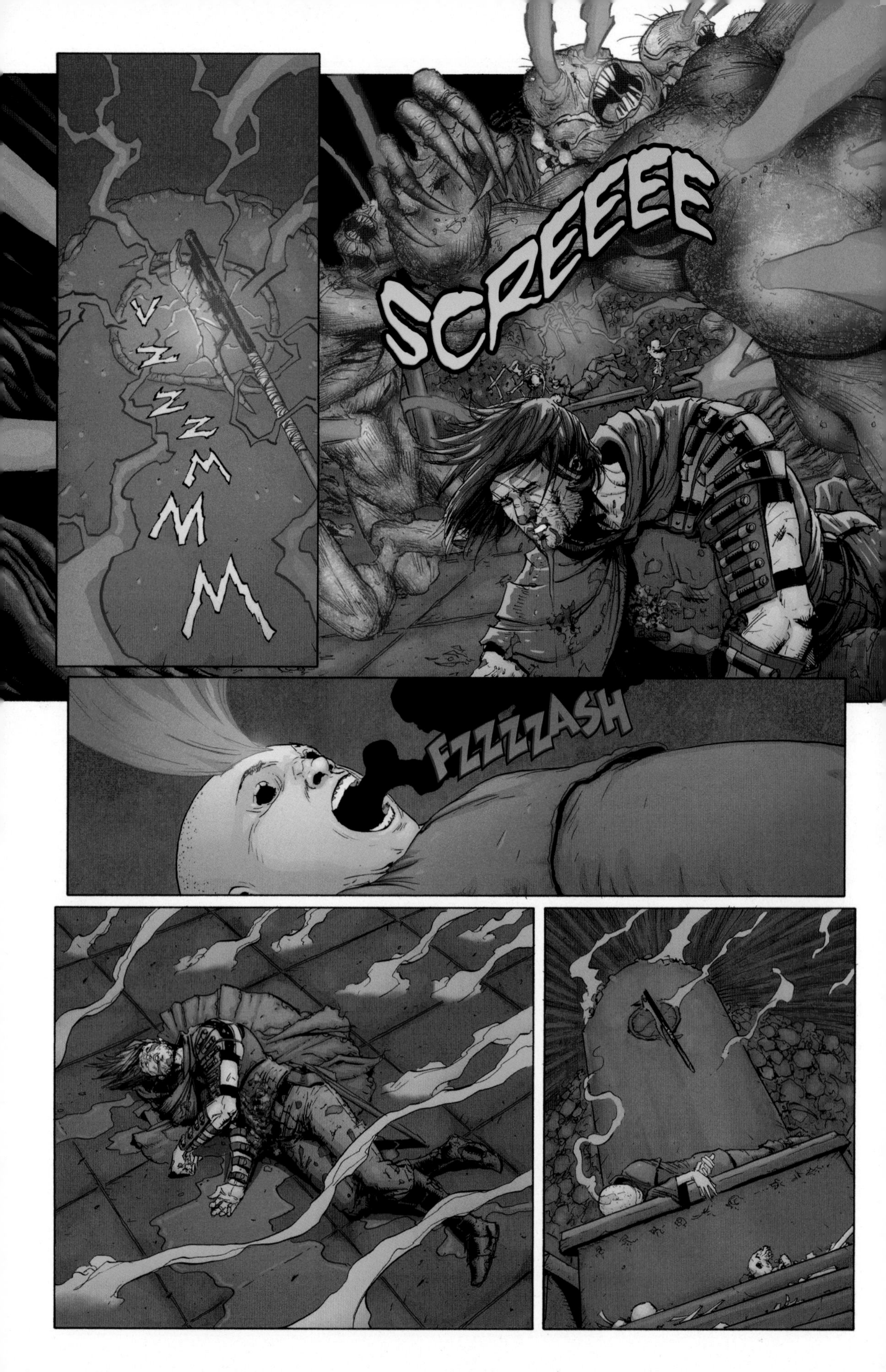
VVZZZMMMM
SCREEEEE
FZZZZASH

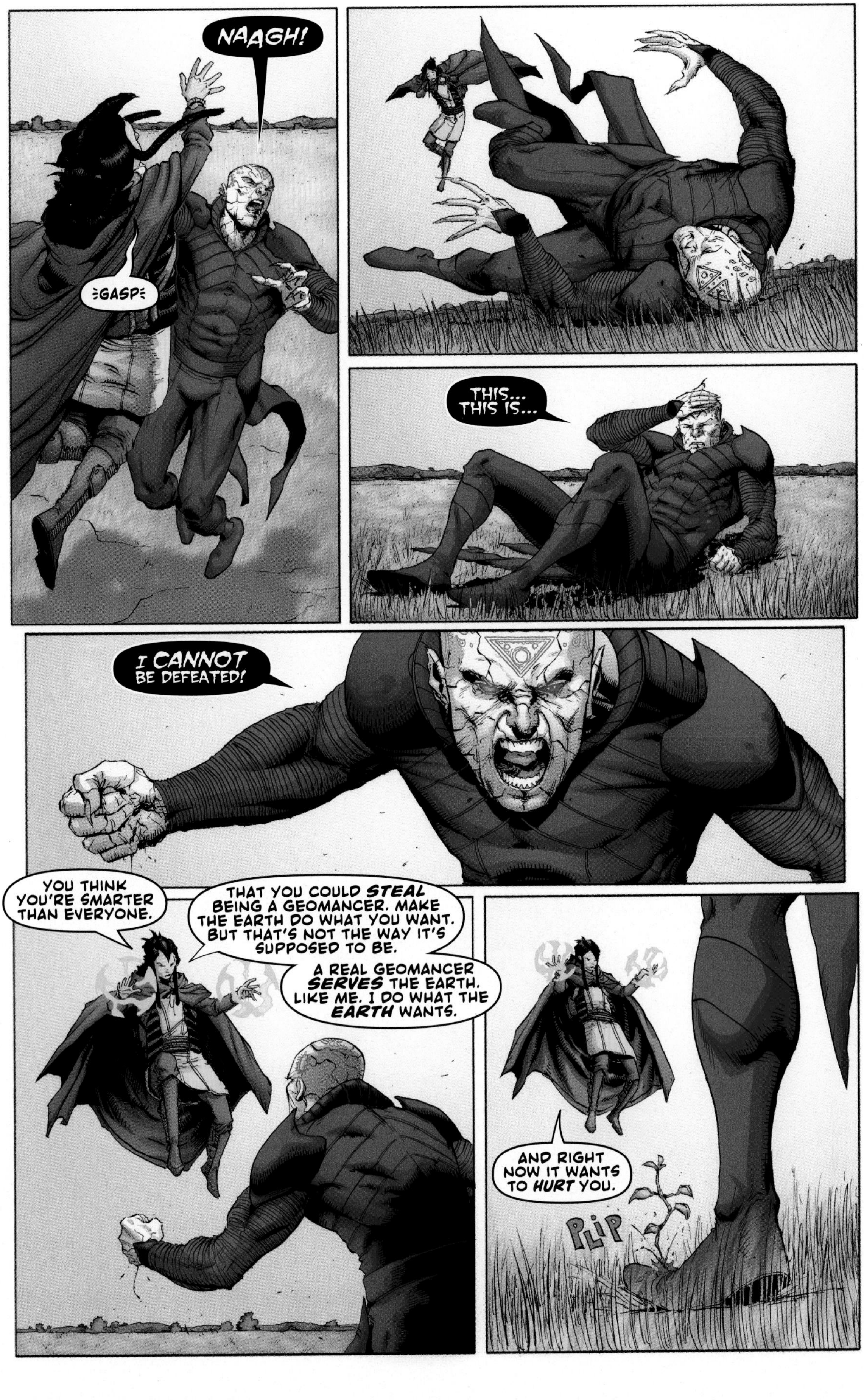
NAAGH!
GASP
THIS... THIS IS...
I CANNOT BE DEFEATED!
YOU THINK YOU'RE SMARTER THAN EVERYONE.
THAT YOU COULD STEAL BEING A GEOMANCER. MAKE THE EARTH DO WHAT YOU WANT. BUT THAT'S NOT THE WAY IT'S SUPPOSED TO BE.
A REAL GEOMANCER SERVES THE EARTH. LIKE ME. I DO WHAT THE EARTH WANTS.
AND RIGHT NOW IT WANTS TO HURT YOU.
PLIP

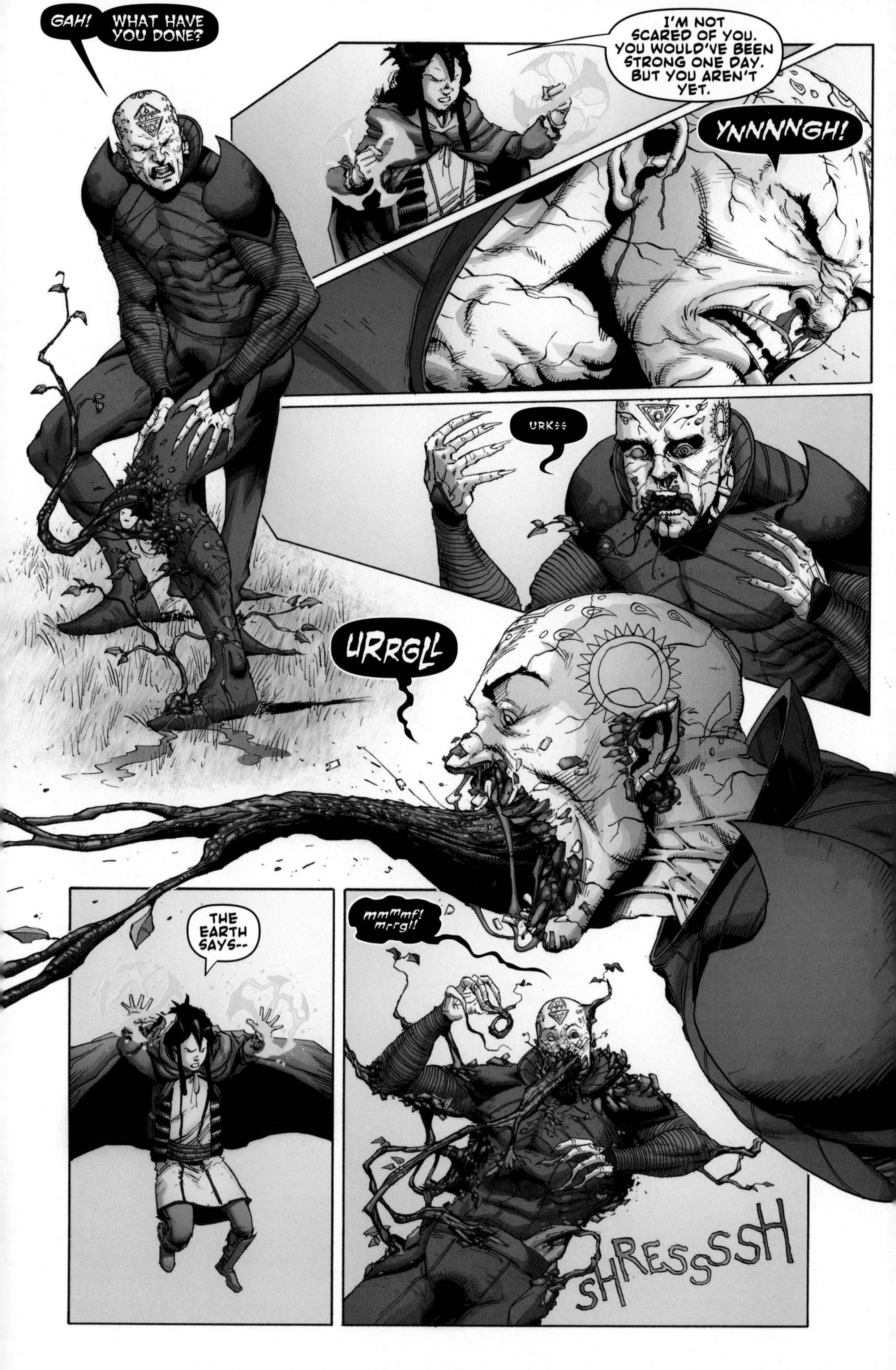
GAH!
WHAT HAVE YOU DONE?
I'M NOT SCARED OF YOU. YOU WOULD'VE BEEN STRONG ONE DAY. BUT YOU AREN'T YET.
YNNNNGH!
URK--
URRGLL
THE EARTH SAYS--
mmmmf! mrrg!!
SHRESSSSH

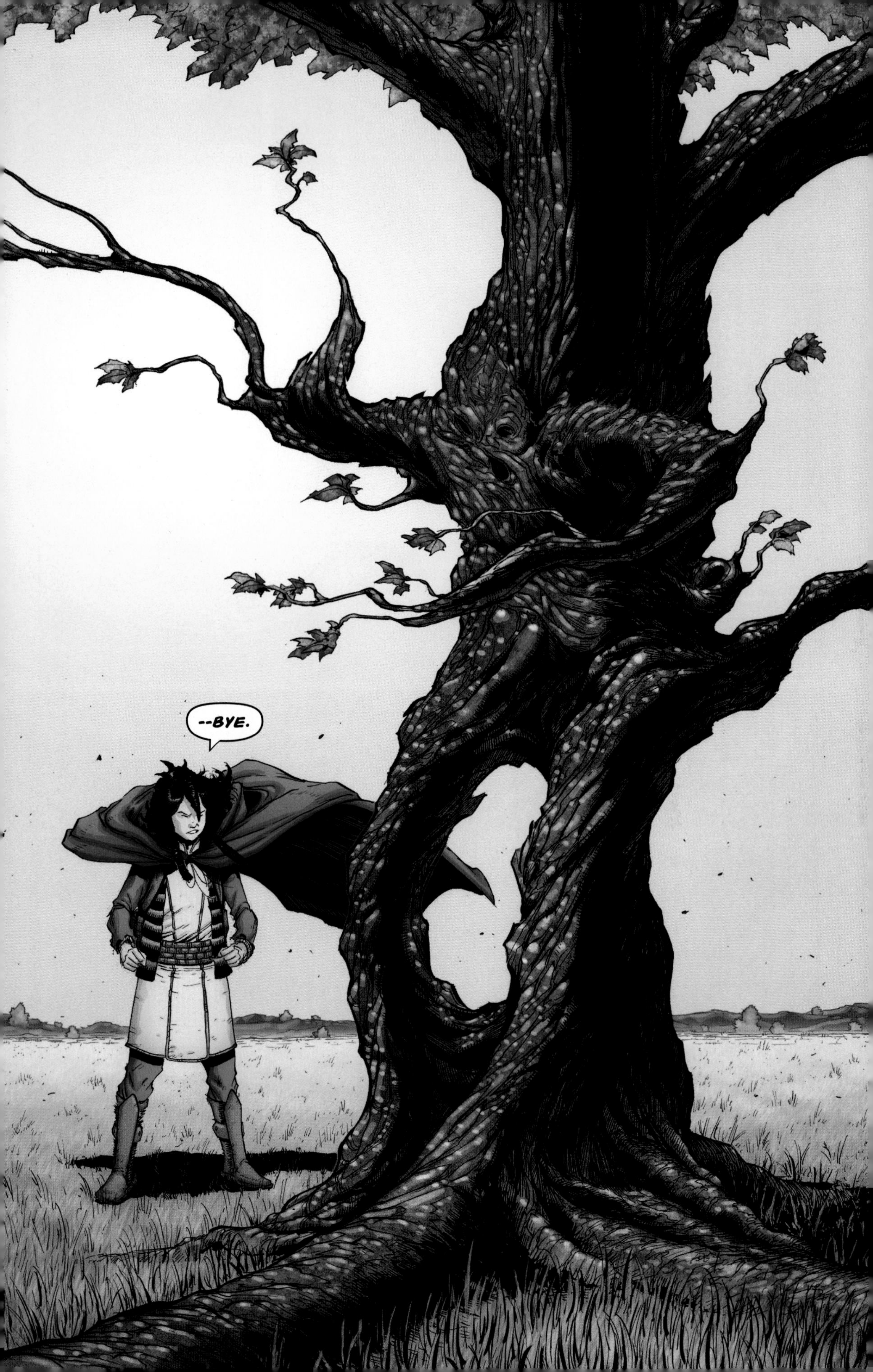
--BYE.

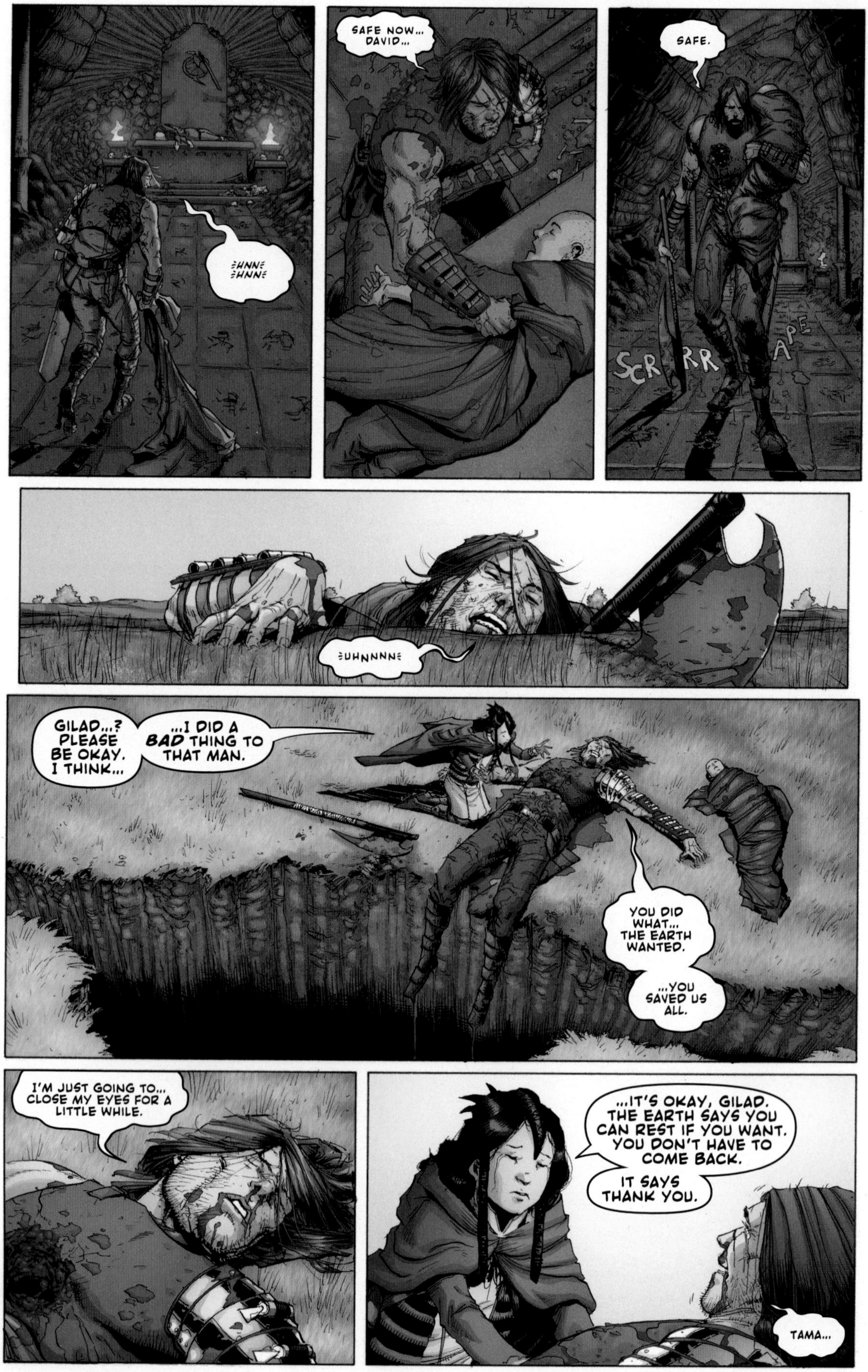
HNN HNN
SAFE NOW... DAVID...
SAFE.
SCRRRAPE
UHNNNN
GILAD...? PLEASE BE OKAY. I THINK...
...I DID A BAD THING TO THAT MAN.
YOU DID WHAT... THE EARTH WANTED.
...YOU SAVED US ALL.
I'M JUST GOING TO... CLOSE MY EYES FOR A LITTLE WHILE.
...IT'S OKAY, GILAD. THE EARTH SAYS YOU CAN REST IF YOU WANT. YOU DON'T HAVE TO COME BACK.
IT SAYS THANK YOU.
TAMA...

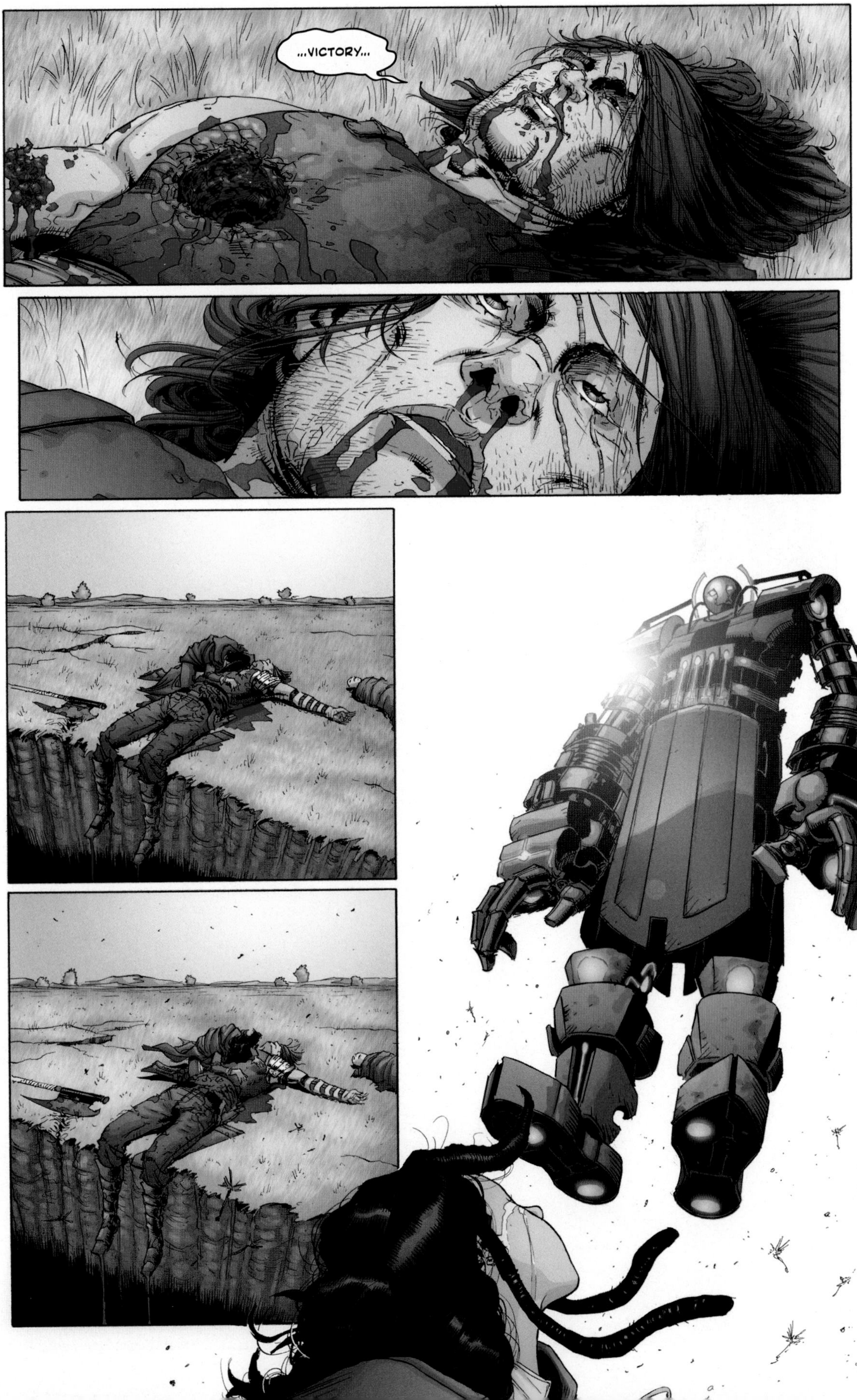
...VICTORY...

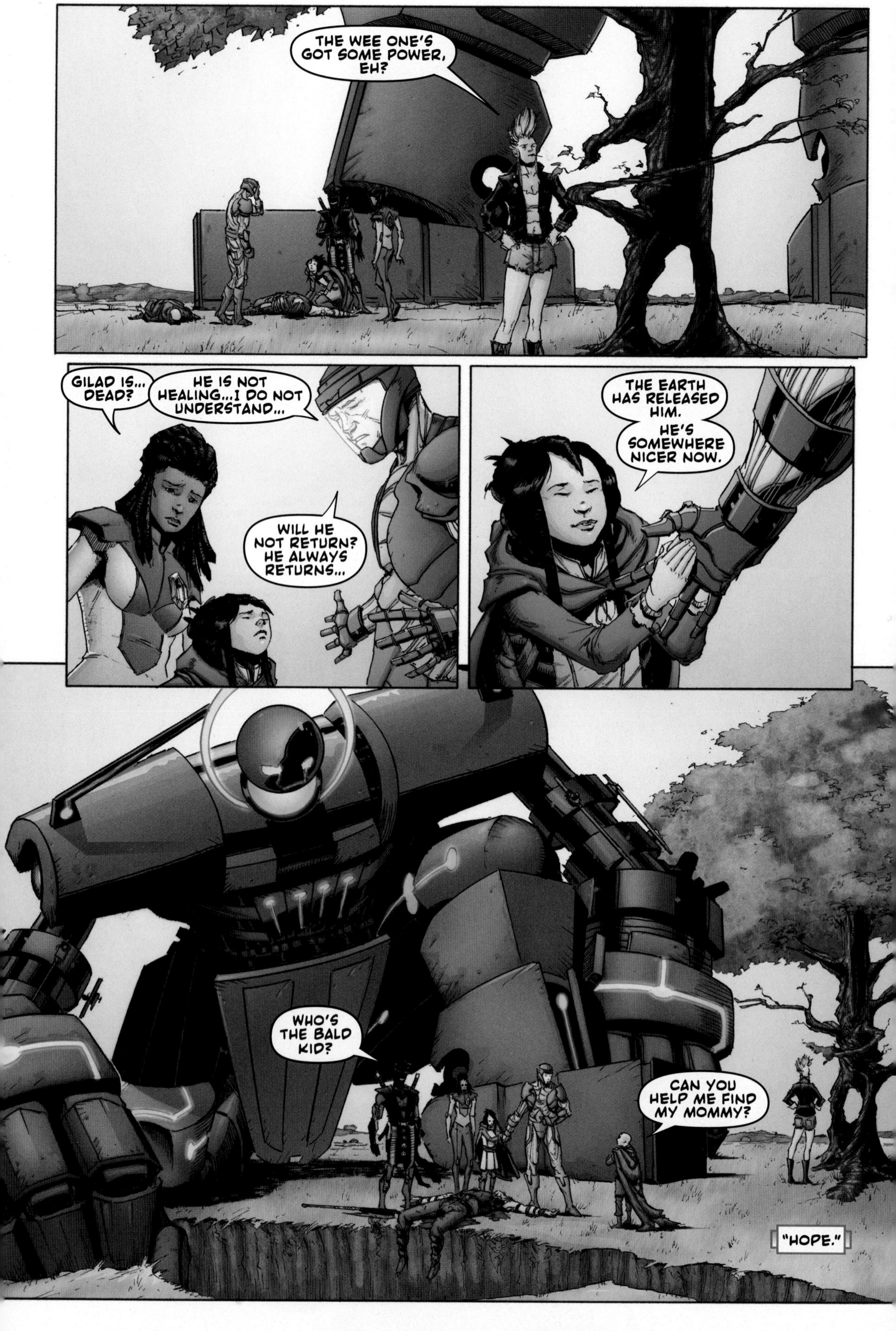
THE WEE ONE'S GOT SOME POWER, EH?
GILAD IS... DEAD?
HE IS NOT HEALING...I DO NOT UNDERSTAND...
WILL HE NOT RETURN? HE ALWAYS RETURNS...
THE EARTH HAS RELEASED HIM.
HE'S SOMEWHERE NICER NOW.
WHO'S THE BALD KID?
CAN YOU HELP ME FIND MY MOMMY?
"HOPE."

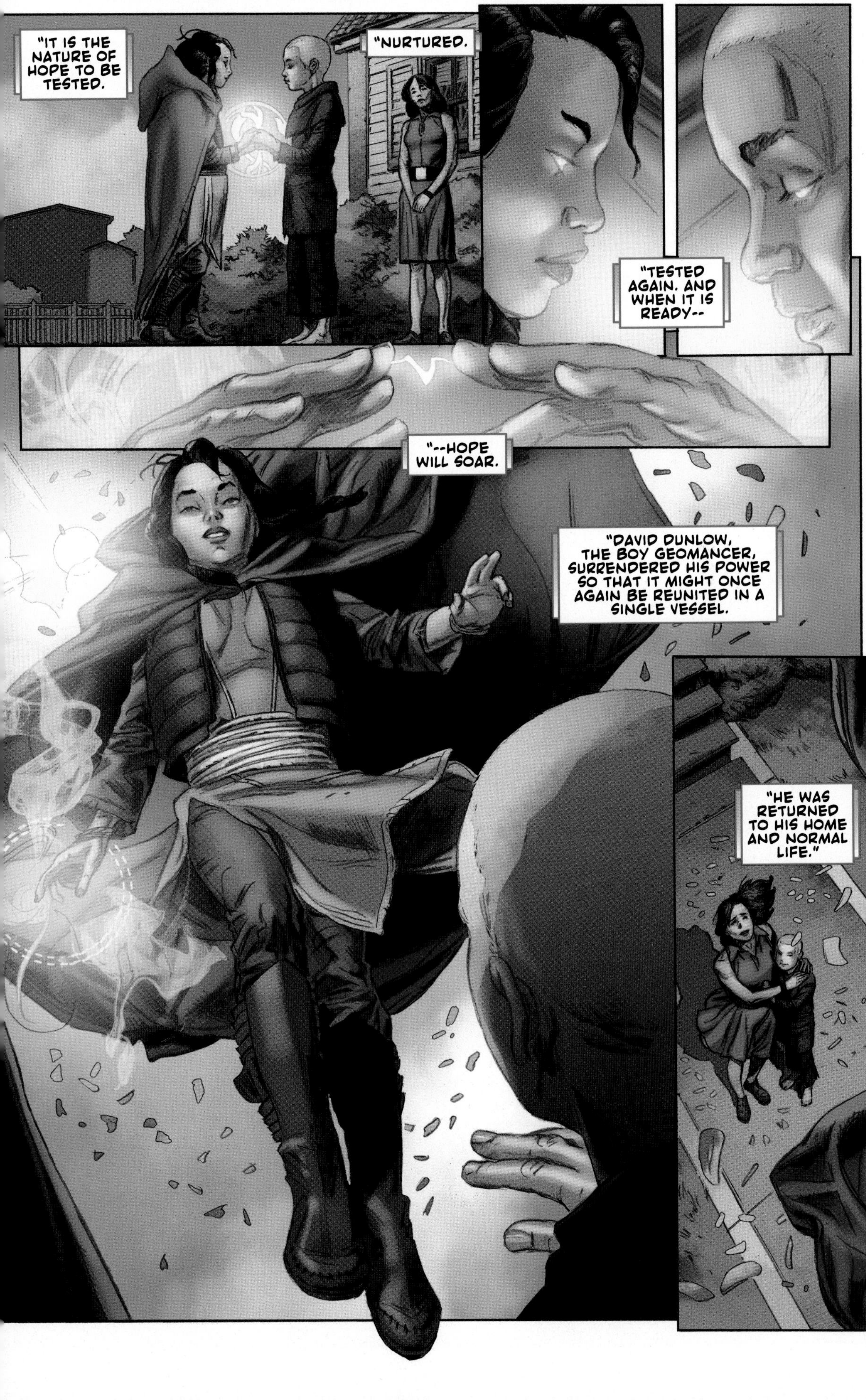
"IT IS THE NATURE OF HOPE TO BE TESTED.
"NURTURED.
"TESTED AGAIN. AND WHEN IT IS READY--
"--HOPE WILL SOAR.
"DAVID DUNLOW, THE BOY GEOMANCER, SURRENDERED HIS POWER SO THAT IT MIGHT ONCE AGAIN BE REUNITED IN A SINGLE VESSEL.
"HE WAS RETURNED TO HIS HOME AND NORMAL LIFE."

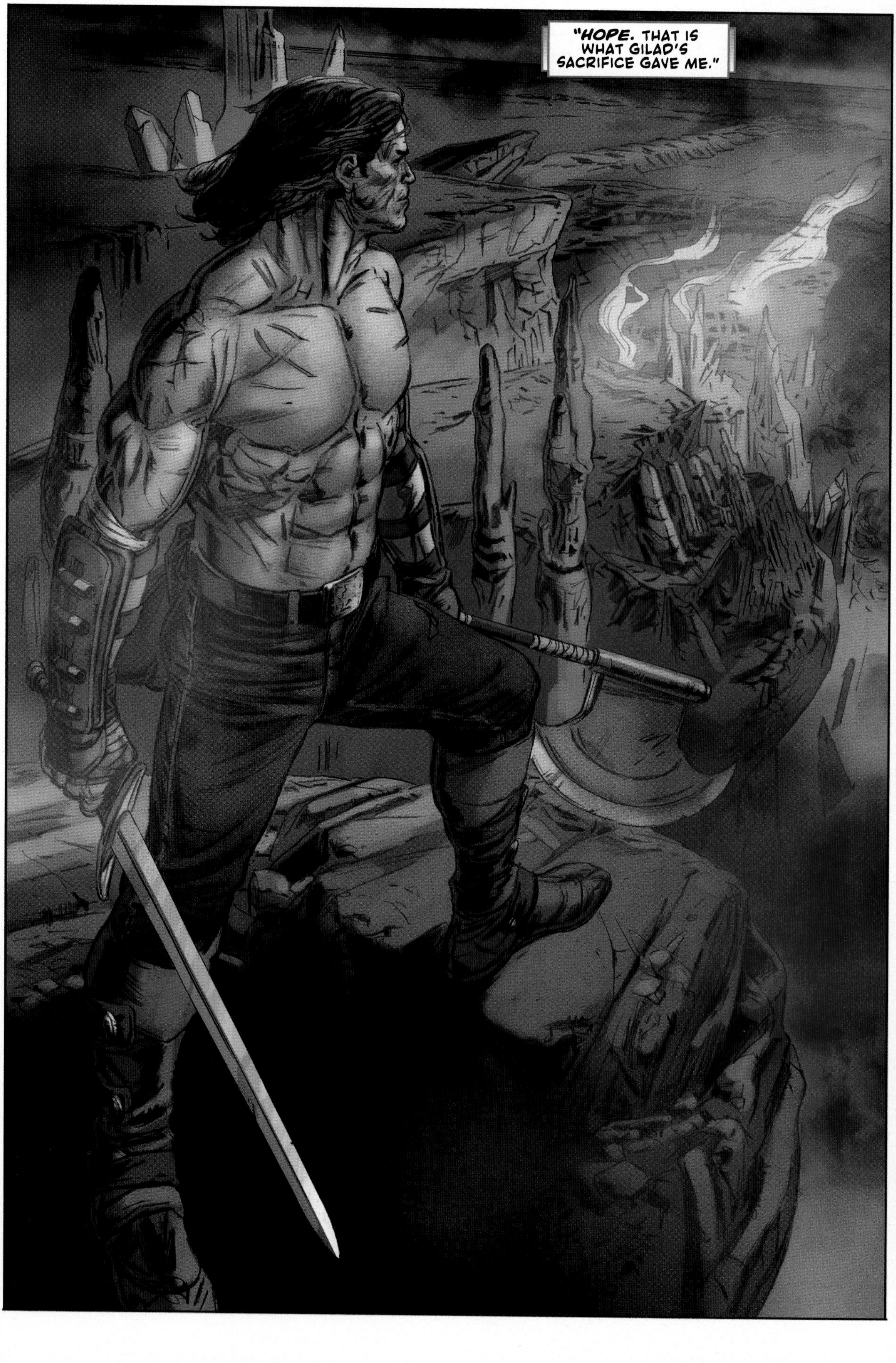
"HOPE. THAT IS WHAT GILAD'S SACRIFICE GAVE ME."

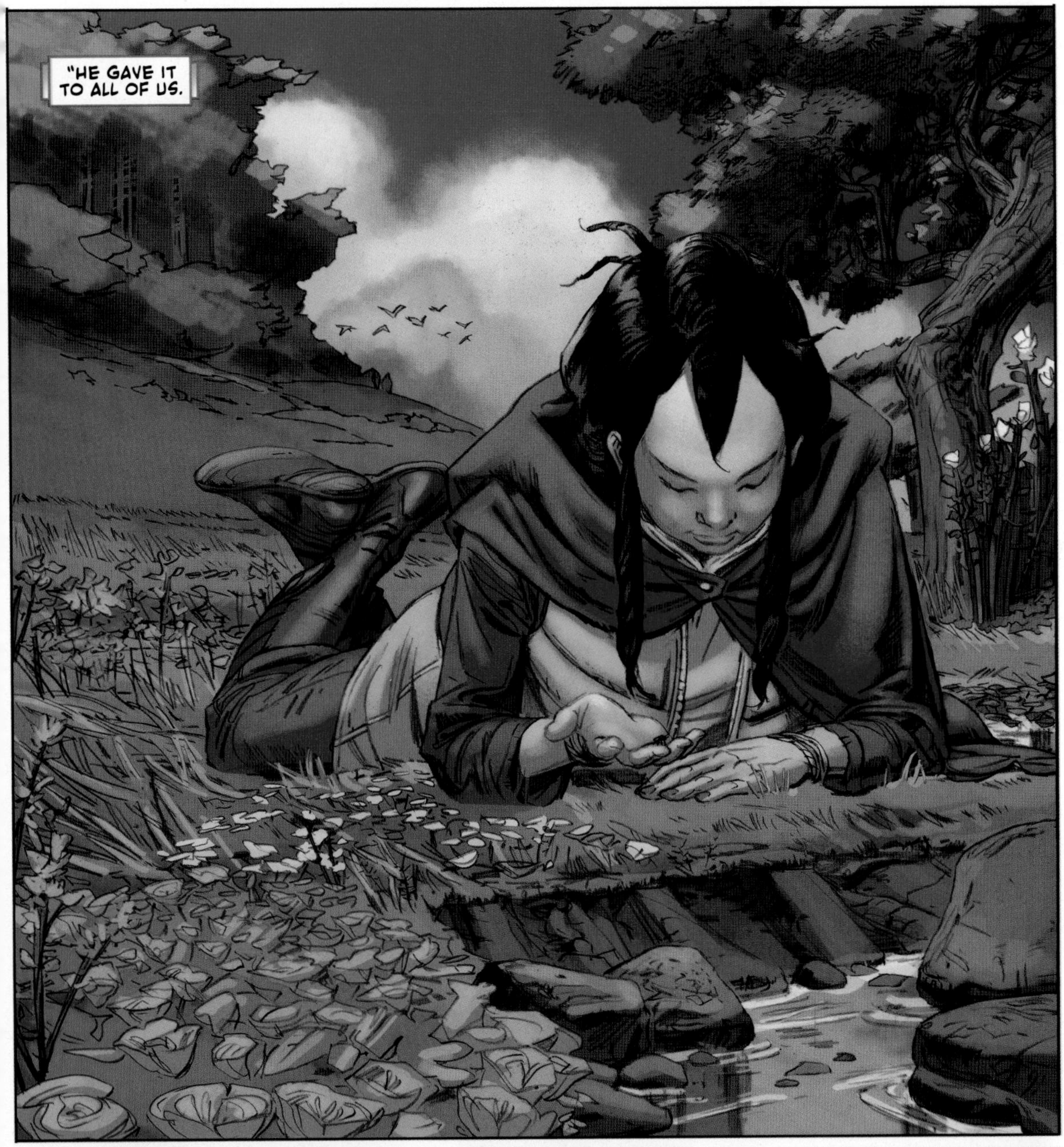
"HE GAVE IT
TO ALL OF US.

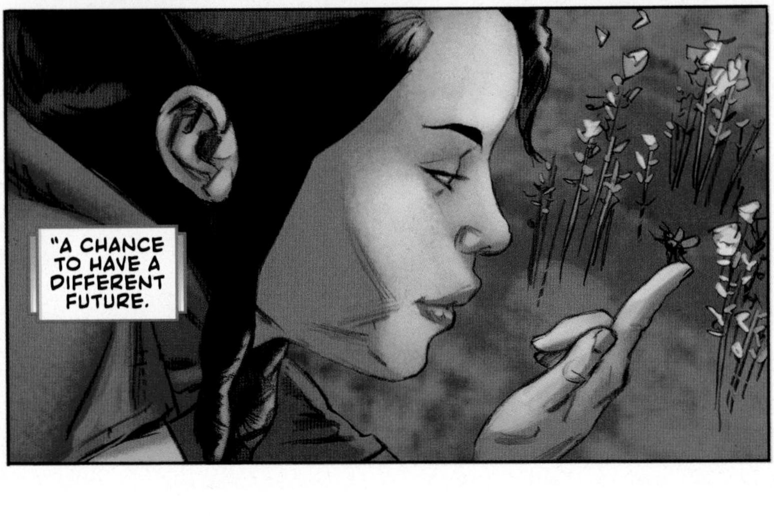
"A CHANCE
TO HAVE A
DIFFERENT
FUTURE.

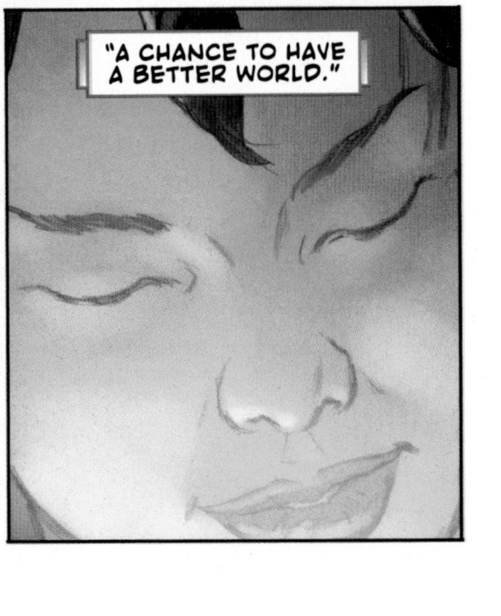
"A CHANCE TO HAVE
A BETTER WORLD."

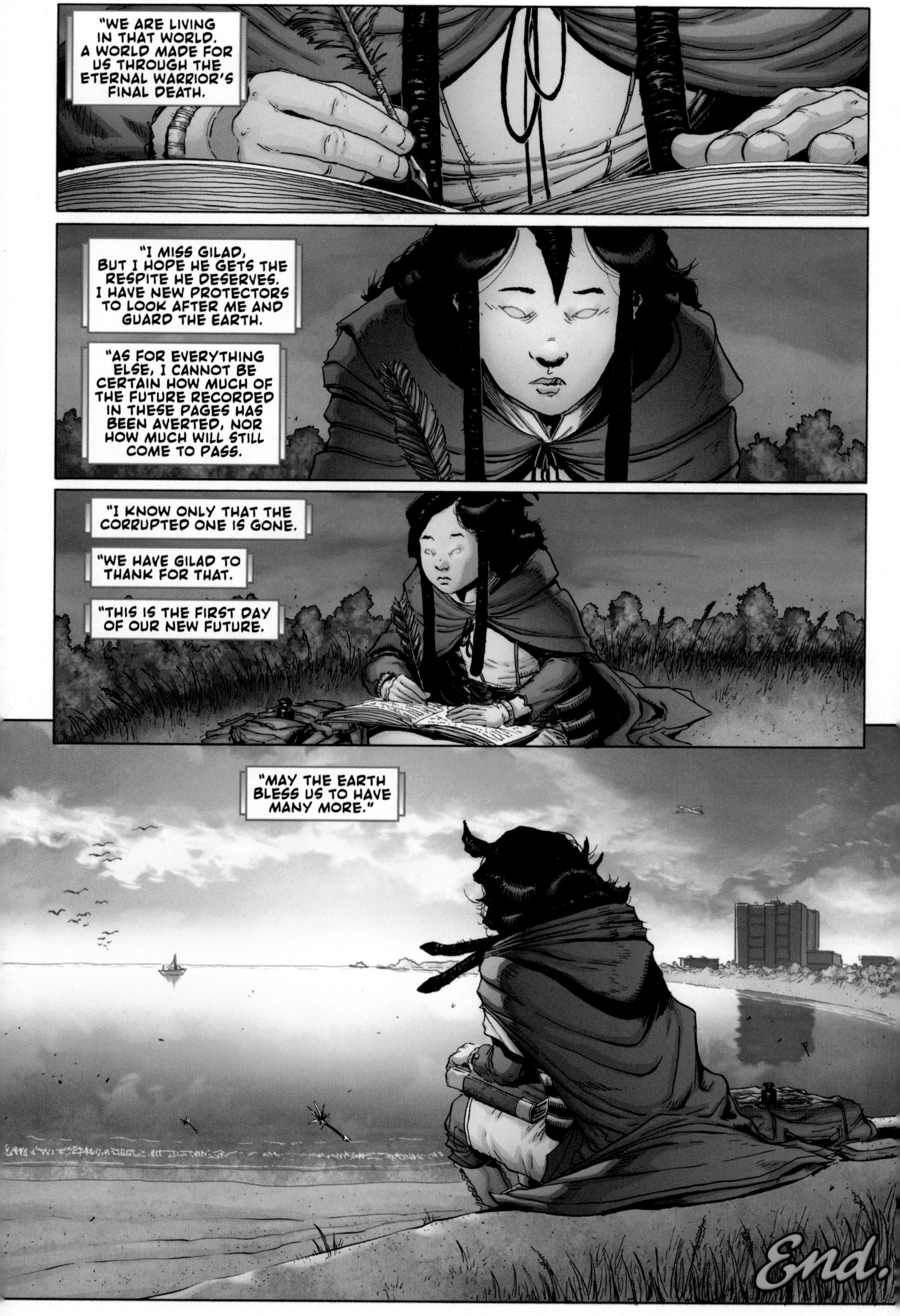
"WE ARE LIVING IN THAT WORLD. A WORLD MADE FOR US THROUGH THE ETERNAL WARRIOR'S FINAL DEATH.
"I MISS GILAD, BUT I HOPE HE GETS THE RESPITE HE DESERVES. I HAVE NEW PROTECTORS TO LOOK AFTER ME AND GUARD THE EARTH.
"AS FOR EVERYTHING ELSE, I CANNOT BE CERTAIN HOW MUCH OF THE FUTURE RECORDED IN THESE PAGES HAS BEEN AVERTED, NOR HOW MUCH WILL STILL COME TO PASS.
"I KNOW ONLY THAT THE CORRUPTED ONE IS GONE.
"WE HAVE GILAD TO THANK FOR THAT.
"THIS IS THE FIRST DAY OF OUR NEW FUTURE.
"MAY THE EARTH BLESS US TO HAVE MANY MORE."
End.

GALLERY

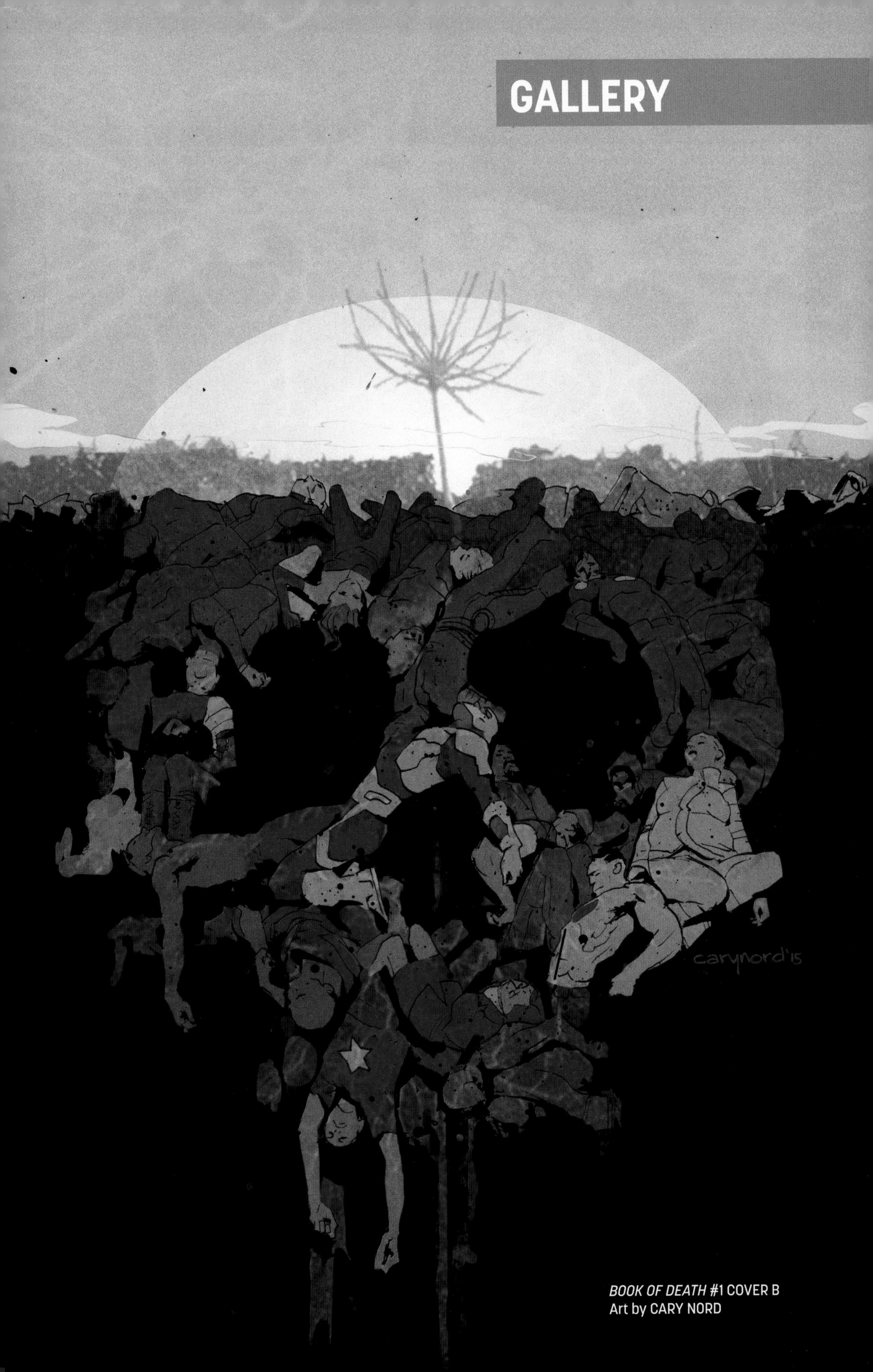
carynord'15

BOOK OF DEATH #1 COVER B
Art by CARY NORD

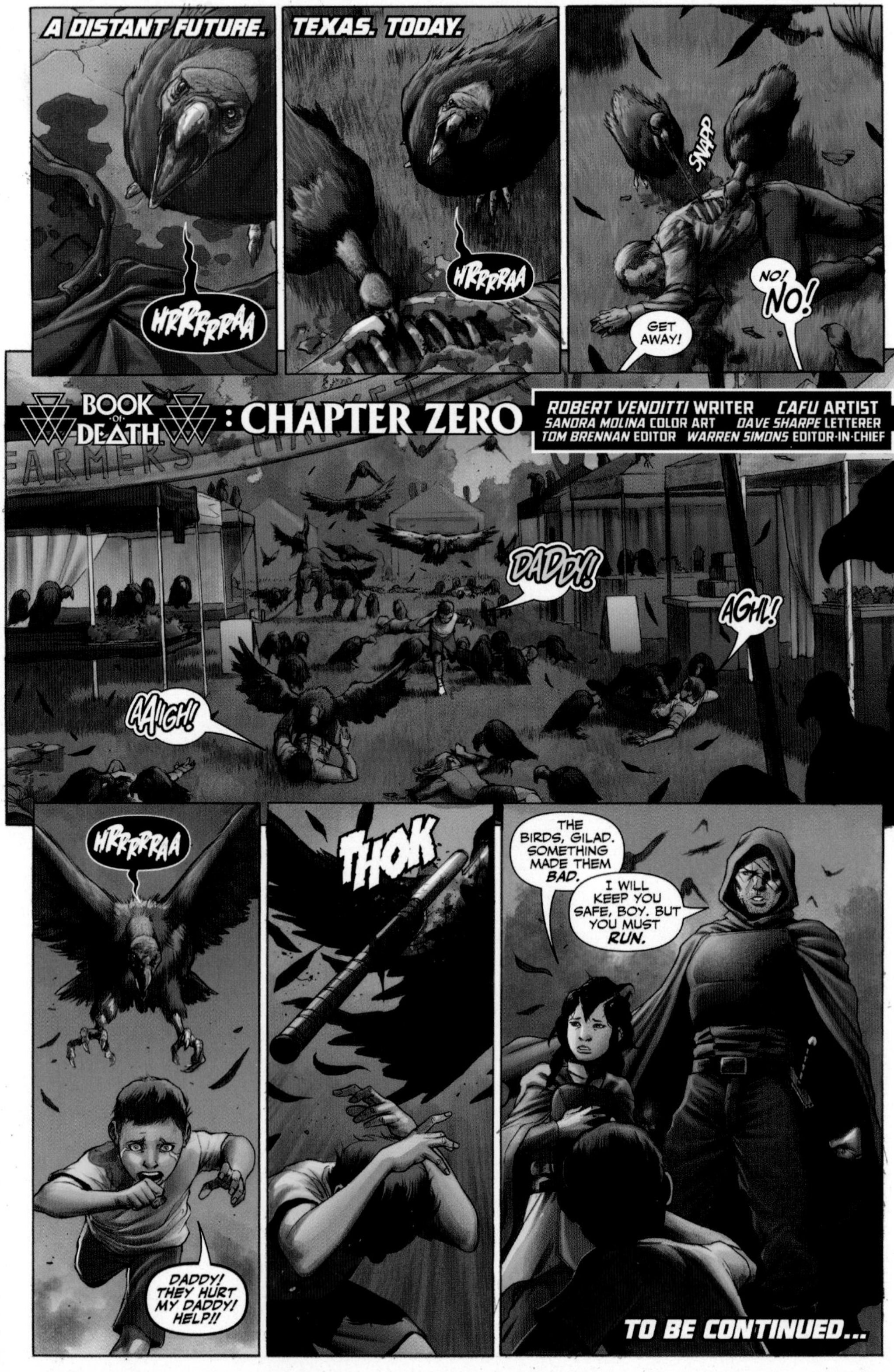
A DISTANT FUTURE.
HRRRRRAA
TEXAS. TODAY.
HRRRRAA
SNAPP
GET AWAY!
NO! NO!
BOOK OF DEATH
: CHAPTER ZERO
ROBERT VENDITTI WRITER CAFU ARTIST
SANDRA MOLINA COLOR ART DAVE SHARPE LETTERER
TOM BRENNAN EDITOR WARREN SIMONS EDITOR-IN-CHIEF
DADDY!
AGH!
AAIIGH!
HRRRRRAA
DADDY! THEY HURT MY DADDY! HELP!!
THOK
THE BIRDS, GILAD. SOMETHING MADE THEM BAD.
I WILL KEEP YOU SAFE, BOY. BUT YOU MUST RUN.
TO BE CONTINUED...

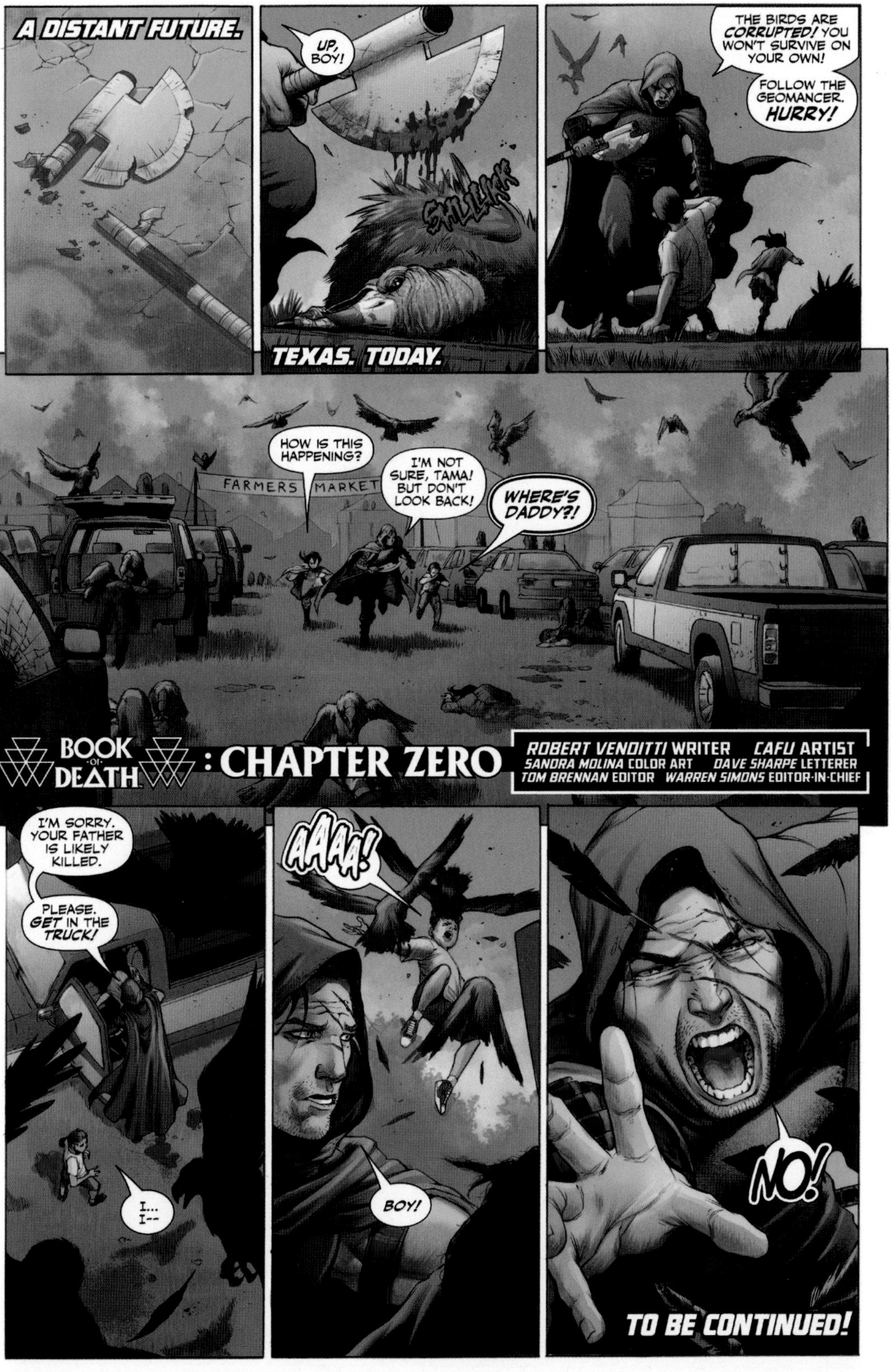

A DISTANT FUTURE.
UP, BOY!
SHLLUKK
TEXAS. TODAY.
THE BIRDS ARE CORRUPTED! YOU WON'T SURVIVE ON YOUR OWN!
FOLLOW THE GEOMANCER. HURRY!
FARMERS MARKET
HOW IS THIS HAPPENING?
I'M NOT SURE, TAMA! BUT DON'T LOOK BACK!
WHERE'S DADDY?!
BOOK OF DEATH : CHAPTER ZERO
ROBERT VENDITTI WRITER CAFU ARTIST
SANDRA MOLINA COLOR ART DAVE SHARPE LETTERER
TOM BRENNAN EDITOR WARREN SIMONS EDITOR-IN-CHIEF
I'M SORRY. YOUR FATHER IS LIKELY KILLED.
PLEASE. GET IN THE TRUCK!
I... I--
AAAA!
BOY!
NO!
TO BE CONTINUED!

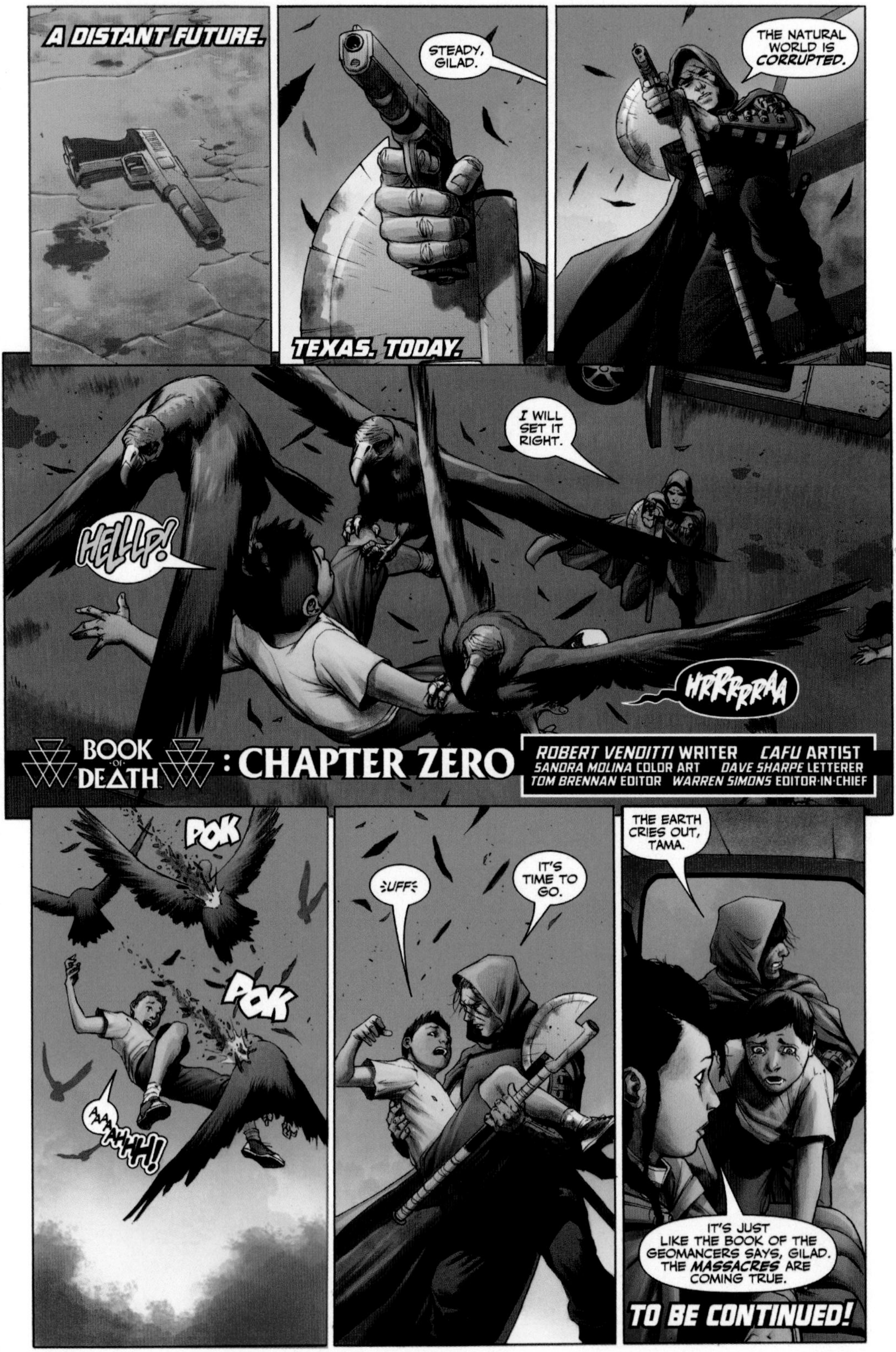
A DISTANT FUTURE.
STEADY, GILAD.
TEXAS. TODAY.
THE NATURAL WORLD IS CORRUPTED.
I WILL SET IT RIGHT.
HELLLP!
HRRRRRAA
BOOK OF DEATH : CHAPTER ZERO
ROBERT VENDITTI WRITER CAFU ARTIST
SANDRA MOLINA COLOR ART DAVE SHARPE LETTERER
TOM BRENNAN EDITOR WARREN SIMONS EDITOR-IN-CHIEF
POK
POK
AAAAHHH!
UFF
IT'S TIME TO GO.
THE EARTH CRIES OUT, TAMA.
IT'S JUST LIKE THE BOOK OF THE GEOMANCERS SAYS, GILAD. THE MASSACRES ARE COMING TRUE.
TO BE CONTINUED!

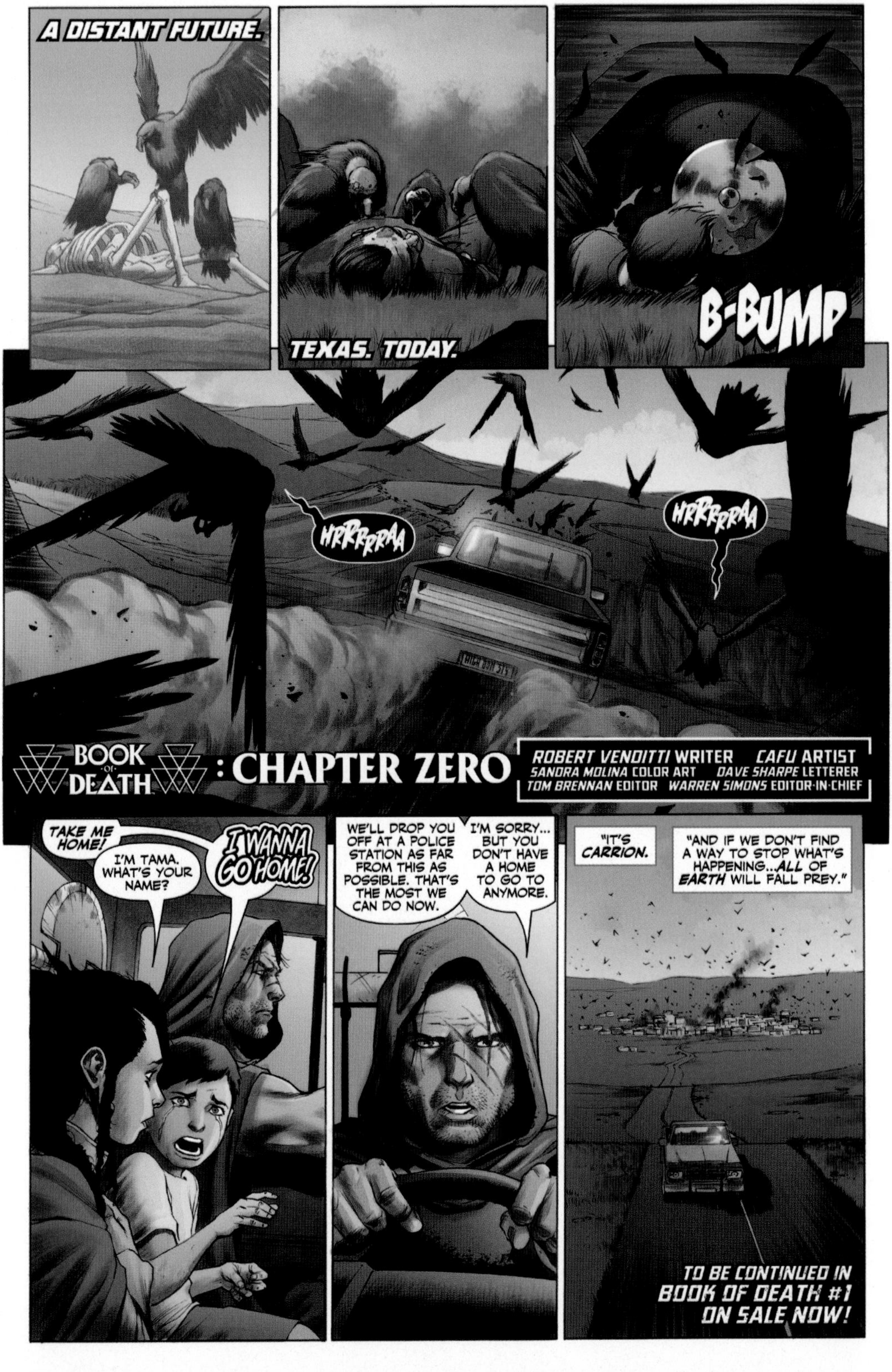
A DISTANT FUTURE.
TEXAS. TODAY.
B-BUMP
HRRRRRAA
HRRRRRAA
BOOK of DEATH
: CHAPTER ZERO
ROBERT VENDITTI WRITER CAFU ARTIST
SANDRA MOLINA COLOR ART DAVE SHARPE LETTERER
TOM BRENNAN EDITOR WARREN SIMONS EDITOR-IN-CHIEF
TAKE ME HOME!
I'M TAMA. WHAT'S YOUR NAME?
I WANNA GO HOME!
WE'LL DROP YOU OFF AT A POLICE STATION AS FAR FROM THIS AS POSSIBLE. THAT'S THE MOST WE CAN DO NOW.
I'M SORRY... BUT YOU DON'T HAVE A HOME TO GO TO ANYMORE.
"IT'S CARRION.
"AND IF WE DON'T FIND A WAY TO STOP WHAT'S HAPPENING...ALL OF EARTH WILL FALL PREY."
TO BE CONTINUED IN BOOK OF DEATH #1 ON SALE NOW!

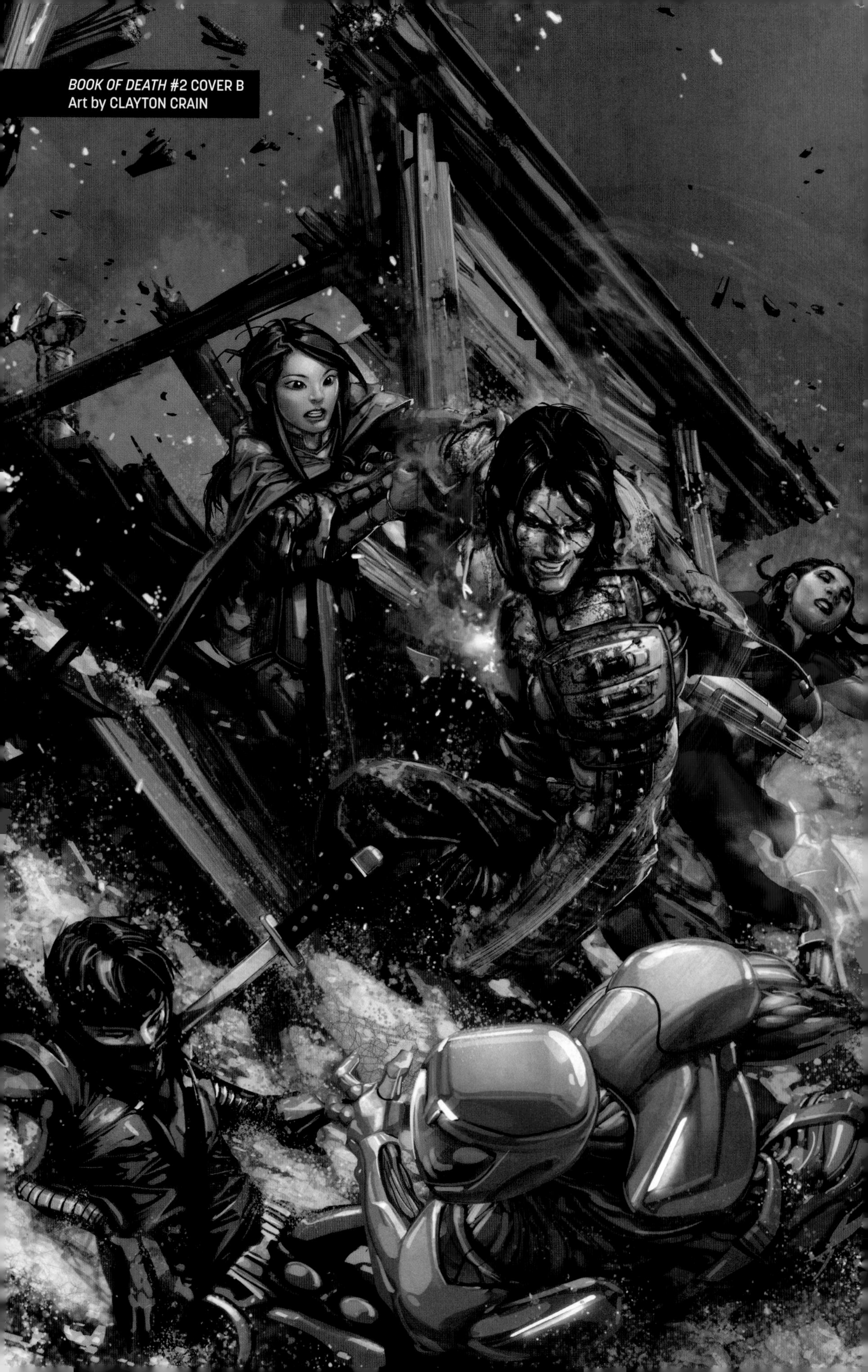

BOOK OF DEATH #2 COVER B
Art by CLAYTON CRAIN

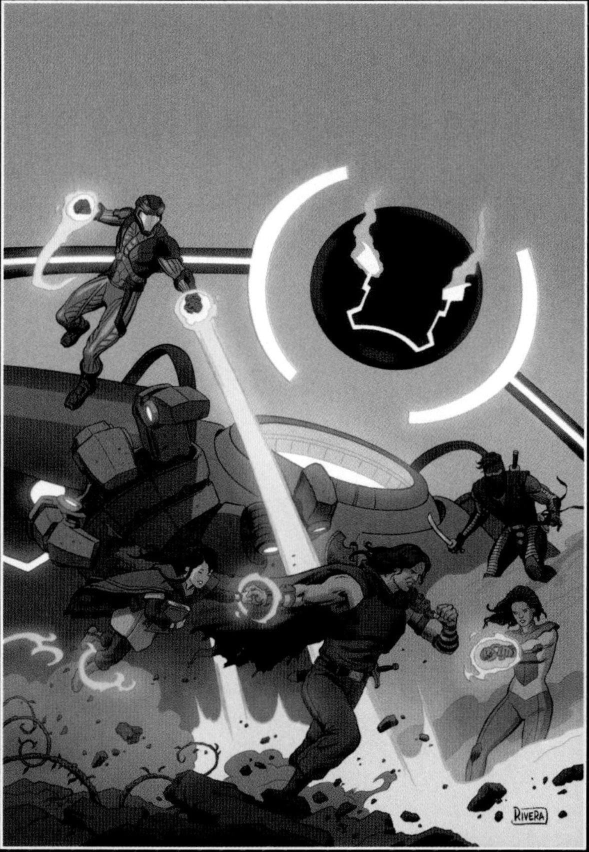
RIVERA

BOOK OF DEATH #2 VARIANT COVER
Art by PAOLO RIVERA

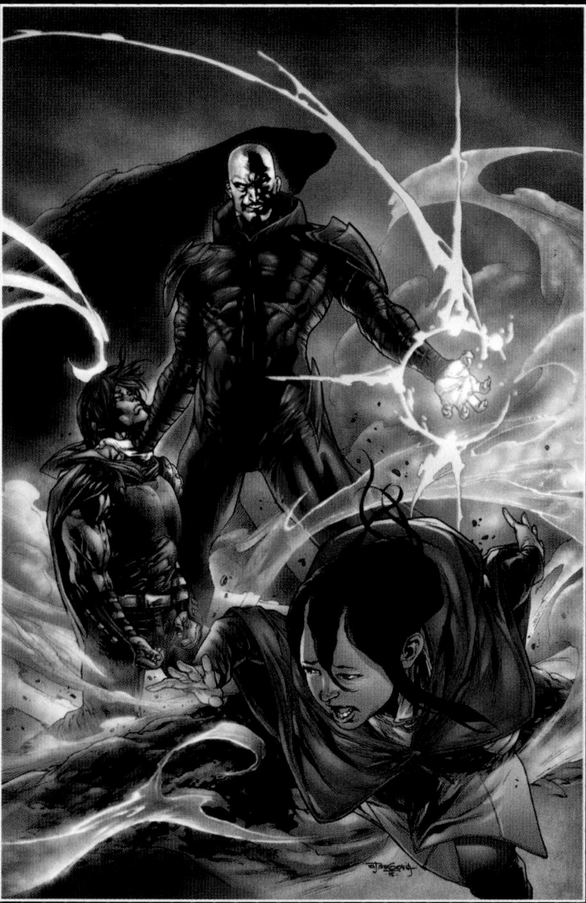

BOOK OF DEATH #3 COVER C
Art by STEPHEN SEGOVIA with ULISES ARREOLA

BOOK OF DEATH #3 VARIANT COVER
Art by PAOLO RIVERA

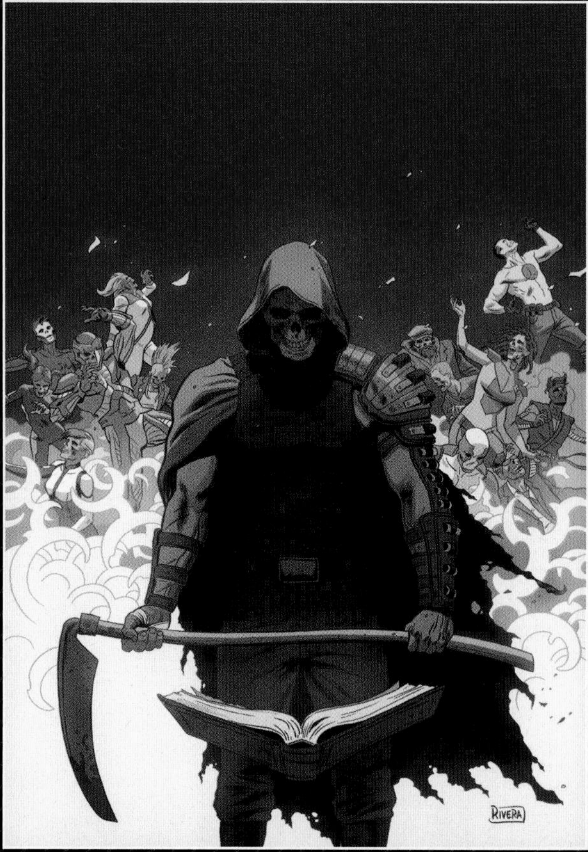
RIVERA

BOOK OF DEATH #4 VARIANT COVER
Art by PAOLO RIVERA

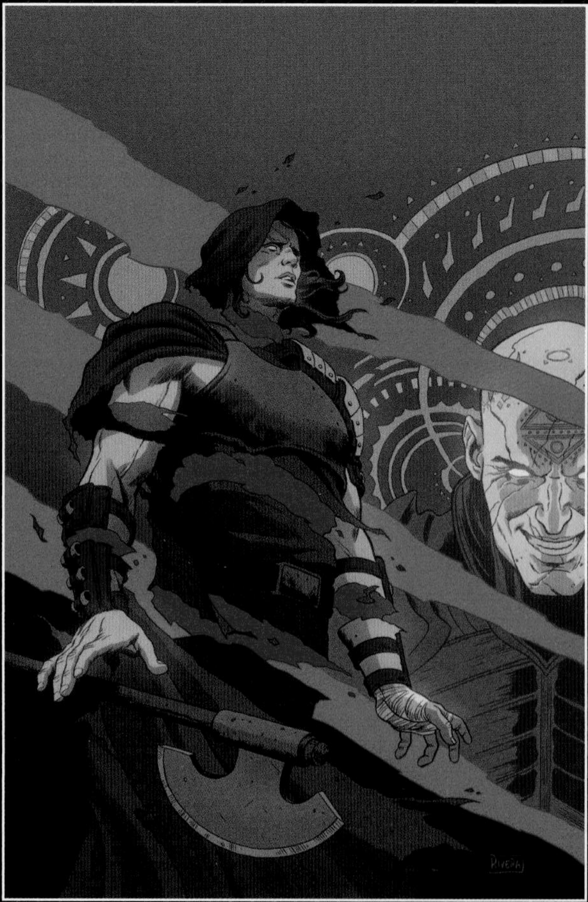
RIVERA

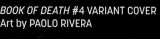

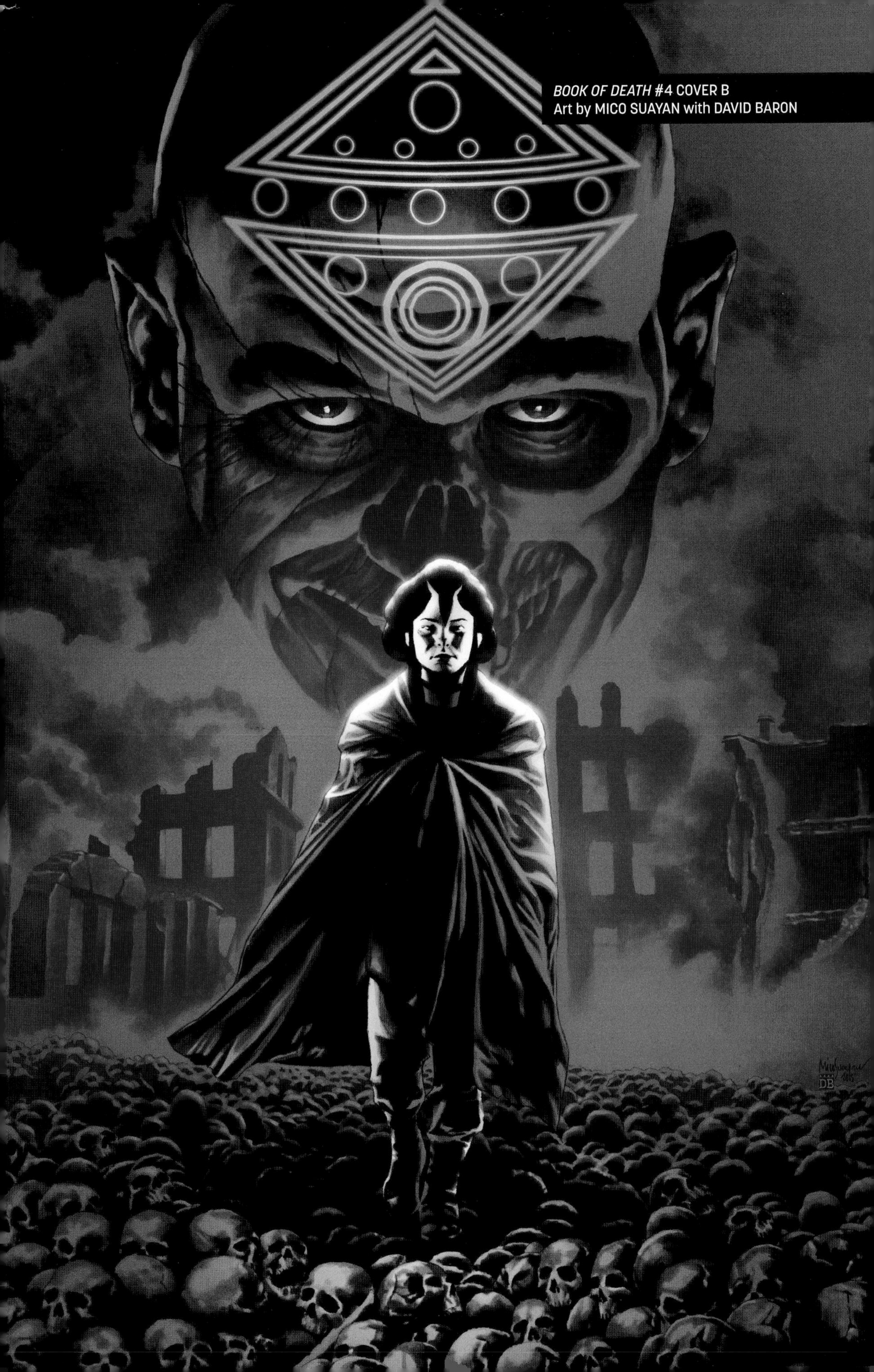

BOOK OF DEATH #4 COVER B
Art by MICO SUAYAN with DAVID BARON

BOOK OF DEATH #1, pages 12-13
Art by DOUG BRAITHWAITE

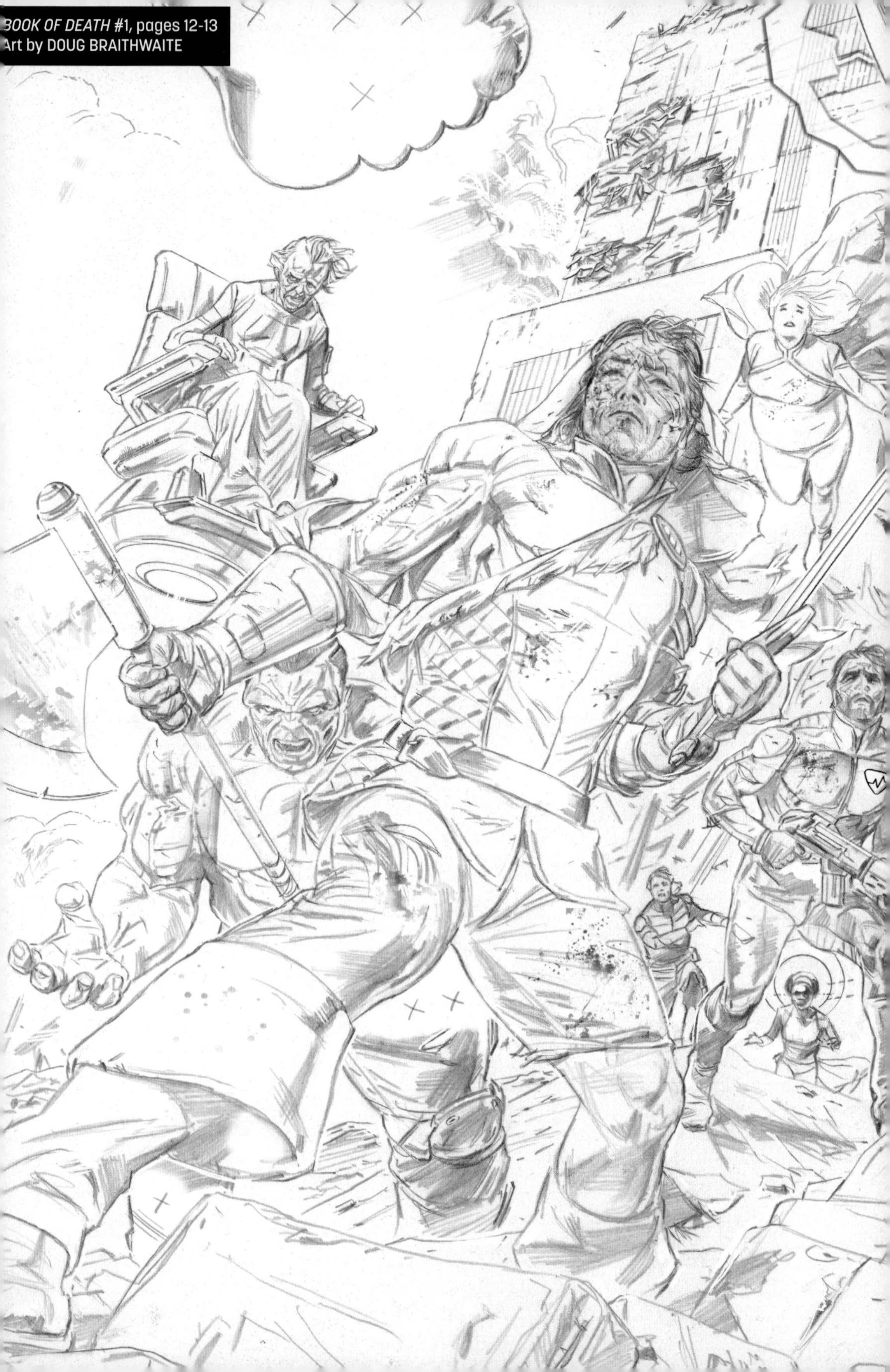

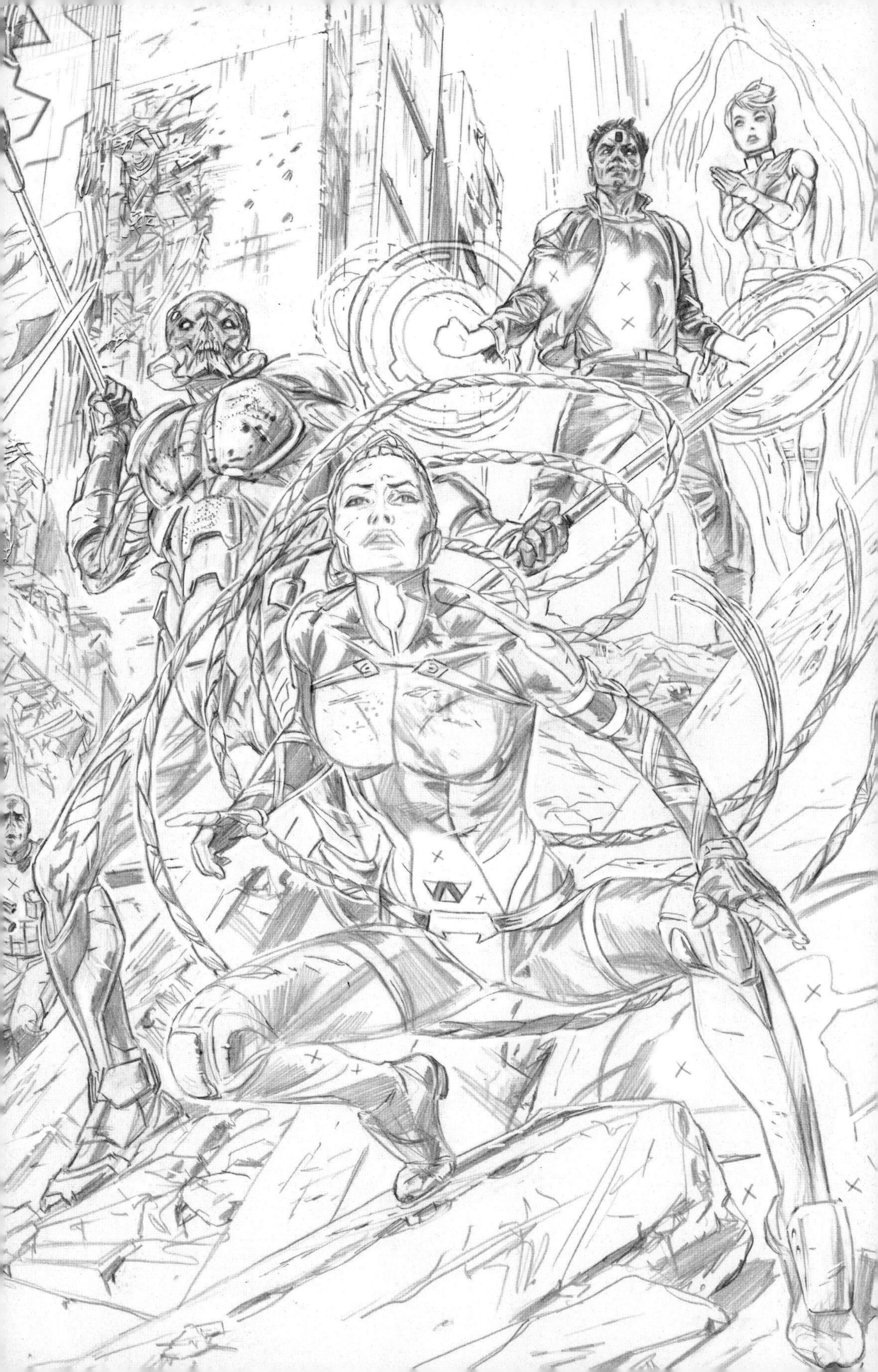

BOOK OF DEATH #2, p. 27
Art by DOUG BRAITHWAITE

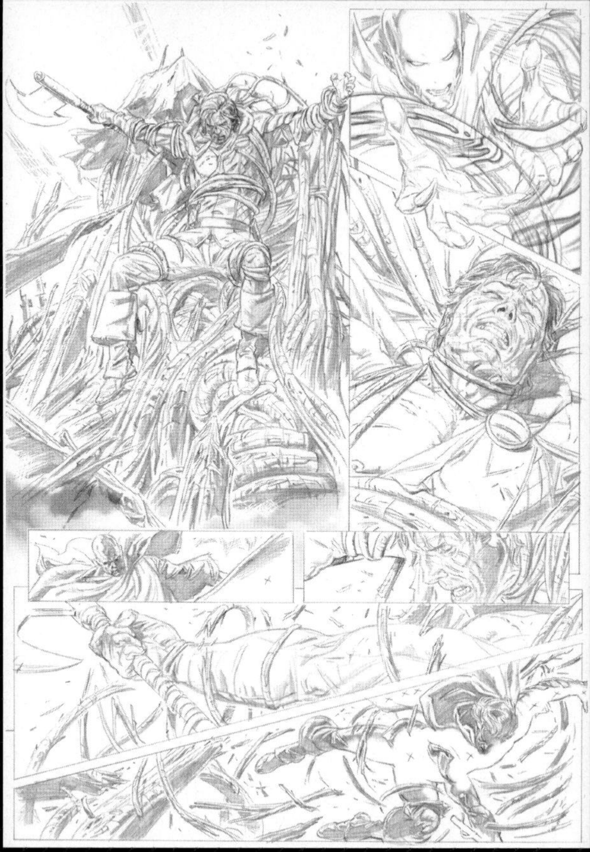

BOOK OF DEATH #2, p. 28
Art by DOUG BRAITHWAITE

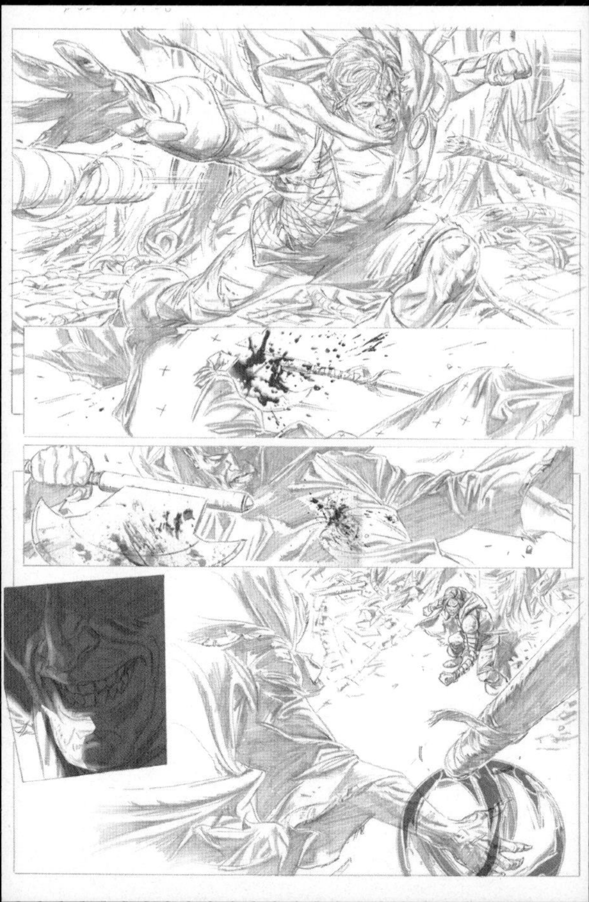

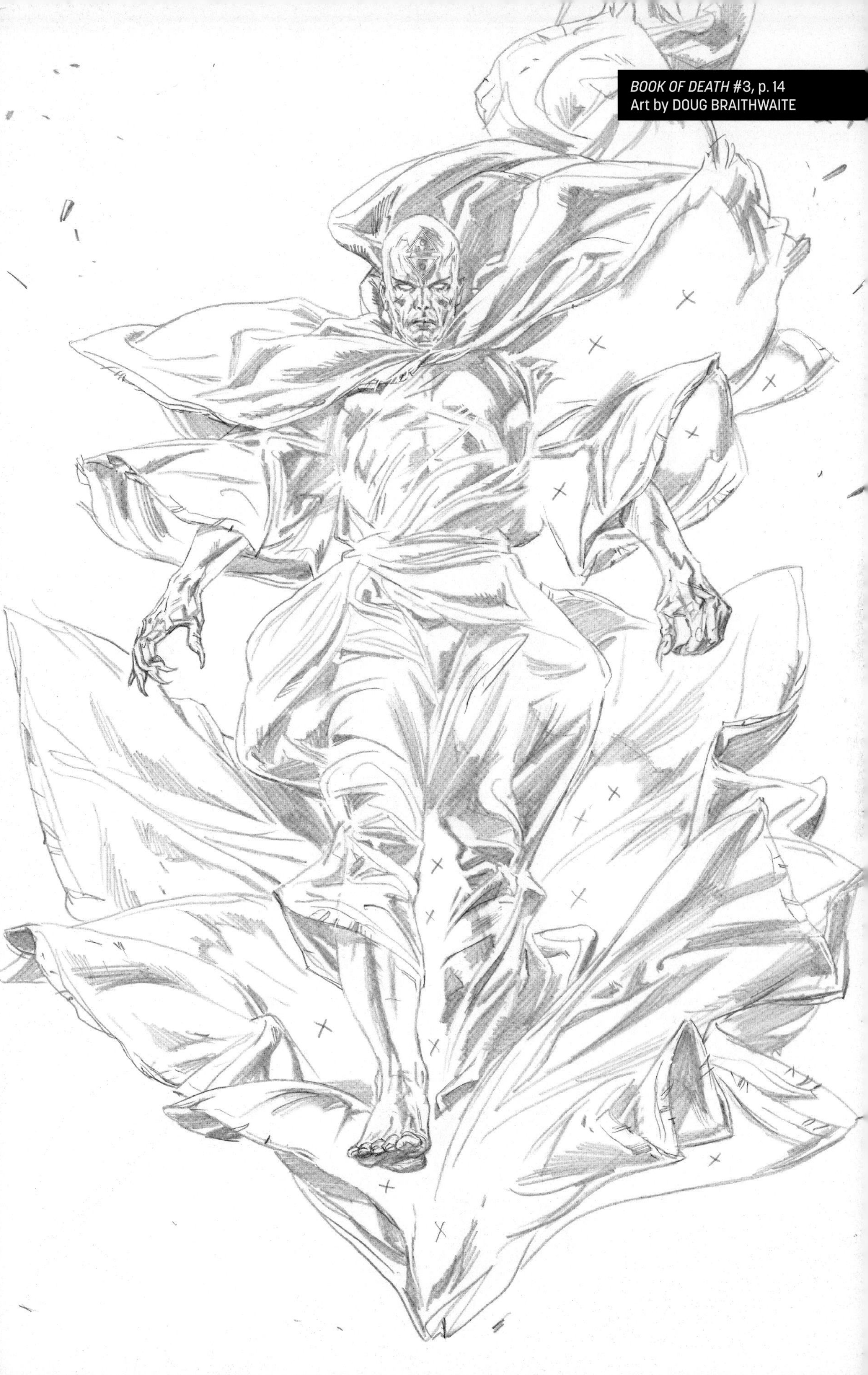

BOOK OF DEATH #3, p. 14
Art by DOUG BRAITHWAITE

EXPLORE THE VALIANT UNIVERSE

VALIANT
THE MICHELANGELO CODE
ARCHER & ARMSTRONG

VALIANT
SETTING THE WORLD ON FIRE
BLOODSHOT

VALIANT
OMEGA RISING
HARBINGER

VALIANT
BY THE SWORD
X-O MANOWAR

VALIANT
THE WORLD'S WORST SUPERHERO TEAM
QUANTUM AND WOODY!
KLANG

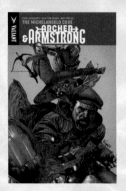

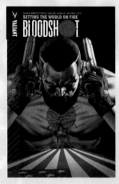

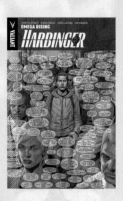

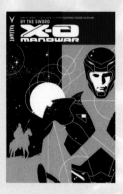

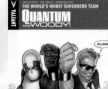

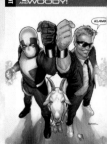

ARCHER & ARMSTRONG

Volume 1: The Michelangelo Code
ISBN: 9780979640988

Volume 2: Wrath of the Eternal Warrior
ISBN: 9781939346049

Volume 3: Far Faraway
ISBN: 9781939346148

Volume 4: Sect Civil War
ISBN: 9781939346254

Volume 5: Mission: Improbable
ISBN: 9781939346353

Volume 6: American Wasteland
ISBN: 9781939346421

Volume 7: The One Percent and Other Tales
ISBN: 9781939346537

ARMOR HUNTERS

Armor Hunters
ISBN: 9781939346452

Armor Hunters: Bloodshot
ISBN: 9781939346469

Armor Hunters: Harbinger
ISBN: 9781939346506

Unity Vol. 3: Armor Hunters
ISBN: 9781939346445

X-O Manowar Vol. 7: Armor Hunters
ISBN: 9781939346476

BLOODSHOT

Volume 1: Setting the World on Fire
ISBN: 9780979640964

Volume 2: The Rise and the Fall
ISBN: 9781939346032

Volume 3: Harbinger Wars
ISBN: 9781939346124

Volume 4: H.A.R.D. Corps
ISBN: 9781939346193

Volume 5: Get Some!
ISBN: 9781939346315

Volume 6: The Glitch and Other Tales
ISBN: 9781939346711

BLOODSHOT REBORN

Volume 1: Colorado
ISBN: 9781939346674

Volume 2: The Hunt
ISBN: 9781939346827

DEAD DROP

ISBN: 9781939346858

THE DEATH-DEFYING DOCTOR MIRAGE

ISBN: 9781939346490

THE DELINQUENTS

ISBN: 9781939346513

DIVINITY

ISBN: 9781939346766

ETERNAL WARRIOR

Volume 1: Sword of the Wild
ISBN: 9781939346209

Volume 2: Eternal Emperor
ISBN: 9781939346292

Volume 3: Days of Steel
ISBN: 9781939346742

HARBINGER

Volume 1: Omega Rising
ISBN: 9780979640957

Volume 2: Renegades
ISBN: 9781939346025

Volume 3: Harbinger Wars
ISBN: 9781939346117

Volume 4: Perfect Day
ISBN: 9781939346155

Volume 5: Death of a Renegade
ISBN: 9781939346339

Volume 6: Omegas
ISBN: 9781939346384

HARBINGER WARS

Harbinger Wars
ISBN: 9781939346094

Bloodshot Vol. 3: Harbinger Wars
ISBN: 9781939346124

Harbinger Vol. 3: Harbinger Wars
ISBN: 9781939346117

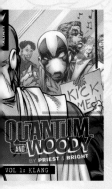

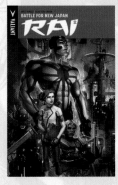

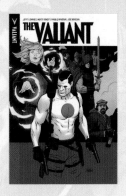

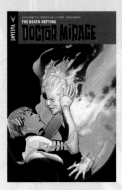

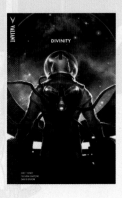

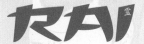

EXPLORE THE VALIANT UNIVERSE

KICK ME
QUANTUM AND WOODY
BY PRIEST & BRIGHT
VOL 1: KLANG

VALIANT
BATTLE FOR NEW JAPAN
RAI

VALIANT
THE VALIANT

VALIANT
THE DEATH-DEFYING
DOCTOR MIRAGE

VALIANT
DIVINITY

インピリアム MPERIUM

olume 1: Collecting Monsters
;BN: 9781939346759

olume 2: Broken Angels
;BN: 9781939346896

NINJAK

olume 1: Weaponeer
;BN: 9781939346667

olume 2: The Shadow Wars
;BN: 9781939346940

QUANTUM AND WOODY!

'olume 1: The World's Worst Superhero Team
SBN: 9781939346186

'olume 2: In Security
SBN: 9781939346230

olume 3: Crooked Pasts, Present Tense
SBN: 9781939346391

'olume 4: Quantum and Woody Must Die!
SBN: 9781939346629

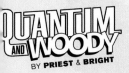

QUANTUM AND WOODY BY PRIEST & BRIGHT

lume 1: Klang
BN: 9781939346780

lume 2: Switch
BN: 9781939346803

lume 3: And So...
BN: 9781939346865

lume 4: The Return
BN: 9781682151099

RAI

Volume 1: Welcome to New Japan
ISBN: 9781939346414

Volume 2: Battle for New Japan
ISBN: 9781939346612

Volume 3: The Orphan
ISBN: 9781939346841

SHADOWMAN

Volume 1: Birth Rites
ISBN: 9781939346001

Volume 2: Darque Reckoning
ISBN: 9781939346056

Volume 3: Deadside Blues
ISBN: 9781939346162

Volume 4: Fear, Blood, And Shadows
ISBN: 9781939346278

Volume 5: End Times
ISBN: 9781939346377

Ivar, Timewalker

Volume 1: Making History
ISBN: 9781939346636

Volume 2: Breaking History
ISBN: 9781939346834

UNITY

Volume 1: To Kill a King
ISBN: 9781939346261

Volume 2: Trapped by Webnet
ISBN: 9781939346346

Volume 3: Armor Hunters
ISBN: 9781939346445

Volume 4: The United
ISBN: 9781939346544

UNITY (Continued)

Volume 5: Homefront
ISBN: 9781939346797

Volume 6: The War-Monger
ISBN: 9781939346902

THE VALIANT

ISBN: 9781939346605

VALIANT ZEROES AND ORIGINS

ISBN: 9781939346582

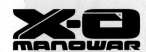

X-O MANOWAR

Volume 1: By the Sword
ISBN: 9780979640940

Volume 2: Enter Ninjak
ISBN: 9780979640995

Volume 3: Planet Death
ISBN: 9781939346087

Volume 4: Homecoming
ISBN: 9781939346179

Volume 5: At War With Unity
ISBN: 9781939346247

Volume 6: Prelude to Armor Hunters
ISBN: 9781939346407

Volume 7: Armor Hunters
ISBN: 9781939346476

Volume 8: Enter: Armorines
ISBN: 9781939346551

Volume 9: Dead Hand
ISBN: 9781939346650

Volume 10: Exodus
ISBN: 9781939346933

EXPLORE THE VALIANT UNIVERSE

VALIANT
JOSHUA DYSART | BARRY KITSON | CLAYTON HENRY
KHARI EVANS | RAFA SANDOVAL
HARBINGER
DELUXE EDITION 2

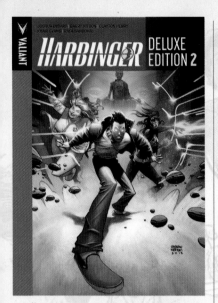

Omnibuses

Archer & Armstrong: The Complete Classic Omnibus
ISBN: 9781939346872
Collecting ARCHER & ARMSTRONG (1992) #0-26, ETERNAL WARRIOR (1992) #25 along with ARCHER & ARMSTRONG: THE FORMATION OF THE SECT.

Quantum and Woody: The Complete Classic Omnibus
ISBN: 9781939346360
Collecting QUANTUM AND WOODY (1997) #0, 1-21 and #32, THE GOAT: H.A.E.D.U.S. #1, and X-O MANOWAR (1996) #16

X-O Manowar Classic Omnibus Vol. 1
ISBN: 9781939346308
Collecting X-O MANOWAR (1992) #0-30, ARMORINES #0, X-O DATABASE #1, as well as material from SECRETS OF THE VALIANT UNIVERSE #1

VALIANT
ROBERT VENDITTI MATT KINDT JOSHUA DYSART JOE HARRIS ROBERT GILL
DOUG BRAITHWAITE DIEGO BERNARD TREVOR HAIRSINE STEPHEN SEGOVIA
ARMOR HUNTERS
DELUXE EDITION

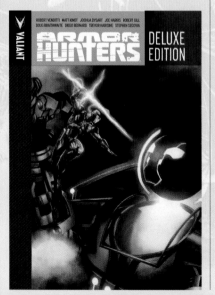

Deluxe Editions

Archer & Armstrong Deluxe Edition Book 1
ISBN: 9781939346223
Collecting ARCHER & ARMSTRONG #0-13

Archer & Armstrong Deluxe Edition Book 2
ISBN: 9781939346957
Collecting ARCHER & ARMSTRONG #14-25, ARCHER & ARMSTRONG: ARCHER #0 and BLOODSHOT AND H.A.R.D. CORPS #20-21.

Armor Hunters Deluxe Edition
ISBN: 9781939346728
Collecting Armor Hunters #1-4, Armor Hunters: Aftermath #1, Armor Hunters: Bloodshot #1-3, Armor Hunters: Harbinger #1-3, Unity #8-11, and X-O MANOWAR #23-29

Bloodshot Deluxe Edition Book 1
ISBN: 9781939346216
Collecting BLOODSHOT #1-13

Bloodshot Deluxe Edition Book 2
ISBN: 9781939346810
Collecting BLOODSHOT AND H.A.R.D. CORPS #14-23, BLOODSHOT #24-25, BLOODSHOT #0, BLOODSHOT AND H.A.R.D. CORPS: H.A.R.D. CORPS #0, along with ARCHER & ARMSTRONG #18-19

Divinity Deluxe Edition
ISBN: 97819393460993
Collecting DIVNITY #1-4

Harbinger Deluxe Edition Book 1
ISBN: 9781939346131
Collecting HARBINGER #0-14

Harbinger Deluxe Edition Book 2
SBN: 9781939346773
Collecting HARBINGER #15-25, HARBINGER: OMEGAS #1-3, and HARBINGER: BLEEDING MONK #0

Harbinger Wars Deluxe Edition
ISBN: 9781939346322
Collecting HARBINGER WARS #1-4, HARBINGER #11-14, and BLOODSHOT #10-13

Quantum and Woody Deluxe Edition Book 1
ISBN: 9781939346681
Collecting QUANTUM AND WOODY #1-12 and QUANTUM AND WOODY: THE GOAT #0

Q2: The Return of Quantum and Woody Deluxe Edition
ISBN: 9781939346568
Collecting Q2: THE RETURN OF QUANTUM AND WOODY #1-5

Shadowman Deluxe Edition Book 1
ISBN: 9781939346438
Collecting SHADOWMAN #0-10

Shadowman Deluxe Edition Book 2
ISBN: 9781682151075
Collecting SHADOWMAN #11-16, SHADOWMAN #13X, SHADOWMAN: END TIMES #1-3 and PUNK MAMBO #0

Unity Deluxe Edition Book 1
ISBN: 9781939346575
Collecting UNITY #0-14

The Valiant Deluxe Edition
ISBN: 97819393460986
Collecting THE VALIANT #1-4

X-O Manowar Deluxe Edition Book 1
ISBN: 9781939346100
Collecting X-O MANOWAR #1-14

X-O Manowar Deluxe Edition Book 2
ISBN: 9781939346520
Collecting X-O MANOWAR #15-22, and UNITY #1-4

VALIANT
JIM SHOOTER | DAVID LAPHAM
CHILDREN OF THE EIGHTH DAY
HARBINGER
VALIANT MASTERS

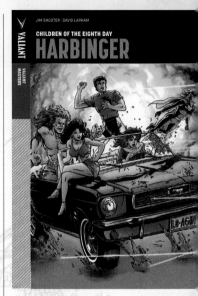

Valiant Masters

Bloodshot Vol. 1 - Blood of the Machine
ISBN: 9780979640933

H.A.R.D. Corps Vol. 1 - Search and Destroy
ISBN: 9781939346285

Harbinger Vol. 1 - Children of the Eighth Day
ISBN: 9781939346483

Ninjak Vol. 1 - Black Water
ISBN: 9780979640971

Rai Vol. 1 - From Honor to Strength
ISBN: 9781939346070

Shadowman Vol. 1 - Spirits Within
ISBN: 9781939346018

VALIANT
KEVIN VANHOOK | DON PERLIN
BLOOD OF THE MACHINE
BLOODSHOT
VALIANT MASTERS

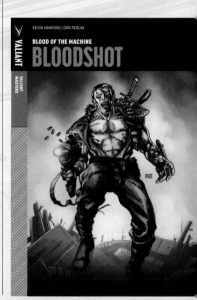

BOOK OF DEATH
THE FALL OF THE VALIANT UNIVERSE

SO LET IT BE WRITTEN, SO LET IT BE DONE...

The dawn of the new Dark Age foretold in BOOK OF DEATH continues right here with a glimpse into the future of the Valiant Universe in four visionary tales of present and future ripped directly from the pages of the Book of the Geomancer! An all-star cast of creators chronicle the ultimate fate of Valiant's most indelible heroes. From the modern day to the far future, the destinies of Bloodshot, Ninjak, the Harbinger Renegades, X-O Manowar, and more will stand revealed in these four essential, standalone chapters at the epicenter of the blockbuster Valiant event of the year.

Writers Jeff Lemire (BLOODSHOT REBORN), Matt Kindt (NINJAK), Joshua Dysart (HARBINGER), and Robert Venditti (X-O MANOWAR) join superstar artists Doug Braithwaite (ARMOR HUNTERS), Trevor Hairsine (DIVINITY), Kano (THE DELINQUENTS), and Clayton Henry (ARCHER & ARMSTRONG) as they foretell the deadly future and final days of the greatest heroes of the Valiant Universe.

Collecting BOOK OF DEATH: THE FALL OF BLOODSHOT #1, BOOK OF DEATH: THE FALL OF NINJAK #1, BOOK OF DEATH: THE FALL OF HARBINGER #1, BOOK OF DEATH: THE FALL OF X-O MANOWAR #1.

TRADE PAPERBACK
ISBN: 978-1-939346-98-8

LEMIRE | KINDT | DYSART | VENDITTI | BRAITHWAITE | HAIRSINE | KANO | HENRY
BOOK OF DEATH
THE FALL OF THE VALIANT UNIVERSE
VALIANT

WRATH OF THE ETERNAL WARRIOR

VOLUME ONE: **RISEN**

New York Times best-selling writer Robert Venditti (BOOK OF DEATH, X-O MANOWAR) and visionary artist Raúl Allén (NINJAK, *Hawkeye*) forge a new legend for Valiant's master of war!

For five millennia, the Eternal Warrior has shaped history at the end of his sword. He's razed empires, toppled civilizations, and broken armies as an immortal soldier in service to the Earth.

But now, the Eternal Warrior has been torn from the world he once protected and finds himself stranded in a hostile alien landscape unlike any he's faced before. Separated from his earthly environs, can history's deadliest soldier survive a realm far older, far deadlier, and fare more ruinous than anything he's ever encountered? Beyond Earth lies eternity...

Collecting WRATH OF THE ETERNAL WARRIOR #1-4

TRADE PAPERBACK
ISBN: 978-1-68215-123-5

ROBERT VENDITTI | RAÚL ALLÉN
RISEN
WRATH OF THE ETERNAL WARRIOR
VALIANT

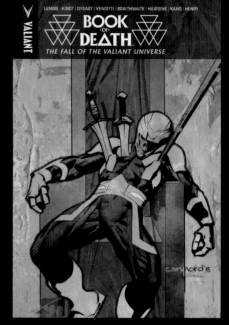